Rethinking Peace and Conflict Studies

Series Editors
Oliver P. Richmond
University of Manchester
Manchester, UK

Annika Björkdahl
Department of Political Science
Lund University
Lund, Sweden

Gëzim Visoka
Dublin City University
Dublin, Ireland

This agenda-setting series of research monographs, now more than a decade old, provides an interdisciplinary forum aimed at advancing innovative new agendas for peace and conflict studies in International Relations. Many of the critical volumes the series has so far hosted have contributed to new avenues of analysis directly or indirectly related to the search for positive, emancipatory, and hybrid forms of peace. Constructive critiques of liberal peace, hybrid peace, everyday contributions to peace, the role of civil society and social movements, international actors and networks, as well as a range of different dimensions of peace (from peacebuilding, statebuilding, youth contributions, photography, and many case studies) have been explored so far. The series raises important political questions about what peace is, whose peace and peace for whom, as well as where peace takes place. In doing so, it offers new and interdisciplinary perspectives on the development of the international peace architecture, peace processes, UN peacebuilding, peacekeeping and mediation, statebuilding, and localised peace formation in practice and in theory. It examines their implications for the development of local peace agency and the connection between emancipatory forms of peace and global justice, which remain crucial in different conflict-affected regions around the world. This series' contributions offer both theoretical and empirical insights into many of the world's most intractable conflicts, also investigating increasingly significant evidence about blockages to peace.

This series is indexed by Scopus.

Noah B. Taylor

Existential Risks in Peace and Conflict Studies

Noah B. Taylor
Universität Innsbruck
Innsbruck, Austria

ISSN 1759-3735   ISSN 2752-857X (electronic)
Rethinking Peace and Conflict Studies
ISBN 978-3-031-24314-1   ISBN 978-3-031-24315-8 (eBook)
https://doi.org/10.1007/978-3-031-24315-8

© The Editor(s) (if applicable) and The Author(s), under exclusive licence to Springer Nature Switzerland AG 2023

This work is subject to copyright. All rights are solely and exclusively licensed by the Publisher, whether the whole or part of the material is concerned, specifically the rights of translation, reprinting, reuse of illustrations, recitation, broadcasting, reproduction on microfilms or in any other physical way, and transmission or information storage and retrieval, electronic adaptation, computer software, or by similar or dissimilar methodology now known or hereafter developed.

The use of general descriptive names, registered names, trademarks, service marks, etc. in this publication does not imply, even in the absence of a specific statement, that such names are exempt from the relevant protective laws and regulations and therefore free for general use.

The publisher, the authors, and the editors are safe to assume that the advice and information in this book are believed to be true and accurate at the date of publication. Neither the publisher nor the authors or the editors give a warranty, expressed or implied, with respect to the material contained herein or for any errors or omissions that may have been made. The publisher remains neutral with regard to jurisdictional claims in published maps and institutional affiliations.

This Palgrave Macmillan imprint is published by the registered company Springer Nature Switzerland AG.
The registered company address is: Gewerbestrasse 11, 6330 Cham, Switzerland

To all who have come before, and all those yet to

Acknowledgments

The journey of this book was helped, knowingly and unknowingly, by many along the way. To Nerea, I want to express gratitude from the bottom of my heart for your support, accompaniment, kind ears, and keen eyes. A big thank you to Shawn for your friendship over all these years and the sound boarding sessions for this book. A deep thank you to Wolfgang for his guidance, mentorship, and inspiration over this decade and a half; you have had a profound influence on my thinking and my life. Thank you to Nobert, Josefina, and many more in my extended peace family for your support and camaraderie. A deep thank you to Esthi for your love and support. All my love to my family Karen, Bruce, Patti, Judy, Dan, Laura, Ben, and Barrett. I would also like to thank Habiba and Arden, at 80,000 Hours, for helping me work out this book's initial idea and for feedback on the first draft.

Contents

1 Introduction   1
2 Foundations   5
3 At the Intersection of PCS and ERS   41
4 Great Powers Conflict   63
5 Peace, Pandemics, and Conflict   85
6 Climate Change Peace and Conflict   109
7 Emerging Technologies, Risk, Peace, and Conflict   139
8 Totalitarianism Risk and Peace   191
9 Conclusion   205

Index   211

CHAPTER 1

Introduction

> Some say the world will end in fire,
> Some say in ice.
> From what I've tasted of desire
> I hold with those who favor fire.
> But if it had to perish twice,
> I think I know enough of hate
> To say that for destruction ice
> Is also great
> And would suffice.
> (Frost, 1920)

I have thought about the end of the world for as long as I can remember. When I was young, a fear of death drove my fascination with the apocalypse. For me, the tragedy of death, myself or my loved one, was that we must go on without the other. The idea of the end of the world held freedom from fear because there would be nothing nor no one to miss or to be missed. Over time I began to study how the world may end. My namesake, Noah, is known for saving life from a prototypical antediluvian existential risk.

Robert Frost's poem "Fire and Ice" was the first poem I memorized in school. The poem introduces two classical Greek elements; the first, fire, often used to symbolize power, action, and the gift Prometheus stole, here is equated to a fate through the consumption by desire. No doubt, in part, an echo of the moment of its writing, one year after the end of World War I. The second element, water in the form of ice, and the image of a frozen apocalypse, is anecdotally inspired by a conversation with the astronomer Harlow Shapley about the universe's ultimate fate. For Frost, influenced by Dante's *Inferno*, the destructive force of ice equates to hatred. Heraclitus, the weeping philosopher, understood the soul as a mixture of fire and water. For Frost, the world's fate sits between a fiery apocalypse spurned by desire and a frozen wasteland resulting from hate.

The spirit of this book is based upon the ultimate end of humankind, our role in determining that fate, and what that means in the present moment.

Many years after I memorized that poem I went into studying, and later practicing, Peace and Conflict Studies (PCS). It seemed a useful tool to understand and try to overcome the roots of one of our tendencies as species: destroying each other. PCS is concerned with understanding the causes and impacts of violence, how conflicts can be transformed, and how humans can relate to each other and the world in a way that allows the unfolding of potential. Coming back to Frost's poem, PCS is a discipline seeking to transform hate. But, what about desire? What about fate? Where is the fire? This is where Existential Risk Studies (ERS) came into place. While the essence of PCS is how we relate to each other, ERS is concerned with our medium, long, and very long-term future: the possibilities of humanity, the chances that we will not make it.

As I dived deeper into this recently developed discipline, the fact that there were points of convergence between PCS and ERS that were not being explored became increasingly clear. PCS and ERS have similar roots, aims, and ethos. Both fields are, in a way, a reaction to destruction in the past and concern for the future. However, both disciplines have not been in dialogue with each other; as often happens in academia, they develop in silos, unaware of each other. In this book I aim to reveal ways of thinking of risks to our existence together with Peace and Conflict Studies. I hope that bringing together these two fields contributes to understanding how our future can be shaped, peaceful, and long.

I wrote this book amidst the COVID-19 pandemic, worsening climate change, a new war in Europe, and the ever-present specter of nuclear war. At the outset, it feels no leap of the imagination to posit that peace and human survival are interlinked. Further, it is no longer radical to posit that we are not prepared for the worst that can happen.

This book explores the topic of peace and the long-term survival of the human species. The departure point for this text is that both fields could benefit from each other. PCS would benefit from the future emphasis that comes from ERS, while ERS could benefit from the relational focus of PCS. To this end, this text draws from the field of ERS, which has been developed precisely to find ways of envisioning humanity's long-term future, possible threats to human survival, and methods for addressing those risks. This text lays out a theoretical framework for drawing on perspectives from ERS to contribute new ways of thinking about the future of peace research. Experts in PCS need to be involved in discussions regarding the future. PCS offers perspectives that will be complementary to better decision-making on issues that will affect the future.

I begin with a brief history of both fields focusing on the historical contexts in which they developed. I then summarize the current state of the art in both fields and engage with critical philosophical questions at the intersection between PCS and ERS. The second question examines the intersection between these two fields focusing on each field's understanding of time, prioritization, and values.

With the overall frame of the discussion established, I make the case for five research topics in PCS that are both current topics of concern yet require a substantial understanding of existential risks and frameworks for looking toward the future. Each of these topics is defined and discussed. Current perspectives on these issues in PCS are outlined, how they are understood in ERS, and what approaches would be beneficial to adapt and integrate into PCS. Each section concludes with a reflection on what questions may be relevant for developing a body of research at this intersection between these two fields. The book concludes with a discussion of PCS and long-term thinking in the context of threats to existence.

This book adds new ways of thinking to discussions about the future. When considering the long-term future, the question needs to be asked, "how do we still relate to each other in the here and now?" I often imagine that last being at the edge of the last black hole as the final star goes dark and wonder what their reflections would be. I position this book between the present moment and the long-term future in what Elise Boulding, one of the early founders of PCS, called the "long-present," which invokes the idea of any of us living mid-history, at the intersection of the lives preceding us, and those that will precede from us. In this book, I build an epistemological bridge between how to think about threats to the future and how to peace in every single present without contradiction.

In 1925 (five years after Frost's "Fire and Ice"), T.S. Eliot wrote "The Hollow Men." The poem also has an apocalyptic tone. The narrator describes himself as being one of the hollow men, those empty people living in a desolate and broken world, neither living nor dead. His image echoes the horrors of that World War I and prophecies: "This is the way the world ends / Not with a bang but a whimper" (128). Written 20 years before the first nuclear bomb was dropped, I wonder if he would have still placed his bets on "whimper."

References

Eliot, T. S. 1925. Eliot's Poems: 1909–1925. London: Faber & Faber.
Frost, Robert. 1920. "A Group of Poems by Robert Frost." Harper's Magazine, December.

CHAPTER 2

Foundations

PEACE AND CONFLICT STUDIES

Ancient Concerns, Modern Discipline

Peace and Conflict Studies (PCS) and Existential Risk Studies (ERS) are both simultaneously old and new. Concerns about war, peace, and survival are as old as human civilization and, at the same time, have only recently crystallized into distinct fields of research and practice. The history of humanity is often told as the history of conflicts. For example, both the *Mahābhārata* and Thucydides' *History of the Peloponnesian War* were written centuries ago to address the above-mentioned concerns and still have contemporary religious and political influence.

PCS does not have a single definition; there are many camps with different emphases and perspectives. Broadly speaking, these different focuses are security and conflict management, conflict resolution, conflict transformation, applied, and transdisciplinary approaches. What connect these different camps are efforts to understand conflict, violence, and peace. Specifically, PCS examines the causes, dynamics, and effects of different types of conflict and what factors and processes contribute to peace and reduce violence and suffering. In its transdisciplinary nature, PCS draws from Political Science, Philosophy, International Relations (IR), Sociology, Anthropology, Psychology, Religious Studies, Contemplative Traditions,

Peace Movements, and our collective history of conflicts and experiences of peace.

The beginning of Peace and Conflict Studies as an academic field is placed at different moments in history by scholars: the founding of the first Peace Studies Program in 1948 at Manchester College in Indiana (Harris et al. 1998); the work of Johan Galtung who is the founder of Peace Research Institute Oslo (PRIO) in 1959 and the *Journal of Peace Research* in 1964 and his popularization of many foundational ideas in the field such as positive and negative peace, peace research, and structural and cultural violence (Galtung and Fischer 2013a); or the work of Adam Curle and the establishment of the Department of Peace Studies at the University of Bradford in the UK in 1974 (Woodhouse 2010). While these are important moments in the history of the field, rather than definitive founding moments they represent moments in a longer story. Many scholars and practitioners have built the field of PCS. It has been shaped by the movements of history, resulting in an ongoing synthesis of different streams of thought.

The emergence of PCS has its roots in disillusionment with previous ways of understanding conflict and approaches to building peace during World Wars I and II. The Treaty of Versailles marked the end of the World War I at the beginning of the twentieth century. A consensus emerged that new ways of thinking needed to be developed and supported by the founding of institutions to scientifically study the causes of war and how it could be prevented in the future. This resulted in the development of the field of International Relations (IR) to guide newly formed institutions, such as the League of Nations in 1920, the American Institute of International Affairs (later the Council of Foreign Relations), and the British Institute of International Affairs (later the Institute of International Affairs), both in 1922. The aim of the field of IR and the mission of these institutions was to apply a scientific approach to understanding relationships between countries at a global level to prevent another world war. World War I was seen as an aberration in an otherwise peaceful system. It was believed that future global conflicts could be prevented by understanding and managing the relationships between nation-states as they were seen as the primary actors in conflicts and have a monopoly on the use of force (Dietrich 2012). At this time the field of IR was shaped by the competing perspectives of Realism and Idealism. Both voices argued for ways of understanding the world that were not based on religious faith but rather on philosophical assumptions about the nature of humankind, society, and the state.

Despite the lofty aims of trying to understand conflict to prevent another global war, World War II erupted just 21 years later. The failure of the League of Nations to prevent the invasion of Manchuria (1931) and World War II (1939–1945) cast doubt on the ability of theories of International Relations to prevent war. These failures can be understood as the beginning of the disillusionment that arose after World War II. The horrors of the Nazi concentration camps, Soviet gulags, and the use of nuclear weapons fractured the faith in previous ways of understanding conflicts and their ability to deliver on the promise of peace.

The development and use of nuclear weapons were influential factors in the emergence of PCS. The destruction wrought on Hiroshima and Nagasaki became, to many, a symbol of the inevitable conclusion of devotion to modern thinking and the destructive potential that technology could bring, and the mistrust of the systems of governance that wield that power. Further, the voices of those in the scientific community concerned with these developments became an important force in the development of PCS throughout the 1940s–1950s. These voices came together in the Russell-Einstein Manifesto, which is regarded as the "impulse document for peace studies as a discipline" (Dietrich 2012, 181). This manifesto, authored by Bertrand Russell, Albert Einstein, and nine other scientists,[1] warns of the disastrous potential ramifications of the use of Hydrogen Bombs and calls for humanity to decide against armed conflict. It was published in July of 1955 at the beginning of the nuclear arms race and was a radical call for nuclear disarmament on all sides.

The Russell-Einstein Manifesto gave rise to the Pugwash movement beginning in 1957, with many of the signatories to the Russell-Einstein Manifesto becoming prominent Pugwashites. The creation of the Pugwash movement was also supported by the newly formed Bulletin of Atomic Scientists (the Bulletin), whose co-founders include scientists who worked on the Manhattan Project: J. Robert Oppenheimer, Leo Szilard, and Hans Bethe. The Bulletin is a nonprofit organization that seeks to educate fellow scientists about atomic weapons, especially the connections between their scientific work and national and international politics. An additional aim of the Bulletin is to educate US citizens about the potential risks

---

[1] Max Born, Percy Bridgman, Leopold Infeld, Frédéric Joliot-Curie, Hermann Muller, Linus Pauling, Cecil Powell, Joseph Rotblat, and Hideki Yukawa.

posed by nuclear energy in its application to warfare. They are also the keepers of the Doomsday Clock, an artistic metaphor for the dangers and urgency posed by manmade threats to humanity.

Since its creation, the Pugwash movement has become a series of international conferences and workshops. In these spaces, scientists come together to discuss questions of global security, armed conflict, nuclear weapons, and other weapons of mass destruction and the responsibility of those working in the sciences with regard to working for war or peace. Some of the most noteworthy accomplishments of this movement were the nuclear test ban in 1963, the Nuclear Non-Proliferation Treaty in 1968, the Anti-Ballistic Missile Treaty of 1972, and the ban on chemical and nuclear weapons in 1972 (Kraft et al. 2018). In 1995 the Pugwash movement was awarded the Nobel Peace Prize to commemorate these accomplishments (Nobel Prize Outreach 2022).

From these initial foundations, the field of Conflict Resolution began in earnest at the height of the Cold War between 1950 and 1960. People came together from different disciplines concerned about escalating geopolitical tensions, the nuclear arms race, and the specter that war between superpowers could threaten human survival. These pioneers recognized a common vision in developing rigorous and scientifically grounded approaches to studying conflict. Early systems theories by Ludwig von Bertalanffy, Anatol Rapoport, Ralph Gerard, Kenneth Boulding, and Elise Boulding brought cross-disciplinary perspectives and methods to the field of Peace Studies as it developed in the USA. The multidimensional approaches developed from their early work were built on a radically different starting point than previous ways of understanding conflict. Their approach was based on the observation that the vast majority of all social conflict occurs nonviolently and that the minority of human activity is related to war. From this perspective, researching peace requires an understanding built from peace rather than conflict, war, or violence (Dietrich 2012).

In the 1980s, the Harvard Negotiation Project popularized, particularly through Fisher and Ury's *Getting to Yes* (1981), many of the principles of negotiation and mediation, such as separating people from problems and distinguishing between interests and positions. These approaches shaped interventions in the struggle to end Apartheid in South Africa, developing problem-solving workshops to support peace processes in the Middle East and taking community-oriented approaches to resolving conflict in Northern Ireland. Additionally, many development and humanitarian agencies, particularly in Africa and Southeast Asia, began to focus on understanding conflict and mainstream Conflict Resolution as an essential component of their activities (Ramsbotham et al. 2016).

Another important development in PCS was the UN Security General Boutros Boutros-Ghali's "An Agenda for Peace: Preventative Diplomacy, Peacemaking, and Peace-Keeping" (1992), which marked the changing nature of conflict in the global political system at the end of the Cold War. The inception of the Agenda for Peace was a request made by the UN Security Council for an analysis of and recommendations for strengthening the practices of peacemaking and peacekeeping in light of these political changes and of recent failures that had made the flaws in peacekeeping practices increasingly visible. The Agenda for Peace outlines how the UN should respond to conflicts in the new post-Cold War era. Among the key points of the document was the establishment of methods of preventive diplomacy that could be used before or during peacekeeping operations. It also defined and differentiated between peacemaking and peacekeeping. Further, it introduced and defined the concept of "post-conflict peacebuilding."

Conflict Management, Conflict Resolution, and Conflict Transformation

The field of PCS is often subdivided into different approaches of Conflict Management, Conflict Resolution, and Conflict Transformation. Even though these perspectives have developed over time, they should not be understood as a linear development or mutually exclusive perspectives. These approaches can be differentiated by their answers to five foundational questions.

Human nature: *What is the view of human nature at the core of this approach? Are humans inherently violent or peaceful, or is our nature ambivalent?*

The nature of conflict: *What is conflict, why does it happen, and what function does it serve?*

The primary actor: *According to this perspective, who is the ideal actor to work in conflicts?*

Method of peace work: *What is the main approach for working on conflict from this perspective?*

The goal of peace work: *From this perspective, what is the overall aim of peace work?*

Conflict Management approaches are built on the assumption that conflict is inherent in human nature and cannot be avoided, and thus, the most logical approach for working with conflict is to try to prevent or manage it. Peace work, in this understanding, is left to those actors (usually nation-states) powerful enough to manage other parties' conflict.

Conflict Resolution approaches take an ambiguous view of human nature where we are neither inherently prone to violence nor peace. They posit instead that conflicts arise through a lack of understanding and communication. This approach involves skilled neutral mediators who engage with conflicting parties to come to an official resolution to the "problem" of conflict through a better understanding of themselves and a clearer ability to communicate with the other.

Conflict Transformation starts from the same ambiguous view of human nature and takes a different view of the nature of conflict, which is understood to be a fundamental driver of transformation and change. Conflicts occur at all levels, from the individual to the global, and result from the relational dynamics among those involved in the conflict. Thus, the task of the peace worker is to operate as a facilitator, seeking to guide transformational processes in the relationships present in the conflict to reduce violence and build peace.

Approaches to Conflict Transformation are further subdivided into prescriptive and elicitive approaches. These terms refer to "ideal types" of approaches, and in real life, a pure version of either is likely not to exist. In a prescriptive approach, a peace worker, here imagined in the role of a trainer, is understood as an expert, and the training event is conceptualized around the transmission of their specialized knowledge and experience to the participants. The goal of the encounter is the mastery of a piece of knowledge, or a set of skills, where the participants try to emulate the expert's work. The concept of Elicitive Conflict Transformation was introduced into PCS in the 1990s to expand approaches to the understanding of the dynamics of peace and conflict. This approach seeks to draw out, or elicit, existing knowledge about how conflicts are addressed by a specific group of people in a specific time and place. This approach then facilitates the catalyzation of these existing practices of dealing with conflict to guide a transformation process between individuals, groups, and communities. In an elicitive approach, the peace worker is understood as a process facilitator, rather than an expert trainer. The process is aimed at the discovery, creation, and rarefication of models of understanding that come from the participants in the encounter, who are seen as vital resources for grounded contextual knowledge. The facilitator functions as a catalyst, holding and guiding the process whereby those involved determine the outcomes (Lederach 2015).

With changes in the understanding of peace work, there have been subsequent changes in how timescales are viewed when working for peace. Conflict Management approaches have the narrowest timescale, focusing on discrete episodes of conflict and developing power-based strategies to reach a formal agreement. Conflict Resolution approaches expand the temporal view by seeking to understand the deeper root causes of the conflict, and come to solutions that build a more sustainable peace. Conflict Transformation approaches paradoxically hold both the narrowest and the farthest-reaching view of time, integrating a multigenerational perspective on approaches to transforming systems of relationships with the importance of a focus on the present moment with the people in the room. Peace scholar, John Paul Lederach, calls this balancing act the 200-year present (Lederach 2005).

Many forces have continued to shape the field of Peace and Conflict Studies. Globalization has had a host of influences including increasing access to information on conflicts around the world, the expansion of identities that reach further than they have before while at the same time contributing in some cases to more localized identities. Shifts in the geopolitical order, particularly by the USA which has come to think of itself as the leader in a monopolar world, have had a significant impact on International Relations. The nature of war has shifted from warfare between professional militaries of nation-states to hybrid wars fought with a mixture of state and nonstate forces. These wars are often fought for goals that are different from the past, with more attention to identity issues over ideology (Kaldor 2012).

Defining Peace and Conflict Studies

A precise definition of Peace and Conflict Studies is difficult to articulate beyond the tautological "peace and conflict studies" is the "study of peace and conflict." Nonetheless, there are some core definitional criteria for the field. A critical analysis of the key terms of peace, conflict, and violence has been deemed appropriate and necessary. As the field has developed, many voices have been brought into this discussion, adding further depth and nuance. Whatever is meant by peace is an incomplete understanding if it is defined only as the absence of violence (Galtung and Fisher 2013b). The conditions that need to be present for there to be peace are at the heart of the field.

Some generally agreed-upon characteristics can describe the field: PCS has roots in a postmodern field of study fueled by disillusionment with the grand explanatory narrative. The field tends to cast a critical eye on how peace and conflict issues are understood. PCS is transdisciplinary, drawing from and transcending the disciplinary boundaries of many fields (Political Science, International Relations, Philosophy, Sociology, Anthropology, Psychology, Religious Studies, peace movements, our collective history of conflicts, and experiences of peace). It is also multilevel in that while International Relations had an explicit focus on elite-level actors, governments, and militaries and sought to find strategies to prevent war at the nation-state level, PCS took an expanded view on who can work to prevent violence and build peace. PCS is multicultural. While a clear influence of particular cultures and places shaped its origins as a field, as it has grown and developed, increasing attention has been placed on bringing experiences from different cultures, religions, ethnicities, sexes, genders, and sexual orientations into its theory and methodology. The field is analytical, seeking to utilize various methods and frames to understand the nature and dynamics of peace, conflict, and violence. PCS is also a normative discipline. Similar to medicine, few doctors would think of themselves as neutral. They are on the side of the patient seeking a particular outcome. PCS maintains a clear bias toward reducing violence and increasing peace. Finally, PCS emphasizes the linkage between theory and practice. Effective peace work and research depend on each other for their validity. The efficacy of peace work is important because the subjects of research are the lives of people.

State of the Art

The state of the art in PCS is growing and changing. There are a few key trends that define PCS that are particularly relevant to the topic of the long-term survival of humanity and peace. The early history of PCS as a defined field of inquiry was characterized by disillusionment with previous approaches to dealing with the problem of conflict. The further development of this field has followed this essential motivation, taking what has been learned through successes and failures, and going beyond the confines of previous approaches. At the same time, the changing nature of violent conflict has also necessitated changes in theory and practice. One set of interpretations traces the development of peace thinking through the "Liberal Peace" and posits different ideas for what comes next.

Here liberal peace refers to an understanding of peacebuilding that emerged after the end of the Cold War. It focuses on the importance of "external interventions that are intended to reduce the risk that a State will erupt into or return to war" (Barnett et al. 2007, 37). There is a consensus that this type of liberal peacebuilding rests on the principles of democratization and the liberalization of markets (O.P. Richmond 2011, 2015). A precondition for sustainable peace is that a wide range of social, economic, and institutional reforms must be put in place to support these principles and ensure the presence of a strong system of democratic politics. This understanding and approach to peace have shown their limitations, and much of the research in contemporary PCS is attempts to go beyond this initial understanding. What lies beyond a liberal peace has variously been termed "Post-liberal Peace" (O.P. Richmond 2011, Richmond and Mitchell 2012), "Hybrid Peace" (O.P. Richmond 2015; Mac Ginty and Richmond 2015), "Everyday Peace" (Mac Ginty 2014, 2021), and "Transrational Peace" (Dietrich 2012, 2013, 2017, 2021). Within these different conceptions are key themes of complexity (de Coning 2016, 2018; von Bertalanffy 1972), systems thinking (CDA 2016; Gallo 2012; Ropers 2008), and resilience (de Coning 2016, 2018; Cote and Nightingale 2011).

The term "hybrid peace" has been used to describe a Post-liberal Peace and refers to the complex and multileveled dynamics of peace that straddles the local to the international. A hybrid piece is observed at the in-betweens, at the intersections of local understandings and practices of peace and the national and international norms that guide and govern international relations and development. These kinds of peace first emerge in the tension of the opposition between the local and the international until some kind of accommodation and, at least, a tacit agreement is reached that this kind of peace and those actors who work toward building and maintaining it have legitimacy at both local and international levels (O.P. Richmond 2015; Mac Ginty 2014). Attempts at moving toward this kind of hybridity are found in the Agenda for Peace, the Millennium Development Goals, and the Responsibility to Protect doctrine.

The concept of "Everyday Peace" is one of these hybrid turns which focuses peace research on the everyday practices that individuals and groups use to navigate their dynamics when society is deeply divided. The rationale for coining the term is to designate a more human-focused and vernacular approach to understanding experiences of peace and conflict. Examples of these practices of everyday peace range from coping mechanisms, such as avoiding hot topics in mixed company, concealing identities, rituals of politeness, concern with ascertaining the social identifications of others, to deferring blame to those outside of the context. This everyday peace is the bottom-up organizations of local agency in conflict-affected societies that are mechanisms and practices that address grievance, conflict, and difference in ways that allow communities to live together. Though, at first glance, this conception of peace may seem to be conflict avoidance by a different name, these strategies often overlap into a complex system that is aimed at survival through minimizing risk while potentially building the ground and necessary calm for gradually working on the differences that have led to the conflict (Mac Ginty 2014).

Another future development in PCS follows a different line in understanding peace that does not follow through a progression from "liberal" to "post-liberal." The "transrational approach" developed by Wolfgang Dietrich in his "Many Peaces Tetralogy"[2] takes a different history and vision of peace. Dietrich identifies his approach as "Transrational Peace Philosophy." This perspective's origin is two-fold. An understanding of peace requires a perceiving subject to have meaning. It thus is more accurate to describe peace in the plural, as "peaces" than as a single "peace." Even though this can, and does, on one level, suggest that there are as many interpretations of peace as perceiving subjects, it is possible to group understandings of peace into general categories. These categories he describes as "peace families," denoting the fuzzy delineations between different groups of interpretations of peace. This type of categorization also suggests that although these different families have developed over time, one should not read it in an evolutionary sense where one perspective excludes the other. These peace families are the energetic, moral, modern, postmodern, and transrational (Dietrich 2012, 2013).

The energetic peace family comprises immanent understandings of peace rooted in the human perception of dualities: hot and cold, dark and

---

[2] Dietrich, Wolfgang. 2012. *Interpretations of Peace in History and Culture*. New York: Palgrave Macmillan.

—. 2013. *Elicitive Conflict Transformation and the Transrational Shift in Peace Politics*. New York: Palgrave Macmillan.

—. 2017. *Elicitive Conflict Mapping*. New York: Palgrave Macmillan

—. 2021. *Der die das Frieden. Nachbemerkung zur Trilogie über die vielen Frieden*. Wiesbaden: Springer VS.

light, wet and dry. The core value of this understanding of peace is the striving to unite these dualities, not into a final state but a balance of homeostatic equilibrium. Energetic peace is peace out of harmony (Dietrich 2012, 2013).

The moral peace family begins with the same perception of duality but draws different conclusions by positing an ultimate transcendent point outside the experience of imminence. Since this point is situated outside the world of experience, it becomes the referent for ethical rulings and the establishment of norms. Here peace becomes a gift given to the good by a creator God. Moral peace is peace out of justice (Dietrich 2012, 2013).

The modern peace family is structurally similar to the moral. The norms that govern human relations are interpreted through a transcendental referent point, but this point becomes a secular one. God is replaced by Reason, and the world is reduced to the material and understood as mechanical. Visions of a utopia on earth replace the promise of a paradise in the afterlife if we are just rational enough. Since this view of the world only validates what can be seen, held, and measured, those same valuable things can be taken away. This becomes a call for defense, and the modern understanding of peace becomes peace through security (Dietrich 2012, 2013).

These modern peaces are those that lost their draw after the horrors of World War II had revealed what unbridled devotion to rational progress could bring. This wounding of the story that was once held to be true resulted in disillusionment and disenchantment with all grand narratives that claimed explanatory power on who we are as a people, where we are going, and how we should get there. With this collapse of the orienting narratives, the question of truth, or rather truths, became paramount in the postmodern peace family (Dietrich 2012, 2013).

The transrational peace family is named because this perceptive acknowledges that human beings possess rational faculties but that we are so much more than those. The term "transrational" is used because this perceptive applies the rationality of modern science, while, at the same time, transgressing its limits to embrace the entire sphere of human nature and experience. A transrational perspective of peace integrates subjective experiences of harmony, behavioral understanding of security, cultural considerations of truth, and social perceptions of justice. These four elements do not constitute discreet parts of an overarching singular understanding of a transrational peace but rather a dynamic and contextualized peace. As a research practice, a transrational approach focuses on encounters, relationships, and communication styles—understanding humans as "contact boundaries at work" (Dietrich 2012, 2013, 2017).

As understandings of peace and conflict have developed, complexity has become a central component in describing the dynamics of conflict and, in response, systems thinking and resilience as two concepts to guide the development of conflict transformation and peacebuilding initiatives.

Complexity here refers to a few key qualities of a system. The first is the existence of emergent properties that are qualitative of a system that is only made manifest at certain thresholds of complexity. This implies that a system cannot be best understood in a reductionist manner, where the complex system is reduced to the sum of its parts, but rather that a system needs to be understood as more than the sum of its parts. The second quality of a complex system pertaining to peace and conflict is the functioning of non-linear dynamics. The system components do not necessarily have a direct relationship to each other, but rather, interact in complex modulated forms of feedback. Finally, all systems have an inherent tendency to seek a homeostatic equilibrium. In a conflict system, this often shows up as a form of self-organization where the complex system itself seeks to regulate itself without an outside agent inputting energy into the system (de Coning 2016).

As a result of recognizing complexity as a core element of conflict, systems thinking has become an increasingly vital tool in peace research and practice. This development is related to several reasons. First, both conflicts and the actors responsible for addressing them have become increasingly more complex. Second, advancements in peace theory and conflict analysis have shown that the dynamics of conflict are more complex than previously thought. And finally, the understanding of what the overall goal is for working with conflict has evolved from signing a peace agreement to solving the root problems, to working on building relationships that foster a more sustainable peace.

Systems thinking, briefly stated, is a perspective that came about as a reaction to prevailing tendencies in scientific thinking, which focused on deconstructing complex wholes in order to better understand them through their parts. Instead, a systems perspective argues that, especially for complex phenomena, it is equally if not more important to focus on the whole system as the whole is more than the sum of its parts. A systems perspective focuses on understanding complex networks of relationships and the dynamics of feedback loops within a system. This perspective also includes an expanded view of time, recognizing that the complexities of a system are dynamics, and their effects are seen on different timescales. It also recognizes that systems are often characterized by complex, rather than linear, relationships between cause and effect, and overall emergent phenomena are unique to different levels of complexity within the system. Lastly, a system perspective also recognizes that it is perspective-dependent, and thus it is a map that will never be the territory (Ropers 2008).

The advantage of incorporating a systems perspective in peace research and practice is that it provides an increased ability to grasp the complexity of the system of interest. In particular, this kind of perspective helps shed light on the deeper dynamics of conflict intractability and provides an approach for understanding the difficulties encountered by peace processes. A systems perspective offers flexibility and creativity as a tool for conflict analysis and intervention design. In most cases, the ability of any peacebuilding or conflict transformation organization to change an actor or organization in a conflict is extremely unlikely. However, by shifting the perspective from actors to relationships, a systems approach can highlight which relationship, if focused on, stands the best chance of producing the desired change in the system. Further, an asset of a systems approach is that it is not possible to be working on a system of conflict and not be part of it; this helps to situate the individual or the organization into the system they are working on, often assisting in revealing implicit assumptions and moving implicit understanding to explicit knowledge (Coleman 2006; CDA Collaborative Learning Projects 2016).

The use of complexity theory and systems thinking in PCS has highlighted the importance of the concept of resilience. Though the concept has existed for a long time in different fields, it has recently become an important topic for academics and practitioners, especially to imagine peace work beyond the failings of liberal peace (Juncos and Joseph 2020). A resilience approach to peacebuilding and conflict transformation can have several interrelated meanings. At its basic level, drawing from understandings of resilience from ecology, it can be understood as "the capacity of a system to absorb disturbance and reorganize while changing to still retain essentially the same function, structure, identity, and feedback" (Walker et al. 2004). When adapted to PCS, resilience can be understood as the capacity to recover from, or diminish, the effects of violent shocks and stressors on the system to maintain an overall state of peace (van Metre and Calder 2016). More specifically, concerning Conflict Transformation and Peacebuilding approaches, resilience can be understood as a group's capacity to transform conflictive relationships into sources of change, growth, and adaptation, rather than let the conflicts manifest as violent episodes. This capacity can be referenced at the horizontal level, that is, between individuals and groups, and on the vertical level between the people and the state.

Applying systems thinking and complexity theory to conflicts has led to an increased focus on resilience in peace research. Resiliency is the emergent and self-organized capacity for complex systems to balance, adapt, and evolve after a disruption. A systems perspective is necessary to see how resiliency arises, not due to any specific component of the system, but as a result of the system as a whole (Capra 1983). A resilient system is more likely to handle acute shocks to the system and prolonged stresses. The fragility of a system can be understood as a lack of sufficient resiliency in the system (de Coning 2016). When considered in the context of a violent conflict, a resilient society is one where the quality of the relational dynamics, meaning-making systems, and economic and political institutions can maintain a dynamic equilibrium of harmony, truth, justice, and security to ensure the disruptions from the violent episodes can be absorbed, sustained, and transformed with integrity and coherence.

A focus on resilience can be a challenge to liberal peacebuilding perspectives. If a social system is considered in its complexity, it cannot be approached in the rather mechanist view of many peacebuilding approaches where international actors come from outside the system to build peace from above. If sustainable peace is understood in terms of resiliency, then an appropriate peacebuilding approach would seek to facilitate the capacity of a society to self-organize and adapt to a high enough degree to transform the shocks and adapt to the stressors.

Already some of the paradoxes in PCS have started to emerge. If everything is connected in a complex set of relationships, where is the line drawn between the local and the international? Even if this line is disambiguated, how can international actors outside of a conflict do anything to help contribute to peace in another place? Especially because one could take a systems-complexity view on resiliency to mean that any external interference could be detrimental to the emergence of the self-organizing capacity of the system to adapt. If this is the case, then is it best to do nothing? How to approach these questions and their underlying tensions are at the vanguard of the current state of the art in peacebuilding and conflict transformation and has direct links with the field of existential risk.

"Adaptive Peacebuilding" has been proposed as an approach to working toward peace from a perspective informed by "complexity, resilience and local ownership" (de Coning 2018, 5). In this way of thinking, if complex systems cope with changes in the environment by evolving in tandem with it, so too, then should peace theory and practice. The core frame of application should of process facilitation, similar to Elicitive Conflict Transformation. In a peacebuilding context, a Theory of Change needs to be made explicit in a partnership between external actors and local stakeholders, laying out a hypothesis of which series of actions are likely to lead to the desired outcome. These interventions are monitored and evaluated, both about their intended and unintended consequences. After a given time, those affected by the programs and those who designed the interventions decide together which ones should continue, allowing for a type of natural selection process. The learning results then need to be disseminated as broadly as possible within the system, so other initiatives can integrate this information into their theory-planning-action-reflection cycle. The external actors then use the finding to frame the processes that they facilitate in ways that foster the capacity for self-organization and thus the strengthening of resilience (de Coning 2018).

Concerns about peace and conflict are ancient. The academic study of the causes and dynamics of conflict and the nature and conditions of peace is new. Born from a fusion of our collective experiences of peace and conflict with the specific historical context of the end of World War II, the field of Peace and Conflict Studies emerged. It holds a set of overlapping objectives: to explore different understandings of what peace is or could be, to learn from previous conflicts and all the moments where violence did not happen, and to envision new ways of relating to each other. At its core, PCS is about how the energetic potential in conflicts can be transformed into an engine for change rather than a source of violence.

EXISTENTIAL RISK STUDIES

The understanding of the concept of risk has changed over time. As a concept, risk is likely traced back to prehistoric times and was thought of in terms of danger. To frame the discussion of the field of Existential Risk Studies, I will first touch on the development of the notion of risk as it is currently used in English. From there, I will highlight some of the historical shifts that were necessary for the idea of humanity's extinction to emerge. I will then discuss a brief history of ERS.

The contemporary understanding of the concept of risk dates back roughly a thousand years. Dr. Karla Mallette, a professor of Italian and

Mediterranean Studies at the University of Michigan, traces, in her article "How 12th-Century Genoese Merchants Invented the Idea of Risk" (2021), the origin of the concept of "risk" in Western Europe through its Latin cognate *resicum* to the twelfth century. The term referred to the Mediterranean practice of splitting the profits between ship captains and investors at the end of a successful shipping journey. It was necessary because the law forbade usury, so the *resicum* was considered a bonus paid to investors. Historians believe that *resicum* is derived from a much older Arabic word *al-rizq*, a Quranic Arabic word that refers to god's provision for creation. In its contemporary English usages, risk, both as a noun and as a verb, carries connotations of the possibility of loss, danger, or injury (Oxford University 2010; Merriam-Webster 2016)

Contemporary usage of the term "risk" has often been used to help estimate the probability of loss in a given venture or in reference to safety when assessing the probability of danger. When the qualifier "existential" is included in the concept of risk, it draws on those elements of "loss, danger, or injury." It scales those concerns to the level of existence itself. In the field of Existential Risk Studies (ERS), existential risks are those that "threaten the destruction of humanity's long-term potential" (Ord 2020, 6) or "threaten the extinction of intelligent life on earth" (Bostrom 2013, 15). Global catastrophic risks is a closely related concept referring to those risks that "have the potential to inflict serious damage to human well-being on a global scale" (Bostrom and Ćirković 2011, 1). These risks, despite being severe, do not necessarily threaten all human existence. Put differently, all existential risks are global catastrophic risks, but not all global catastrophic risks are existential risks. The nuances in these distinctions and their importance in studying these risks will be discussed in this chapter.

The systematic study of these risks is a new academic field, and the precise terminology has not yet been standardized. This book will follow the convention used by Simon Beard and Phil Torres (2020) of using the term "Existential Risk Studies" (ERS) as an umbrella term covering topics of existential risks and global catastrophic risks, as well as the research that focuses on understanding the nature and dynamics of these risks (Existential Risk Research) as well as the research on what can be done about these risks (Existential Risk Mitigation) (2).

Humanity's Destruction—Thinking About the End

Concerns about the ultimate fate of the world and humanity are both an ancient concern and a newly crystalizing field of study. Eschatology, derived from the Greek *eschatos* meaning the "study of the final end of things, the ultimate resolution of the entire creation" (Walls 2008, 4), has long been the domain of religious speculation and finds its expression in many of humanity's oldest stories. Stories of past endings pervade mythology and religious texts. The preponderance of flood myths across the world points to this fact. Stories from the Hebrew texts of Noah, the Sumerian Ziusudra, the Greek Deucalion, and the Indian Manu all tell a similar tale—the world has become corrupt; therefore, a great flood comes to end the world, to literally wash it away and mark the beginning of a new, better world (Dundes 1988).

Another end story is found in the *Vaishnavite* Hindu tradition where time is cyclical and divided into four *yugas*. A complete set of yugas spans approximately 4.32 billion years. As the cycle of time progresses through the yugas, there is a marked decline in the goodness of life. This decline progresses until the final and current *Kali Yuga*, where *Kalki*, the tenth and final avatar of the God Vishnu, comes into being (Dalal 2011). Seated on a white horse with a flaming sword, *Kalki* dissolves the remnants of the world, after which existence enters a phase of rest known as *pralaya*, after which the world is reborn into a golden age the cycle repeats (McFarland 2009; Dalal 2011).

The Book of Revelation in the Christian bible also depicts the end of times. It tells a narrative that begins with a warning to heed the author's words to survive the apocalypse. The book describes a vision of Jesus encouraging the faithful to continue to believe in him even when they are being persecuted. God then reveals that seven seals will be opened, and with each seal will come disasters—rivers of blood and plagues. Chaos continues to spread until a final judgment happens and the faithful will ascend into the kingdom of heaven (Resseguie 2020).

This fascination with "the end" continues today. Post-apocalyptic dystopia has its own genre of film. *The Hunger Games* (Ross 2012; Lawrence 2013, 2014, 2015), *The Matrix* (Wachowskis 1999, 2003a, b), *World War Z* (2013), *Mad Max: Fury Road* (Miller 2015), and *The Book of Eli* (Huges and Huges 2010) are movies that all are built upon apocalypse or post-apocalyptic themes and have grossed between $94.4 and $424.67 million each (IMDB 2016). The popularity of the apocalypse in the collective imagination may be a retelling of old myths in a new medium or may be a means by which fiction is used to process collective fears and insecurities about the present and the future. The apocalyptic narrative in film or print reassures the audience that there might still be meaning in the face of such a horrible proposition. The ongoing curiosity with "the end" indicates its importance in human thought.

It is worth noting that even though the notion of apocalypse seems to have perennially occupied our collective consciousness, in these tellings, the story does not end. Some "things" survive most of the "great flood" myths; the end of the *Kali Yuga* ushers in a rebirth of the universe, and a subsequent golden age, and monotheistic "final judgments" still purport a transcendental plane after the end of time. In Hollywood movies, the crisis is usually averted in some way by the hero. Even in the edgier domains of speculative and science fiction, the stories rarely end with the absolute extinction of earth-originating intelligent life. After all, such an ending would not be a compelling narrative because humans are the audience for this media. Considering the possible reality of our own extinction does seem to be relatively new.

Pondering the possibilities of human extinction, how it might happen, and what might be able to be done about it is the task of Existential Risk Studies (ERS). ERS takes a secular approach grounded in a scientific worldview and builds models on the laws of nature, observations of human behavior, and statistical probability. The "end" that is the subject of investigation ranges from complete extinction of the human species to a societal collapse on such a scale and magnitude that there would be no hope of getting anywhere back to where we once were.

The Emergence of Existential Risk Studies

The development of ERS shares some similarities with the origins of PCS. Both fields arose following scientific revelations that the existence of humanity could be threatened and, further, that it may be threatened by the ways in which humans act, organize, and govern themselves. Simon Beard and Phil Torres' article "Ripples on the Great Sea of Life: A Brief History of Existential Risk Studies" (2020) provides an overview of the development of ERS organized as developing through three interrelated waves of thought. The emergence of these waves was dependent upon a few essential precursors.

These antecedents illustrate that while the possibility of an apocalypse is not a new idea, the possibility of human extinction is. Beard and Torres argue that the general realization that humanity could become extinct required four main events. The first two of these events are connected to relatively recent scientific discoveries in the natural sciences and the acceptance of those findings. In 1815, the French Zoologist Georges Cuvier (1769–1832) published his *Essay on the Theory of the Earth* which helped to convince the scientific community that not only is it possible for species to go extinct, but it has happened many times throughout history (Cuvier 2009). The second of these discoveries was that humanity is, in fact, part of the natural order of the biological world. The acceptance of this idea was driven by the publication of Charles Darwin's, *On the Origin of Species* (Darwin 1859). At this point in history, acceptance was growing that humans are a species like any other and that species have and can become extinct. Added to these discoveries was the gradual secularization of thought beginning in the 1960s. Eschatology moved out from the sole purview of religious and theological discussions into other fields of study. Finally, witnessing the use of nuclear weapons and the knowledge in the 1980s that a nuclear winter may be possible and would pose a grave threat to humanity gave the scientific community a kill switch, a mechanism by which the extinction of humanity, by our own hands, is possible (Beard and Torres 2020).

Beard and Torres (2020) identify two driving forces that build upon these precursors and set the stage for the emergence of ERS. The first of these forces is speculative fiction, where some of the earliest thoughts about human extinction can be found. Authors such as Lord Byron (1788–1824), Mary Shelley (1797–1851), Jean-Baptiste Cousin de Grainville (1746–1805), Alexander Winchell (1824–1891), Jules Verne (1827–1905), and H.G. Wells (1866–1946) brought the notion of human extinction into the public imagination through their now well-known novels. The second force, and similar to the development of PCS, was the communities of concerned scientists that emerged after World War II, primarily in response to the use of nuclear weapons. Their concern found its most effective articulation in the already mentioned Russel-Einstein Manifesto of 1955 which led to the establishment of the Pugwash Conferences and their work on addressing weapons of mass destruction and other threats to the globe (Beard and Torres 2020).

The publication of Nick Bostrom's paper "Existential Risks: Analyzing Human Extinction Scenarios and Related Hazards" (2002) is often noted as the beginning of ERS as a field of study. Bostrom is a Professor of Philosophy at Oxford University and the founding Director of the Future of Humanity Institute. Bostrom's work set the stage for the first wave of ERS, defined by its dual philosophical foundations of Transhumanism and Utilitarianism. Transhumanism is the belief that humanity can, and should, evolve beyond its physical and mental limits through scientific and technological interventions (Bostrom 2008). Total Utilitarianism is a philosophical position that maintains that ethical acts are those that increase the total prosperity in the universe. This logic scales as the human population increases. The more people there are, the greater number of people can experience well-being. Estimates of how many potential future humans there could vary wildly due to the starting assumptions and definitions used in the calculation. If humanity remains as it currently is and stays on earth, Carl Sagan estimated that there could be upwards of 500 trillion future humans (Sagan 1983). If humans were to colonize the galaxy, Milan Ćirković estimates that the Virgo Supercluster would be able to support approximately 10^{10} future humans (2002). Bostrom (2003) extends these calculations further, estimating that if a posthuman state of being (e.g., in a simulation) is considered, then there could be upwards of 10^{38} future humans in our supercluster per century (Beard and Torres 2020).

This first-wave ERS has a teleological momentum toward a type of techno-utopia. This future utopia would be inhabited by beings that, very likely, would be quite unlike ourselves. Proponents of this wave of ERS placed the emphasis of their hope and faith in technology, particularly artificial intelligence, genetic engineering, and nanotechnology, to lead humanity into a type of posthuman state where the divisions between the physical, virtual, mechanical, and biologic blur.

This utopia is seen as our cosmic potential, and any failure to achieve it would doom countless future humans (biological or otherwise) to nonexistence. To this end, Bostrom coined a type of guiding principle, which became known as the "Maxipok rule," which states that one should "maximize the probability of an okay outcome, where an okay outcome is any outcome that avoids existential disaster" (Bostrom 2002, 8). This type of approach can be understood as "etiological," where the focus of the inquiry is on individual existential risks according to their cause. By drawing logical connections between an existential risk and its likely cause, scholars seek to determine interventions to mitigate the risk. This type of methodological approach is most effective if there are a small number of factors that would bring about the catastrophe that can progress in a more or less straightforward manner (Beard and Torres 2020).

The second generation of ERS built on this foundational work and incorporated many aspects of the Effective Altruism (EA) movement. With this integration of EA thinking, the importance of Transhumanism was less emphasized (Beard and Torres 2020). The question at the heart of the EA movement is how to do as much good as possible for the greatest number of people possible. This central ethos shapes the priority of the EA movement to an explicit focus on the long-term future. There are many more possible people in the future. Thus, if you want to maximize the total amount of good done for the most amount of people, then a focus on the long-term future is essential. In the EA logic, this long-term perspective has been neglected in efforts to do good in the world. When assessing how to do good in the world while reducing existential risk, a long-term time horizon implies that even small decreases in existential risks could save millions or billions of lives. This emphasis on looking to improve the long-term future has led to the second wave of ERS to eschew the narrow threat-based approaches in favor of broader strategies to reduce risk such as the reduction of poverty and improving education (Beard and Torres 2020).

Beard and Torres (2020) point toward a newly emerging third wave of ERS primarily defined by its movement away from analyzing risks based on their most direct cause (what they call the etiological approach) to an increased emphasis on ethical pluralism. In this expanded perspective on understanding existential risks, the larger systems of causes and contexts that lead to risks must be understood. This approach also places emphasis on increasing the number and diversity of viewpoints that help define and classify existential risks and devise methods for their study. The third-wave approaches generally favor a systems perspective that embraces the complex systems that give rise to existential risks as emergent phenomena and are subjected to systems of feedback loops. A systems perspective brings the importance of including vulnerabilities and exposures into the existential calculus of existential risks (Beard and Torres 2020).

By acknowledging and embracing complexity, third-wave approaches seek to shift attention to epistemically messy scenarios in which the links between cause and effect are not immediately obvious. This type of perspective is well-suited for addressing issues such as climate change and loss of biodiversity within the context of existential risks. Scholars following these approaches also have placed the importance on including discussions of medium-term risks in the ERS scholarship. Third-wave approaches also move away from utilitarian ethics. An existential catastrophe would be negative not because humanity would not fulfill its technological utopian destiny, as first-wave approaches hold dear, nor that the catastrophe would be detrimental because of the effects it would have on future not-yet-existing humans, as second-wave scholars hold, but rather it would be bad because of the immense amount of suffering it would cause to those humans who are currently alive (Beard and Torres 2020).

It is likely that these three phases often represent overlapping approaches to understanding and addressing existential risks, and each will continue to go grow and develop over time. The continued evolution of this line of thinking is demonstrated by the number of recently established research centers with high levels of funding, the growth of the Effective Altruism movement, and the number of scholars from different backgrounds who are being brought into these discussions.

Classifying Risks to Existence

Given the wide range of events or phenomena that could threaten human extinction, it is necessary to find ways of breaking down and categorizing these risks into smaller domains of analysis. Since its inception, refining the possible definitions of existential risks and ways in which they could be grouped has been a key concern of ERS. Perhaps the most instinctive way of grouping these kinds of risks is separating them into natural or anthropogenic sources of risk.

Humanity has contended with a host of natural existential risks since the dawn of time. These risks arise from natural vulnerability and occur independently of our existence on the planet (Bostrom 2019). Existential risks of this variety are events such as a comet or asteroid strike, a supervolcanic eruption, or a stellar explosion. These risks have always been there; yet we have only relatively recently become aware of them. Before we began to understand astrodynamics, it would have been difficult to imagine, let alone calculate, how likely it would be for an asteroid to strike the planet or assess the level of destruction such a strike might cause.

How dangerous are naturally occurring existential risks? Estimates on this vary. In his book *The Precipice: Existential Risk and the Future of Humanity* (2020), Toby Ord, places his current estimate on the total likelihood of all natural risks posing a threat to human extinction within the next 100 years at 1 in 10,000 (167).

Despite our seeming inability to affect natural events, these advancements in scientific understanding and technology have given us the potential to mitigate some of the death and destruction they may bring. Effective evacuation plans can be made for earthquakes. Robust systems of detection and early warning for tsunamis have been constructed. Organizations such as the International Asteroid Warning Network and the United Nations Office for Outer Space Affairs have even been constructed to track objects in space and calculate the likelihood of an impact on the earth (UNOOSA 2020; IAWN 2020; Ord 2020).

Anthropogenic risks are those that are directly related to our existence on this planet. These risks emerge as a result of our influence on the planet such as climate change, pollution, and loss of biodiversity and do not necessarily imply malicious intent. They can be a byproduct of the current ways in which humans live on earth, for example, habitat loss, globalization, and inadequate preparedness mechanisms for theoretically manageable problems such as the COVID-19 pandemic. These types of risks can also be a result of our technologies; most notably, the development of nuclear weapons leading to warfare shifting from a relatively low risk of existential catastrophe to the specter of annihilation now thought possible with any potential act of aggression involving a nuclear-armed state.

How likely is an anthropogenic risk? Ord (2020) estimates a 1 in 6 chance of an anthropogenically generated existential catastrophe in the next 100 years. What then is the total risk posed by both these types of risks, natural and manmade? Toby Ord (2020) estimated of total existential risk in the next century as 1 in 6 or as he wrote: "Russian roulette" (2020, 62). This estimate fits into Nick Bostrom's statement that a typical range based on subjective surveys among experts is between a 10% and 20% chance of existential catastrophe in the same time period (Sandberg and Bostrom 2008, Bostrom 2013). Through writing on civilizational collapse and not existential risk, Sir Martin Rees, Royal Astronomer and co-founder of the Centre for the Study of Existential Risk, estimates that humanity has a 1 in 2 chance of surviving the century (Rees 2003). If these estimates are to be taken at face value, they are striking. Torres (2016) contextualizes the scale of these risks by pointing out that the average US American is 1500 times more likely to die in an extinction event rather than an airplane crash and 4000 times more likely to witness the collapse of civilization (as of 2016). However, it is important to note that there does not seem to be widespread consensus among a wide range of experts on the exact scale of this risk. However, as we will see, squabbling on the precise estimate may not be of much importance given the possible consequences of any of these events coming to pass.

As the field of ERS has grown, the theoretical frameworks and underlying ethics have changed and expanded as have the methodologies for classifying the risks. The classification methods are roughly traced along with the first-, second-, and third-wave paradigms. First-wave approaches to classification are heavily focused on the overall outcome of the risk. This is because, from this perspective, what is most important is the near-infinite number of potential future humans or posthumans that could span the galaxy. Risks are only problematic if they inhibit or significantly delay this trajectory. Bostrom (2002) proposed a system for classification along this line of thought, borrowing two of his categories from T.S. Elliot's "The Hollow Men" (Beard and Torres 2020). Existential risks can be considered "bangs," events such as an asteroid impact, super volcano eruption, badly designed superintelligent artificial intelligence, or a global nuclear war. In a "bang," intelligent life goes suddenly extinct from acts of destruction, either intentional or unintentional. Risks can be "crunches," events such as resource depletion, where the level of resources can no longer sustain advanced technological human civilization or humanity may succumb to dysgenic pressures, where it becomes vastly more fertile but much less intelligent. During a crunch, humanity may survive but our species is forever prevented from reaching the goal of posthuman galactic colonization. Humanity may end in a "shriek," examples of this would be domination by badly designed artificial superintelligence or an uploaded human mind that grows to a superintelligence. In these examples, humanity achieves a degree of its posthuman future, but its effects are not wanted by the vast majority of people. Finally, the world may end in a "whimper," which for Bostrom is either hitting some long-term limit on the expansion of humanity or the abandonment of what makes us human. Humanity could give up every activity: art, leisure, pleasure, family, and friends for the goal of interstellar colonization. In this example, humanity does not biologically die out but has changed to something else. In a whimper, humanity reaches a posthuman future but follows a trajectory where we live lives that humans do not find value in (Bostrom 2002).

Another outcome-oriented classification system later developed by Bostrom proposes a typology of existential risks based on the relationship between the probability of an event and its consequences. Any risk level of scope will be based on how many people are likely to be affected ranging from a single individual to multiple generations across the globe. This risk will also have a likely level of intensity, from being imperceptible to terminal. At the intersection of these two variables—a terminal level of intensity at the transgenerational scope—is human extinction. A step down from this intersection, in either scope (i.e., not transgenerational) or intensity (i.e., less than terminal intensity), would result in a global catastrophic risk. These are events that could be horrendous and could potentially require centuries or more from which to recover but would not result in the final extinction of humanity. Global catastrophic risks have also been defined as "possible events or processes that, were they to occur, would end the lives of approximately 10% or more of the global population or do comparable damage" (Cotton-Barratt et al. 2016). Bostrom's spatial-temporal matrix was an important starting framework in the field of ERS as it implies that at different levels of intensity and scope, different types of strategies to mitigate these risks would need to be developed.

The Necessity, Tractability, and Importance (NTI) Framework, originally developed by the Open Philanthropy Project, is an example of a system of classification that is more in line with the second-wave approaches to ERS. This framework is oriented around the prioritization of focus and is heavily used in the Effective Altruism (EA) movement. If the ethos of EA is to do as much good as possible, then a system is needed to determine which efforts are likely to produce the "most good." In order to do so, the NTI Framework utilizes three factors: how neglected the particular issue is, how tractable is (the likelihood that the issue can be affected), and how important the issue is (Open Philanthropy n.d.). This classification system, though having eschewed the emphasis on a transhuman future, still maintains the importance of longtermism, originally coined by Nick Beckstead 2013, and the qualifier strong longtermism later added that when decisions need to be made and actions taken, they should be done so that they benefit the long-term future and prioritize giving more benefits to the long-term future over the near term (Greaves and MacAskill 2021).

Third-wave approaches for understanding existential risks are those that build on a framework of systems thinking and complexity theory to examine the interplay between many causal factors that may result in an existential risk, while also considering how the levels of resilience, vulnerability, and exposure are understood. Exemplifying this type of approach, Karin Kuhlemann (2019) proposes distinguishing between sexy and unsexy risks. The so-called sexy existential risks grab our attention, imagination, and fascination. By definition, they have a low probability of occurring, but if they do, their disastrous outcome for the human species has the highest possible severity and magnitude. A meteor strike, a highly contagious and deadly pathogen, a nuclear war, and the rise of a hostile superintelligence are all examples of sexy risks. They can also be thought of as epistemically neat in that it is quite clear which academic field they fall under which makes coordinating inter-disciplinary approaches straightforward. To understand the threat and possibility of a meteor strike, we would naturally turn to astrophysicists and emergency managers. For a deadly pandemic we turn to epidemiologists and biologists. For the prospect of nuclear winter, meteorologists and physicists. For possible risks associated with artificial intelligence, we would rely on computer scientists and philosophers. These risks are viewed as having a sudden onset, a knockout punch, where the risk is crystallized in a matter of hours or years. Further, these risks tend to have a significant focus on technology as either the cause and/or solution to mitigating these risks (Kuhlemann 2019). Many of the sexy risks can be attributed to acts of nature (asteroid impact), malicious actors (nuclear weapons and engineered pandemics), or incompetence/lack of foresight and planning (runaway climate change and reckless AI development) (Kuhlemann 2019).

Unsexy risks have a low probability of an existential outcome but have a high probability of a less than existential outcome. These risks are epistemically messy and pose conceptually difficult wicked problems (Head and Alford 2015). Examples of these kinds of risks are the degradation and erosion of topsoil, waning biodiversity, increasing scarcity of freshwater, large-scale problems with unemployment, unsustainable fiscal policies, and overpopulation. These kinds of risks develop gradually and incrementally damage the potential for human flourishing. Unsexy risks arise from people behaving rationally, doing things they normally do, causing an aggregate impact over time that directly contributes to global catastrophic risks or indirectly to existential risks. These risks are messy, creeping, and highly political (Kuhlemann 2019).

Kuhlemann argues that between these two, the unsexy risks warrant more concerted attention than the sexy ones. The choice between the two is based on how one evaluates potential impacts for people currently existing or people in the future. People in the future are, of course, theoretical until they come to exist. It is true that there could be an astronomical number of people in the future on a long enough timeline. If focusing on a sexy or unsexy risk is based purely on the number of people who could benefit from it without regard to when those people exist, then the choice would focus on the sexy risks. Conversely, if equally weighted value is given to the actual living, breathing people, then the choice would be the unsexy risk. Of course, such a choice is hardly ever going to be exclusive, and there would likely be ways to work on unsexy risks that benefit living people that also have positive effects on future people (Kuhlemann 2019).

Following a similar third-wave approach, Avin et al. (2018) propose a system of classification that seeks to point out areas of convergence between possible risks. The first of these areas of convergences looks at how critical systems essential to human survival may be affected by a risk. Critical systems are considered to be those that sustain life on earth and range from physical systems (laws of nature, stability of temperature), through the whole organism (our ability to learn and reproduce), to the socio-technological (our ability to extract resources and influence the world around us). These systems are assessed in terms of boundaries and thresholds to consider what the breaking point may be for each system. The second organizational criteria are the mechanism that would spread that risk to the critical system(s) across the globe. These scale from mechanisms that spread through the biological, cultural, or digital worlds to those dispersal mechanisms that affect the air and water on the planet. Finally, the systems and institutions that could be used to prevent or mitigate these disasters are considered with regard to the possibility that they may fail under pressure. These are considered at the individual, interpersonal, institutional levels, and beyond.

A more immediately useful picture may arise when categorized in this overlapping manner. Because many risks have dissimilar initial causes, this way of thinking can pose different ways of understanding and mitigating risks that may not have been obvious when using different approaches. As Kuhlemann (2019) pointed out, existential risks, especially of the unsexy variety, tend not to be epistemically neat. By looking at risks in this, it may be easier to determine which expertise may be needed for a specific risk and where different kinds of expertise intersect. Finally, this structure, or another built on it, may prove useful for revealing previously unknown areas of neglect and, hopefully, contribute to providing a more resilient Existential Risk Mitigation system in the face of black swan events (Avin et al. 2018), those events that are highly influential and impossible to predict (Taleb 2010). The capacity to absorb the shocks of unpredictable events is critical to the survival of humanity, as target preventative measures cannot be taken.

In their article, "Governing Boring Apocalypses: A New Typology of Existential Vulnerabilities and Exposures for Existential Risk Research" (2018), Liu, Lauta, and Maas argue that focusing on vulnerabilities and exposures over specific existential hazards is a more helpful framework for increasing existential security. This systems perspective is warranted because few existential threats happen in a vacuum, and it is equally, if not more likely, that complex, slow-moving "unsexy" risk will threaten our extinction. Vulnerabilities here are "a weakness in a system that increases the chance that human civilization will collapse in response to pressure or challenge." In their approach, an existential risk results from the interplay between a "hazard," a "vulnerability," and our "exposure." From this way of thinking, when a specific "source of peril" (hazard) meets a vulnerable system and can affect a sufficient number of people, you get an existential risk. Put differently, "[...] a hazard is what kills us, and a vulnerability is how we die. Exposure is the interface or medium between what kills us, and how we die" (7).

They propose four classifications of vulnerabilities relevant to ERS. These are (1) Ontological, those vulnerabilities inherent in existing in a given time and space—human dependence on food and water paired with the ecosystem's need for energy input; (2) Passive, those vulnerabilities that occur because of inaction—lack of a reliable global crisis management organization; (3) Active, those vulnerabilities that occur because of insufficient or misguided actions—insufficient protection of critical infrastructure to solar flares; and (4) Intentional, those vulnerabilities that are intentionally maintained—a centralized nuclear launch authority making it possible for a single actor to launch a nuclear attack (Liu et al. 2018).

Bostrom offers another understanding of vulnerabilities centered on technological development, which he terms "civilizational vulnerability." This type of vulnerability rests on the premise that there is a level of technological development where the devastation of human civilization is almost ensured. This level of development, dubbed the "semi-anarchic default condition," occurs when technological progress meets a limited capacity for control (Bostrom 2019). In this civilizational condition, there are four types of vulnerabilities:

(Type-1) where it becomes very easy for any small number of people to cause mass destruction; for example, advances in biotechnology lower the bar to the creation of virulent and deadly engineered pathogens, so that anyone with a basic understanding of biochemistry and lab procedures could do it;
(Type 2-a) a technology emerges that encourages powerful actors to cause mass destruction; for example, a way of reliably shielding one country

from a nuclear attack could undermine the doctrine of nuclear security, leading to a situation where first strikes become more likely;

(Type 2-b) a technology emerges that causes actors to cause (seemingly) minor damage to the world, where the sum of those destructive acts is civilizational devastation, imagine global warming, but on a much more accelerated timeframe;

(Type 2-c) technology is developed, in which the first use causes a catastrophe; for example, when the first thermonuclear bomb was detonated, there was not 100% confidence that it would not set off a chain reaction and set the atmosphere ablaze (Bostrom 2019).

Generally, the term resiliency was often used in the hard sciences to refer to "the persistence of relationship within a system" and measure the system's ability to absorb variables while maintaining a similar enough identity. The stability of a system then would refer to the "ability of a system to return to equilibrium after a temporary disturbance" (Holling 1973, 17). The term has expanded in its usage, adapting resiliency and stability to describe the systems of interactions between humanity and nature (Maher and Baum 2013). Another helpful definition of resilience is "the capacity of a system to absorb disturbance and reorganize while changing to still retain the same function, structure and feedbacks and therefore identity" (Folke et al. 2010).

In ERS, the concept of resiliency goes hand in hand with "vulnerability." As a species, we may be moving into the unknown. Despite the myriad of threats that could come knocking on our door, it is worth remembering that humanity is a resilient species. Approximately 70,000 years ago, the Lake Toba super volcano erupted, the largest eruption in the history of civilization. As a result, human populations are believed to have been diminished to between three and ten thousand (Currie and Éigeartaigh 2018). From a deep-time perspective, humans have been on earth for less than the blink of an eye, but have overcome innumerable challenges within that blink. The resilience of humanity as a collective has been a major determining factor in why *Homo Sapiens* are the only hominids around.

As the concept is applied in ERS, resiliency refers to the ability of human civilization to survive in extreme scenarios. If the overall vulnerability is below a certain threshold, then adaptation is still possible. Resiliency is our overall ability to adapt to the risks encountered. If a catastrophe were to occur on a global scale that exceeds overall resilience, then recovery from the disaster would not be possible. Resiliency and sustainability are interconnected in this way of thinking (Baum and Handoh 2014). It may be tempting to fall into understandings of sustainability that invoke notions of stasis. However, when considering the presence of existential risks alongside possible future trajectories of human civilization, status quo is the least likely. Understanding sustainability in dynamic terms and overall trajectory is more helpful (2013).

Challenges of Working on Existential Risks

To understand and mitigate existential risks is to face a particular set of challenges. The first involves assessing the probability of a particular risk or a set of risks and then determining what degree of probability would be sufficiently low enough not to warrant attention. Conversely, identifying where the threshold is on the upper bounds is equally challenging: when does action need to be taken? Existential risks are, almost by definition, unprecedented. If one had come to full fruition, we would not be here thinking about them. No one would be here thinking or writing about them. They are challenging to envision or assess when they are not part of our experience.

It is clear that reducing the chance that humans will become extinct is fundamental for most people, but how should the value of reducing vulnerabilities to existential risks be considered? Who will bear the cost, and who will reap the reward? Given the possible timescale creeping risks require current generations to invest heavily for a sense of existential security they will not live to experience. Given that the scope of existential risks almost always threatens on a global scale, international cooperation and trust will be essential to address the vast majority of these risks. Tensions are likely to arise along issues of state sovereignty and the tenability of investment in risk reduction to election cycles. Further, humans can be highly rational creatures, are not solely rational ones, and it can be hard to predict how collective fears and anxieties may alter approaches to understanding and mitigating risks.

The general approach to dealing with problems as a species has tended to be either through trial and error or through building predictive theories. Neither of these approaches can be relied upon for assessing existential risks. With this level of severity and scope, there would likely be no second chances. Humanity has learned to overcome many threats to our existence through its technology and the social, political, and cultural systems and institutions they have developed. However, these institutions were developed for different classifications of threats and different ways of addressing them (Pinker 2019; Ord 2020).

Living is dangerous, and concern with figuring out the extent of that danger has been with humanity for a long time. The observation that catastrophes have happened and will happen in the future is a theme in many of our species' oldest stories. A few critical scientific discoveries instigated this shift: that species can go, and have gone, extinct; that humanity is, in fact, a species and part of the natural world; and the advent of nuclear weapons for the first time provided a tangible example of just how our extinction could happen. It is against this backdrop that the ERS emerged. The field and its theoretical foundations have gone through many interactions in a short time. The story of the discipline can be thought of as three interrelated waves of development. Its first wave rests on ideas of Transhumanism and Utilitarianism, its second on Effective Altruism, and a newly emerging third wave has an emphasis on understanding resilience, vulnerabilities, and exposures. Since its inception, ERS has emphasized defining and clarifying typologies of potential risks to humanity's long-term survival. As the understanding of existential and global catastrophic risks has grown, so too have perspectives on how they interact with and potentially threaten human civilization.

References

Avin, Shahar, Bonnie C. Wintle, Julius Weitzdörfer, Seán S. Ó. Éigeartaigh, and William J. Sutherland. 2018. "Classifying Global Catastrophic Risks." *Futures* 102: 20-26.

Barnett, Michael, Hunjoon Kim, Madalene O'Donnell, and Laura Sitea. 2007. "Peacebuilding: What Is in a Name?" *Global Governance* 13 (1): 35-58.

Baum, S.D., and I.C. Handoh. 2014. "Integrating Planetary Boundaries and Global Catastrophic Risk Paradigms." *Ecological Economics* 107: 12-21.

Beard, Simon, and Phil Torres. 2020. "Ripples on the Great Sea of Life: A Brief History of Existential Risk Studies." *SSRN Electron*.

Beckstead, Nick. 2013. *On The Overwhelming Importance of Shaping the Far Future*. PhD Thesis: Department of Philosophy, Rutgers University.

Bostrom, Nick. 2003. "Astronomical Waste: The Opportunity Cost of Delayed Technological Development." *Utilitas* 15 (3308-314).

Bostrom, Nick. 2013. "Existential Risk Prevention as Global Priority." *Global Policy* 4 (1): 15-31.

Bostrom, Nick. 2002. "Existential Risks: Analyzing Human Extinction Scenarios and Related Hazards." *Journal of Evolution and Technology* 9 (1).
Bostrom, Nick. 2019. "The Vulnerable World Hypothesis." *Global Policy* 4 (10): 455-576.
Bostrom, Nick. 2008. "Why I Want to Be a Posthuman When I Grow Up." *Medical Enhancement and Posthumanity* 107-36.
Bostrom, Nick, and Milan M. Ćirković. 2011. *Global Catastrophic Risks*. Edited by Nick Bostrom and Milan M. Ćirković. Oxford: Oxford University Press.
Capra, Fritjof. 1983. *The Turning Point. Science, Society and the Rising Culture*. New York: Bantam Books.
CDA Collaborative Learning Projects. 2016. *Designing Strategic Initiatives to Impact Conflict Systems: Systems Approaches to Peacebuilding. A Resource Manual*. Cambridge, MA: CDA Collaborative Learning Projects.
Cote, Muriel, and Andrea J. Nightingale. 2011. "Resilience Thinking Meets Social Theory: Situating Social Change in Socio-Ecological Systems (SES) Research." *Progress in Human Geography* 36 (4): 475-489.
Ćirković, Milan. 2002. "Cosmological Forecast and Its Practical Significance." *Journal of Evolution and Technology* 12: 1-13.
Coleman, Peter T. 2006. "Conflict, Complexity, and Change: A Meta-Framework for Addressing Protracted, Intractable Conflicts--III." *Peace and Conflict: Journal of Peace Psychology* 12 (4): 325–348.
Cotton-Barratt, Owmen, Sebastian Farquhar, John Halstead, Stefan Schubert, and Andrew Snyder-Beattie. 2016. *Global Catastrophic Risks 2016*. Stockholm: Global Challenges Foundation.
Currie, Adrian, and Seán Ó Éigeartaigh. 2018. "Working Together to Face Humanity's Greatest Threats: Introduction to the Future of Research on Catastrophic and Existential Risk." *Futures* 102: 1-5.
Cuvier, Georges. 2009. *Essay on the Theory of the Earth*. Translated by Robert Kerr. Cambridge: Cambridge University Press.
Dalal, Roshen. 2011. *Hinduism: An Alphabetical Guide*. London: Penguin Global.
de Coning, Cedric. 2018. "Adaptive Peacebuilding." *International Affairs* 94 (2): 301-317.
de Coning, Cedric. 2016. "From Peacebuilding to Sustaining Peace: Implications of Complexity for Resilience and Sustainability." *Resilience: International Policies, Practices, and Discourses* 4 (3): 166-181.
Dietrich, Wolfgang. 2012. *Interpretations of Peace in History and Culture*. New York: Palgrave Macmillan.
Dietrich, Wolfgang. 2013. *Elicitive Conflict Transformation and the Transrational Shift in Peace Politics*. New York: Palgrave Macmillan.
Dietrich, Wolfgang. 2017. *Elicitive Conflict Mapping*. New York: Palgrave Macmillan.

Dietrich, Wolfgang. 2021. *Der die das Frieden. Nachbemerkung zur Trilogie über die vielen Frieden.* Wiesbaden: Springer VS.

Dundes, Alan. 1988. *The Flood Myth.* Berkeley: University of California Press.

Fisher, Robert, and William Ury. 1981. *Getting to Yes: Negotiating Agreement Without Giving In.* Boston: Houghton Mifflin.

Folke, Carl, Stephen R. Carpenter, Brian Walker, Marten Scheffer, Terry Chapin, and Johan Rockström. 2010. "Resilience Thinking: Integrating Resilience, Adaptability and Transformability." *Ecology and Society* 15 (4).

Gallo, Giorgio. 2012. "Conflict Theory, Complexity and Systems Approach." *Systems Research and Behavioral Science.*

Galtung, Johan, and Dietrich Fischer. 2013a. *Johan Galtung: Pioneer of Peace Research.* New York: Springer.

Galtung, Johan, and Dietrich Fischer. 2013b. *Positive and Negative Peace.* Vol. V, in *SpringerBriefs on Pioneers in Science and Practice*, by Johan Galtung, 173–178. Heidelberg: Springer.

Greaves, Hilary, and William MacAskill. 2021. *The Case for Strong Longtermism.* GPI Working Paper No. 5-2021. Global Priorities Institute.

Harris, Ian, Larry J. Fisk, and Carol Rank. 1998. "A Portrait of University Peace Studies in North America and Western Europe at the End of the Millennium." *The International Journal of Peace Studies* 3 (1).

Head, Brian W., and John Alford. 2015. "Wicked Problems: Implications for Public Policy and Management." *Administration & Society* 4 (6): 711-739.

Holling, C. S. 1973. "Resilience and Stability of Ecological Systems." *Annual Review of Ecology and Systematics* 4: 1-23.

Huges, Albert and Allen Huges, director. 2010. *The Book of Eli.* Warner Brothers Pictures.

IAWN. 2020. "About." *International Asteroid Warning Network.* http://iawn.net/about.shtml.

IMDB. 2016. "Top 20 Highest Grossing Post Apocalyptic Movies." *International Movie Data Base.* 03 16. Accessed 05 15, 2022. https://www.imdb.com/list/ls051539512/.

Juncos, Ana E., and Jonathan Joseph. 2020. "Resilient Peace: Exploring the Theory and Practice of Resilience in Peacebuilding Interventions." *Journal of Intervention and Statebuilding* 14 (3): 289-302.

Kaldor, Mary. 2012. *New and Old Wars: Organized Violence in a Global Era.* Cambridge: Polity.

Kraft, Alison, Holger Nehring, and Carola Sachse. 2018. "The Pugwash Conferences and the Global Cold War: Scientists, Transnational Networks, and the Complexity of Nuclear Histories." *Journal of Cold War Studies* 20 (1): 4–30.

Kuhlemann, Karin. 2019. "Complexity, Creeping Normalcy and Conceit: Sexy and Unsexy Risks." *Foresight* 22 (1): 35-52.

Lawrence, Francis, director. 2013. *The Hunger Games: Catching Fire.* Lionsgate.

Lawrence, Francis, director. 2014. *The Hunger Games: Mockingjay - Part 1*. Lionsgate
Lawrence, Francis, director. 2015 *The Hunger Games: Mockingjay - Part 2*. Lionsgate
Lederach, John Paul. 2015. *Little Book of Conflict Transformation: Clear Articulation Of The Guiding Principles By A Pioneer In The Field*. Brattleboro: Good Books.
Lederach, John Pau. 2005. *The Moral Imagination: The Art and Soul of Building Peace*. Oxford: Oxford University Press.
Liu, Hin-Yan, Kristian Cedervall Lauta, and Matthijs Michiel Maas. 2018. "Governing Boring Apocalypses: A New Typology of Existential Vulnerabilities and Exposures for Existential Risk Research." *Futures* 102: 6-19.
Mac Ginty, Roger. 2014. "Everyday Peace: Bottom-up and Local Agency in Conflict-affected Societies." *Security Dialogue* 45 (6): 548–564.
Mac Ginty, Roger. 2021. *Everyday Peace: How So-called Ordinary People Can Disrupt Violent Conflict*. New York: Oxford University Press.
Mac Ginty, Roger, and Oliver Richmond. 2015. "The Fallacy of Constructing Hybrid Political Orders: a Reappraisal of the Hybrid Turn in Peacebuilding." *International Peacekeeping* 1-21.
Maher, Timothy M., and Seth Baum Baum. 2013. "Adaptation to and Recovery from Global Catastrophe." *Sustainability* 5: 1461-1479.
Mallette, Karla. 2021. "How 12th-century Genoese Merchants Invented the Idea of Risk." *Psyche*. November 02. Accessed 02 20, 2022. https://psyche.co/ideas/how-12th-century-genoese-merchants-invented-the-idea-of-risk.
McFarland, David V. 2009. "End-time, Beliefs in." In *Encyclopedia of Time: Science, Philosophy, Theology, and Culture*, edited by H James Birx, 407-411. Thousand Oaks, California: Sage Publications.
Merriam-Webster, ed. 2016. *The Merriam-Webster Dictionary*. Springfield: Merriam-Webster.
van Metre, Lauren, and Jason Calder. 2016. *Peacebuilding and Resilience: How Society Responds to Violence*. Vol. Peaceworks No. 121. Washington D.C.: United States Institute of Peace.
Miller, George. director. 2015. *Mad Max: Fury Road*. Village Roadshow Pictures.
Nobel Prize Outreach. 2022. "Pugwash Conferences on Science and World Affairs." *Pugwash Conferences on Science and World Affairs – Facts*. August 27. https://www.nobelprize.org/prizes/peace/1995/pugwash/facts/.
Open Philanthropy. n.d. "Cause Selection." *Open Philanthropy*. Accessed 05 16, 2022. https://www.openphilanthropy.org/research/cause-selection.
Ord, Toby. 2020. *The Precipice: Existential Risk and the Future of Humanity*. New York: Hachette Books.
Oxford University. 2010. *Oxford Dictionary of English*. 3rd Edition. Oxford: Oxford University Press.

Pinker, Steven. 2019. *Enlightenment Now: The Case for Reason, Science, Humanism, and Progress*. Penguin Books.
Ramsbotham, Oliver, Tom Woodhouse, and Hugh Miall. 2016. *Contemporary Conflict Resolution*. 4th. Cambridge: Polity.
Rees, Sir Martin. 2003. *Our Final Hour: A Scientist's Warning: How Terror, Error, and Environmental Disaster Threaten Humankind's Future in This Century - On Earth and Beyond*. New York: Basic Books.
Resseguie, James L. 2020. "Narrative Features of the Book of Revelation." In *The Oxford Handbook of The Book of Revelation*, edited by Craig R. Koester, 37-57. New York: Oxford University Press.
Richmond, Oliver P. 2011. *A Post-Liberal Peace*. 2011: Routledge.
Richmond, Oliver P. 2015. "The Dilemmas of a Hybrid Peace: Negative or Positive?" *Cooperation and Conflict* 50 (1): 50-68.
Richmond, Richmond P., and Audra Mitchell. 2012. "Introduction—Towards a Post-Liberal Peace: Exploring Hybridity via Everyday Forms of Resistance, Agency and Autonomy." In *Hybrid Forms of Peace: From Everyday Agency to Post-Liberalism*, edited by Richmond P. Richmond and Audra Mitchell, 1-38. New York: Palgrave Macmillan.
Ropers, Norbert. 2008. "Systemic Conflict Transformation: Reflections on the Conflict and Peace Process in Sri Lanka." In *A Systemic Approach to Conflict Transformation Exploring Strengths and Limitations*, edited by Daniela Körppen, Beatrix Schmelzle and Oliver Wils, 11-41. Berghof Research Center for Constructive Conflict Management.
Ross, Garry, director. 2012. *The Hunger Games*. Lionsgate.
Sagan, Carl. 1983. "War and Climatic Catastrophe: Some Policy Implications." *Foreign Affairs* 62 (2): 254-292.
Taleb, Nassim Nicholas. 2010. *The Black Swan: The Impact of the Highly Improbable*. 2nd Edition. London: Penguin.
Torres, Phil. 2016. "How Likely is an Existential Catastrophe?" *Bulletin of the Atomic Scientists*. 09 17. Accessed 05 17, 2022. https://thebulletin.org/2016/09/how-likely-is-an-existential-catastrophe/#:~:text=For%20example%2C%20by%20studying%20crater,average%20once%20every%20500%2C000%20years.
UNOOSA. 2020. "Roles and Responsibilities." *United Nations Office for Outer Space Affairs*. https://www.unoosa.org/oosa/en/aboutus/roles-responsibilities.html.
von Bertalanffy, Ludwig. 1972. "The History and Status of General Systems Theory." *Academy of Management Journal* 15: 407–42.
Wachowskis, The. directors. 1999. *The Matrix*. Warner Bros.
Wachowskis, The. directors. 2003a. *The Matrix Reloaded*. Warner Bros.
Wachowskis, The. directors. 2003b. *The Matrix Revolutions*. Warner Bros.

Walker, Brain, Crawford Stanley Holling, and Stephen R Carpenter. 2004. "Resilience, Adaptability and Transformability in Social–ecological Systems." *Ecology and Society* 9 (2).

Walls, Jerry L. 2008. "Introduction." In *The Oxford Handbook of Eschatology*, by Jerry L Walls, 3-18. New York: Oxford University Press.

Woodhouse, Tom. 2010. "Adam Curle: Radical Peacemaker and Pioneer of Peace Studies." *Journal of Conflictology* 1 (1).

CHAPTER 3

At the Intersection of PCS and ERS

The fields of Peace and Conflict Studies (PCS) and Existential Risk Studies (ERS) are interwoven by common intellectual roots and are shaped by the same history. As a defined academic discipline, PCS emerged in the aftermath of World War II, driven by the inadequacy of previous approaches to preventing conflict. The field of ERS has its origins in the advent of nuclear weapons, and how with their first use, humanity realized that the potential for its own extinction was its own hands. Both were further developed and refined through the Cold War's history and dynamics and the resulting shifts and restructuring of the geopolitics of power.

It is not surprising that there are commonalities between the two. They can both be said to have a normative orientation at their foundation. A medical doctor does not maintain a stance of neutrality between the disease and the patient: Similarly, PCS and ERS researchers are shaped by what they value. Though interpretations of peace vary greatly, few peace workers and researchers are not in favor of peace: peace research and praxis focus on reducing and transforming violence (i.e., the differences between Conflict Management, Resolution, and Transformation), not increasing or exacerbating it. Differences are found in how peace and conflict are understood. There are disagreements on how violence should be addressed; there is no debate on whether or not to work for peace. Researchers in ERS, and the policy advocates who seek to operationalize insights, do not stand neutral in their vested interest for the survival of the human species.

© The Author(s), under exclusive license to Springer Nature Switzerland AG 2023
N. B. Taylor, *Existential Risks in Peace and Conflict Studies*, Rethinking Peace and Conflict Studies, https://doi.org/10.1007/978-3-031-24315-8_3

Researchers can significantly differ in their understanding of what an existential risk is and the best ways of mitigating them (i.e., the difference between first-, second-, and third-wave approaches). Regardless of their approaches, it would be difficult to find someone working in the field who would be very much in favor of human extinction. ERS and PCS seem to share the same final aim, the survival of humanity.

ERS and PCS have unfortunate similarities in that they both operate in environments of extreme scarcity. Investments of attention and resources into destructive industries and military armaments vastly dwarf the percentage of resources devoted to peace and sustainability. The Stockholm International Peace Research Institute calculates that US$1917 billion was spent on wars in 2019 (SIPRI 2020), with the total economic impact of violence being $14.5 trillion Purchasing Power Parity (PPP) (IEP 2020). This lack of parity between investments in peace and war does not reflect that, generally, investment in peacebuilding efforts has an effectiveness ratio estimated at 1:16 (IEP 2017).

A similar disparity in funding toward areas that arguably could decrease our existential security is a disproportionally small investment in safeguarding it. Global expenditure on research and development is approximately $1.5 trillion, with investment specifically in artificial intelligence at $98 billion, while investment in AI safety is about $10 million. Global investment in the fossil fuel industry is about $1.85 trillion, with only $300 billion going toward renewable energy. Between 2017 and 2019 $748 billion was invested in nuclear weapons, with only between $1 and $10 billion spent on nuclear safety. Tens of billions of dollars were invested in biological sciences companies in 2019, with only $1 billion being invested in preventing extreme pandemics (UNESCO 2017; Snyder 2019; IEP 2017; Gibbs 2020).

Given the similar disparities between investment in the issues that PCS and ERS seek to address, it is clear that sound research and decision-making are needed. It is a call for those who work in these fields to be as precise, strategic, and creative as possible. Most, if not all, of these problems are cheaper and more effective to work on earlier. The prevention or early intervention into conflict is less complicated and expensive and requires less effort to rebuild peace than recovery initiatives after a conflict has occurred (IEP 2020). Investing early into preventing conflicts is, on average, 60 times more cost-effective than intervening after the violence occurs (Brown and Rosencrance 1999). Diplomacy is cheaper and more effective than rebuilding after a global war; measures to prevent a pandemic outbreak are easier than struggling to contain one after it begins to rage. Addressing climate change now is within the realm of possibilities, while it remains unknown what we would have to do to survive on a radically different planet.

This logic is particularly true regarding emerging technologies which will be further discussed in Chap. 6. The further away we are from deploying these new technologies, the more power we have to influence them. This phenomenon, referred to as the "Collingridge Dilemma," also implies that despite the influence that can be wielded at the early stages of technological development, the tradeoff is that we can predict less of that technology's impacts (Collingridge 1980). As a whole, early research, education, and action are better sooner than later regarding existential risks. Earlier efforts provide a higher degree of leverage for change and are simultaneously easily wasted; this is why coherent priorities and strategies are needed (Ord 2020, 185).

Prioritization

The topic of prioritization has been much more an explicit and central concern in ERS. An intuitive approach to prioritizing existential risks could be to look at the likelihood of the risk happening and rank them according to probability. If we were to take Ord's best estimates for existential catastrophe in the next century and rank them by their likelihood, the priorities would be:

1. Unaligned artificial intelligence: 1 in 10
2. Engineered pandemics: 1 in 30
3. Unforeseen anthropogenic risks: 1 in 30
4. Other anthropogenic risks: 1 in 50
5. Other environmental damage: 1 in 1000
6. Nuclear war: 1 in 1000
7. Climate change: 1 in 1000
8. "Naturally" occurring pandemics: 1 in 10,000. (Ord 2020, 167)

Such an approach would likely be unhelpful. Firstly, Ord describes these as his best guess estimates intended to give a sense of the overall gravity of existential risks rather than articulate precise estimates. Secondly, this approach lacks many essential considerations about the specific nature of the problem, how it might be mitigated, what level of resources might be required to work on the issue, and how much attention is currently being paid to it. Further, it is logical that prioritization is done for a specific reason and, in many cases in ERS, that seems to determine research priorities for a particular organization.

The Open Philanthropy Project is an organization concerned with Global and Existential Risks and works by combining research and grantmaking to maximize the impact of giving. They are also the original developers of the aforementioned NTI Framework (Necessity, Tractability, and Importance). Open Philanthropy has utilized its framework to determine the current focus: (1) biosecurity and pandemic preparedness and (2) potential risks from advanced artificial intelligence (Open Philanthropy n.d.).

The nonprofit organization 80,000 Hours is shaped by the Effective Altruism movement: values doing the "most good" and envisions doing good over the most prolonged periods feasible. One of the main objectives of this organization is to provide guidance on which careers are the most likely to have the most considerable positive social impacts. To do this evaluation they use a prioritization methodology influenced by the NTI Framework, which uses scale, level of neglect, and solvability to determine research priorities. The philosophy of longtermism underpins the prioritization of 80,000 Hours. Their two areas of the highest priority are (1) emerging technologies and global catastrophic risks and (2) building capacity to explore and solve problems. Following these, 80,000 Hours ranks nuclear security, improving institutional decision-making, and climate change as the next in line "most-pressing issues" (80,000 Hours 2021).

The Global Priorities Institute (GPI) at the University of Oxford takes a similar approach to determine their organization's research priorities. GPI, similar to 80,000 Hours and the Open Philanthropy Project, is an organization focused on how those who wish to "do good" can do so most effectively. GPI focuses explicitly on how high-caliber academic research may contribute to cross-sectoral efforts to prioritize efforts and resources at the global level to "do good." Rather than focus on specific risks, their research agenda articulates a prioritization of broad research themes:

1. Articulation and evaluation of longtermism
2. The value of the future of humanity
3. Reducing and mitigating catastrophic risk

4. Ways of leveraging the size of the future
5. Intergenerational governance
6. Economic growth, population growth, and inequality
7. Moral uncertainty for longtermists
8. Forecasting the long-term future (Global Priorities Institute 2020)

Approaches in ERS that do not have an explicit focus on prioritization though assessing the severity or likelihood of a risk also may not emphasize determining which actions will increase the amount of "good" in the future. They instead focus on which measures are taken to reduce the overall amount of vulnerability to existential and global catastrophic risks while at the same time increasing our resiliency in critical systems.

Prioritization has not been an explicit issue of concern in PCS. The question of how problems of peace and conflict are prioritized does not have a clear answer. Many organizations and initiatives that fall under the encompassing banner of peace work are largely programmatic, focusing on a wide range of efforts, from conflict analysis, activism, multitrack diplomacy, negotiation, capacity building, education, and diplomacy. There is a logical tendency to focus on a specific episode of conflict, a particular theme, or issue, or to be directed toward the often-amorphous goal of peace itself. Research on peace and conflict issues follows similar trends, being directed by either the ever-evolving landscape of conflicts and peace initiatives or the particular interests of individual researchers. The question of where we can look to derive priorities in PCS may be an initial starting point for examining this question of prioritization in the field.

Academic literature that focuses specifically on the question of defining priorities for peace research is now more than 40 years old. This early literature identified arms control, peace economics, communication, values, freedom, human rights, and legal and psychological peace research as priorities for the field (Boulding et al. 1963; Thee 1979, 1983). No doubt these were and likely are still important issues in the study of peace and conflict, but there is no consensus on how one could succinctly determine if arms control or human rights is a higher priority and by how much.

One approach to determining the priorities in peace research is to look to the works of individual scholars who have tried to answer this question by reviewing the topics of interest in the field itself. Chadwick F. Alger, in *Peace Research and Peacebuilding* (2014), identifies seven trends in peace research:

1. how comprehensive peace strategies can be built
2. how multiple peace efforts can be combined simultaneously
3. the importance of a long-term perspective in peace work
4. the bridging of theory and practice
5. deepening insight into ethnic conflict
6. developing ways of sustaining peace settlements
7. the conditions for conflict prevention. (55)

A similar approach would be to turn to the work of research organizations such as the Berghof Foundation to determine the priorities in peace research. The Berghof Foundation is a nonprofit organization focused on supporting the efforts of people in conflict to build sustainable peace. It runs an ongoing "dialogue" series that seeks to raise critical issues for debate among scholars and practitioners. As of 2022, the foundation has 12 lines of inquiry:

1. Peace and conflict impact assessment
2. Security sector reform
3. The transformation of war economies
4. Social change and conflict transformation
5. System approaches to conflict transformation
6. Peacebuilding in the absence of states
7. Peace work and complexity
8. Human rights and conflict transformation
9. Peace infrastructures
10. Transforming war-related identities
11. Armed social violence
12. Violent extremism. (Berghof Foundation 2020)

It could be reasonable to assume that depending on the methodology used to determine these "critical issues," they reflect the top priorities in peace research.

If the focus is shifted from priorities in "peace research" to "peace work," international organizations such as the United Nations (UN) may be used as a source of distilling priorities. At the beginning of 2020, the UN identified (1) supporting member states at risk of conflict and (2) strengthening the Peacebuilding Commissions' role in advising the Security Council as key priorities (United Nations 2020). Similarly, multi-stakeholder collaborations may indicate the current priorities in PCS. One example of these is the "Dili Declaration," which put forward seven peacebuilding and state-building goals that support the achievement of the Millennium Development Goals in conflict-affected and fragile states:

1. Foster inclusive political settlements and processes and inclusive political dialogue
2. Establish and strengthen basic safety and security
3. Achieve peaceful resolution of conflicts and access to justice
4. Develop effective and accountable government institutions to facilitate service delivery
5. Create the foundations for inclusive economic development, including sustainable livelihoods, employment, and effective natural resources management
6. Develop social capacities for reconciliation and peaceful coexistence
7. Foster regional stability and cooperation. (OECD 2010)

To add further nuance to our inquiry, we can look toward research on the priorities as reflected upon by peace workers. The Reflecting on Peace Practice Project (RPP) is a large-scale research project conducted by Collaborative Learning Projects (CDA), initially launched in 1999 to answer the question "What works—and what doesn't work—in peacebuilding?" The first phase of the project (1999–2002) consisted of 26 case studies and multiple consultation feedback workshops on single program efforts in conflict zones focused on what makes peace work effective. The results were published in *Confronting War: Critical Lessons for Peace Practitioners* (Anderson and Olson 2003). One of their key findings is that people who work in conflict zones are concerned with their peace work effectiveness. Effectiveness is understood regarding the specific programmatic work and how they are achieving their particular goals contributes to the bigger picture or *peace writ large*. Their research derived four criteria for assessing the effectiveness of peace work. These are that the efforts (1) cause participants and communities to develop their own initiatives for peace, (2) result in the creation or reform of political institutions to handle grievances that rule the conflict, (3) prompt people to resist violence and provocations to violence, and (4) increase people's security (Anderson and Olson 2003).

PCS would likely benefit from more engagement with the question of prioritization. While these previously mentioned ways of inferring priorities may hold some validity, they would not be rigorous nor able to be compared to each other. Further, they are backward-looking, and priorities are determined based on what has happened in the past. Similarly, when priorities are inferred from looking at trends in the field itself, the question being answered is "what have we done?" not necessarily "what should we be doing?" Direct engagement with the foundational question: What is important in the field of Peace and Conflict Studies, and how do we know? Assessing what is important and how priorities are determined is critical because there are so many potential issues. Where should the thrust of the efforts be directed? Developing a gaze toward the future will be beneficial for the field to determine what has been learned from the past to develop ways of thinking about the future.

Measurement and Time

PCS and ERS both engage with conceptual and methodological challenges concerning measurement. Peace is hard to measure. Conflicts, particularly violent ones, manifest as discrete episodes which are amenable to investigation. Similarly, highly raised tensions that garner widespread attention, even if they come to a peaceful resolution, are at least possible to contain within a research design. How can peace or all the times and places where no violent conflict happened, when the day unfolded as it usually does, quantify this? Similar situations are encountered in ERS. Estimating the potential scale and likelihood of an existential or global catastrophic risk is possible.

What is more difficult is framing how to understand all of the times humanity has survived extreme disasters. The further back history is examined, the more must be inferred from the evidence that has endured until the present. Similarly, it is difficult to account for the risks we do not yet know exist. For example, it has only been in the last half-century that super volcanos were discovered. The civilization-ending power of these volcanos could only be considered once we know they existed. Underlying these challenges to measurement is the perennial question of how to understand the future. How is the past understood? How much can that understanding be trusted to guide humanity into the future?

Time is the substrate that carries the fruits of actions in the present into the future. It contextualizes meaning in the here and now. Time is also the essential backdrop for working for peace and seeking to mitigate catastrophic disasters. Understanding of peace cannot be divorced from how time is understood, and the type of peace we think we are trying to build shapes how we work for peace. Understanding the nature of time as vectorial or cyclical and the purpose of being-in-time as transcendent or immanent reflects two common ways of understanding peace.

From a Christian perspective, the highest transcendental form of peace could be considered heaven, realized at the end of life or time, where the time vector ends. Similar in structure with a more secular interpretation are understandings of peace tied inextirpable to notions of development or progress. The peace sought after in this understanding is always in the future; when we are developed enough, reasonable enough, and progressed sufficiently, we will have achieved peace in some time that is never today. Peace can be understood in a cyclical and immanent understanding of time where peace exists in being perpendicular or outside of time. From a Buddhist perspective, time exists as endless cycles of suffering, the escape from which is *samādhi*, a state of single-pointed concentration where only the object of attention remains, or *nirvāna*, freedom from having to be reborn (Keown 2003).

One of the tensions in applied peace work is how connecting interventions aimed at the immediate crisis or episode of the conflict, with the deeper past. Combining in this way will hopefully address the root causes of the conflict and try to elicit transformations in the conflict epicenter so that conflicts do not erupt into violence in the future. Put differently, how does one balance Lederach's "200-year present" (2005) while being accountable to the people you work with in the here and now?

ERS has an explicit focus on the long-term future, often very long, often focusing on human civilization, meaning any current or future civilizations that could trace their origin to the current human population. Barring any existential catastrophes, the lower bounds of the possible future of human civilization could be close to a billion years when the earth becomes uninhabitable (Ord 2020). On the upper edges of realms of possibilities, where human civilization has undergone dramatic changes and spreads across the galaxy, potentially the upper bounds are near the heat death of the universe, an astronomical number of years in the future. Far from being solely intellectually humbling thought experiments, conceptualizing the future of humanity on this scale of trajectories is crucial because it is highly likely that many actions taken now will shape the future and the likelihood of these long-term futures.

Baum et al. (2019) laid out four general classes of long-term trajectories for humanity based on a synthesis from many different fields. They write that there are four general trajectories for our future: (1) "status quo trajectories," where our human civilization stays roughly the same as it is into the future; (2) "catastrophic trajectories," where events come to pass that bring significant destruction to human civilization; (3) "technological transformation trajectories," where discoveries are made in science and technology that radically change the direction of human civilization; and (4) "astronomical trajectories," where humanity takes to the stars and spreads to the far corners of the cosmos (Baum et al. 2019, 54). When assessing the likelihood of each of these possible futures, the authors found that it was least likely that humanity is looking at a status quo trajectory. Given what is known about the possible dangers we currently face and are likely to face, we will likely face disaster (trajectory 2) and go extinct or change dramatically (trajectories 3 and 4) to overcome these challenges.

The challenge for ERS may be the reverse of that of PCS. With so much focus on the far future, how can balanced perspectives be conceptualized in the present? Linking the here and now, or even the "moment" of a single human life in the face of vast possibilities of time, may be a question that different interpretations of ERS are grappling with.

Questions for the Future

There are two main foundational questions at this intersection between these two fields. The reasons these questions are essential and the possible answers to them define the spirit of this book.

Why Is Human Extinction Negative?

The question itself may, at first pass, seem absurd, mainly because it is humans asking and contemplating the question. However, it is an essential question to reflect on when considering the relationship between peace and human survival. After laying out the possible scale and scope of potential existential risks, this question has to be addressed to answer the efforts to safeguard our future.

There have been small studies on how the ethics and morality of human extinction are understood. One such study on focus groups in the USA and the UK asked participants to decide between three options: (1) no existential catastrophe, (2) a catastrophe that kills the vast majority of the human population but a sufficient number survive to give a possibility to recovery, or (3) complete human extinction. Not surprisingly, option one was overwhelmingly chosen as the best-case scenario. The results became interesting when participants were asked their rationale for their decisions between options two and three. When looking into how respondents rationalized their ranking of the last two options, the researchers found that people varied in how much weight they gave the importance of the total amount of suffering in the present and the value of the long-term future (Schubert et al. 2019).

It is a safe starting point to assume that most humans agree that human extinction is bad and should be avoided. The literature that addresses this question, "is human extinction bad," tends to break down into a few sub-questions: "why is human extinction bad?" and "how bad is it?" How the answers to these questions are addressed reflects what is valued and what our time perspectives are. Human extinction can be bad because of the harm it would cause to people: the immediate pain and death of those that perish in the immediate aftermath of the shock that kills the species, and the trauma and psychological damage of those who survive that first shock until they die in some other way.

Outside of the destruction wrought in the present, human extinction can also be bad for humans that existed in the past or would have existed in the future. If all humans perish, their scientific, cultural, and artistic achievements will likely fade to dust, to be witnessed by no one again (Finneron-Burns 2017). If there is a moral obligation to all who existed before, extinction could be considered a betrayal of our ancestors. The efforts of the innumerable generations that have struggled against the odds to survive and create and nourish children also come to an end with our extinction. Human extinction can also be bad because it destroys the future. A very large number of people who stand a good chance of living happy lives will never have an opportunity to exist. All the future accomplishments that humanity may achieve will remain unrealized.

These lines of thinking make some assumptions about the nature of the future and the relative "weight" of suffering. Just because humanity endures into the far future does not necessarily mean that that future is the kind we want. Science fiction and research into human survival in extreme situations have entertained many dystopian scenarios. Continued human existence in a nuclear hellscape, under the yoke of some oppressive AI overload, or locked into a subsistence level of existence due to a singleton totalitarian government may be an unimaginable level of human suffering. Since the future can contain vastly more humans than the present, if that future is one of unendurable suffering, then perhaps a quick extinction is better.

It is also important to note that this kind of reasoning only reflects a particular type of secular humanistic thought. It would be interesting how religious scholars, theologians, and devotees would answer these questions. The Abrahamic faiths all place importance on taking care of the earth (and presumably our continued existence on it). Judaism has the concept of *Tikkun Olam*, which refers to actions to repair and protect the world. The Christian notion of stewardship implies that humans are responsible for taking care of it because humankind was created by the same God that created the earth. There is a similar notion in Islam, where humanity is considered the *Khalifah*, the one who looks after something, in this case, the world, and will be judged by Allah by how well they take care of the creation in their charge.

Between secular reasoning and theological speculation, the question of the importance of humanity is a specter that haunts this discussion. If the loss of humanity's future is negative, then the question must be asked: "why?" Unpacking this question requires determining what, if anything, is unique about humanity. The "Fermi Paradox" is often entertained in ERS to discuss the question of the uniqueness of humanity. Named after the physicist Enrico Fermi and anecdotally sourced from a lunchtime discussion in Los Alamos where a group of scientists was discussing how strange it is that we have not yet encountered other life in the universe given the sheer size of the known universe and the number of known Earth-like planets. So the story goes, during the discussion, Fermi stopped and asked, "Where is everyone?"

Two concepts are often used to try to answer the question of why our skies are so silent. The first is the Drake Equation, a series of assumptions that approximate the number of intelligent species in the universe. The second is a concept proposed by the economist Robin Hanso, the "great filter." Hanso put forth that since we have not yet found intelligent life beyond earth, there must be something out there in time and space that, in almost all cases, prevents the emergence of intelligent life (Webb 2015). There are two general types of answers when trying to answer the question "where are they?" through the lens of the great filter. Either they never existed or they are all dead. If humanity has already made it past that significant hurdle that filters out most emerging life, we can be optimistic, "we are not polishing the brass on a doomed ship" (Taylor 2021). We have already made it through what most nascent life could not. If this is the case, humanity is unique because we are alone in the universe and may consider ourselves a point of preciousness in the vast expanse. We may even choose to understand this as a call for action to protect something so fragile. If the filter lies in the future, we may assume that we will soon face the most crucial moment, the filter is coming, and we best be ready (Taylor 2021).

Can There Be Peace Without Us?

A perhaps similar question to why human extinction is negative in the domain of PCS is, "can there be peace without us?" If humanity were to go extinct tomorrow, could the world be said to be at peace? Is peace even a relevant concept without us? The response to these questions begins frustratingly, but necessarily, with "it depends on what you mean by peace."

Suppose peace is understood in connection with violence, Galtung's definition of "negative peace" is the absence of direct violence (Galtung 1960). The relationship between peace and extinction would depend on the time period. There would be no peace during the process of going extinct, which is likely to involve violence in some form or another. If we are referring to the time after humans have gone extinct, there could be direct violence, and thus we could say a negative peace would prevail.

If peace is defined in its positive sense, where violence is understood as that which influences human beings "so that their actual somatic and mental realizations are below their potential realizations" (1960, 168), then the answer would be no; there is no positive peace in our destruction. There is no positive peace because there is no difference between the actual and potential for humanity, so the distinctions between direct, structural, and cultural violence would not be functional (Galtung 1960, 1990). There would have been violence, the violence that destroyed humanity's future.

Dietrich's Transrational Peace Philosophy offers a more comprehensive framework for exploring this question. His theory of the Many Peaces supposes five general categories of interpretations of peace: peace through harmony, justice, truth, security, and the transrational, which is an integration of the previous four (2012, 2017, 2019).

The first peace family, the energetic peaces, understands the world and humanity's place as inextricably connected with all that is. Peace, in this sense, is understood in terms of harmony, a dynamic balance of the cosmic, the natural, and the social manifestations of the world (Dietrich 2012). After the extinction of humanity, the earth would likely recover from the shock that extinguished us and return to a homeostatic equilibrium. The end of the Anthropocene, when seen from the assumed perspectives of other living beings on earth, would likely be mixed. The wild flora and fauna would probably welcome the end of new pollution and environmental damage. Our domestic animals and pets would likely have a rough time initially. If peace is understood as the harmony of the cosmic and natural worlds, then there may be peace.

The moral peace family departs from the imminent world of the energetic through positing a transcendent creator God outside the world. From this, external referent norms of behavior and classifying the good, bad, right, and wrong become possible. Here peace is understood as justice (Dietrich 2012). The question of "peace without us" then becomes nearly impossible to answer because it would, from its logic, require knowing what that creator God thinks about the extinction of humanity. If our extinction is unjust, then peace would not be present; if, on the other hand, our demise is just, then peace would have prevailed.

The modern peace family presupposes a mechanistic world that is ultimately understandable through reducing its complexity to the functioning of its constituent parts. In this secular conception of the world, the faculty of reason is elevated to the utmost importance. Since what is valued can only be in the material world, a security paradox is invoked because what is cherished can be taken, humanity is insecure, and this, in turn, drives concerns for security to become interwoven with understandings of peace (Dietrich 2012). In this case, the question of "peace without us" may become similar in its logic to the energetic peace family. While human existence is being threatened and while we succumb to the extinction process, we are clearly in a state of insecurity and thus in a state of "unpeace." After humanity is gone, it could be argued that peace through security is present because there is no one's security in jeopardy.

The "postmodern peace family" does not hold a transcendental referent of Truth or God for its orientation. Humans are perceiving subjects. Without grounding our grand narratives as a lattice for meaning-making, it becomes the task of the individual in their relations with the collective to decide what is meaningful (Dietrich 2012). In this way of thinking, the plurality and diversity of truths become the landscape's topography from which understandings of peaces are derived. Here the question of "peace without us" becomes easier to answer; it is a clear no. Without anyone to perceive that peace, it has no truth; without it, there is no peace.

A transrational understanding of peace differs from the previous four because it integrates the experience of harmony, perceptions of justice, considerations of truth, and understandings of security into a dynamic understanding of peace grounded in the present moment in a specific context (Dietrich 2012). Peace and the perception of peace cannot be separated; they exist as each other. From this perspective, without this understanding, peace is not meaningful. Peace requires "a perceiving subject that fills the form," or using the language of semiotics, the *signifié* (the content) with the *significant* (the expression) (Dietrich 2019, 253). On the transrational understanding of peace, Dietrich (2012) writes,

> The secret of the peaces, of existing, thus lies in dying before the body dies and so finding out that there is no death at all. The word "existence" has to be understood in the meaning of its Latin root *exsisto*, as a temporary stepping forth out of the All-One, which does not lead to an individual death but toward the return to the All-One. Whatever appears in the manifest world, in the last instance, is only a temporary aspect of the All-One. (240–241)

From this understanding of peace, the question of "peace without us" has two potential answers depending on an initial assumption. Does essence precede existence? Are human beings individual beings part of a complex whole, or are they manifestations of a transcendent all-one? From an immanent understanding of human life, there can be no peace without the perceiving subject. It would have no content nor expression; no one would communicate it to anyone or anything. Humanity would not have accomplished "dying before the body dies" but only annihilation in our extinction. If, on the other hand, the essence of what life is transcendent, then a higher order peace may exist far beyond the concerns of human life.

What Is the Purpose of Peace?

An important but not often addressed question in PCS that is of relevance for the topic of human survival and peace is "what is the purpose of peace?" This question is crucial because it lies at the heart of peace research and conflict transformation. In this values-oriented field of study, why is peace, by whichever understanding, valued? At first glance, the question may appear banal, too much rooted in common sense to be given, though, or perhaps even quasi heretical.

The lack of direct engagement with this question may result from the early origins of PCS. Martin Luther King Jr., Gandhi, Adam Curle, Elise

Boulding, Kenneth Boulding, Johan Galtung, John Paul Lederach, and many of the key thinkers that shaped the field were inspired by strongly held religious or secular humanistic convictions. Many people are still drawn to PCS because of their religious beliefs and moral convictions. These same beliefs inform their understanding of peace. In these cases, the question of the importance of peace may be more straightforward, rooted in the epistemology and ontology of the relationship between the human and the divine.

The answer to the question may not be as straightforward for those not shaped by such a perspective or background. One option is to approach the question of the purpose of peace through the related question, "what does peace do?" One thing peace does, when understood as "negative peace," is the removal of direct violence. Positive peace builds on this to include removing cultural and structural forms of violence, thus allowing the full realization of all human beings' somatic and mental potentials.

Following the discussion of the transrational understanding of peace, one thing that peace "does" as the *signifié* is imbue the *significant* with meaning. In an almost tautological sense, one of the things peace does is to communicate and allow understanding of peace. Peace is an expression of the dynamic interplay of humans as contact boundaries at work, relating without severe blockages in the multitude of ways they relate to each other; where harmony, justice, truth, and security find a dynamic and adaptive equilibrium that is experienced from the interpersonal to the interpersonal through the family, community, nation, region, and the globe.

This book argues that one of the things peace "does" provides the grounds for trust and cooperation. These two facets of our species are deeply rooted elements of our history and can be relied upon as we move into the future. Human relations are complicated and messy because human beings are both capable of dispassionate logic and movements of passion that can push well past or even sidestep the illogical. Being in relation to another will always be constant navigation, negotiation, problem-solving exercise, and opportunity for transformation. It is unlikely that any form of human origination can be achieved without bringing competition and power imbalances. Rather than being a source of constant potential insecurity, it may be navigated with trust and vision that brings us together across distance and time. We know the converse is true; violent conflict reduces the human capacity to trust and shortens our time horizons. This book's foundation is that part of what peace does or can do is contribute to our long-term survival. It can improve our resiliencies and thus reduce our vulnerabilities to those acute threats to our existence and those that creep and build up slowly.

The emergence of PCS and ERS were influenced by similar historical moments and developed with comparable intentions of contributing to a better world; however, that better world may be understood. Both fields have faced similar obstacles—navigating values in research and practice and building a better world with scarce resources. There is a dissimilarity in how these fields have dealt with the issue of prioritization. The topic has not been an explicit focus for PCS, with the field's focus primarily determined by what has happened in the past. On the other hand, ERS has had the topic of prioritization as a more explicit focus and topic of debate since its inception, shaped mainly by concerns about what might happen in the future. Understanding time and measurement has shaped how prioritization is done. Understandings of peace are deeply connected to understandings of time. Determining the best way to work for the long-term future requires conceptualizing that far future and its connection to the present.

Further inquiry into the relationship between long-term human survival and peace brings profound philosophical questions. These questions may be easy enough to let go unexamined, but a robust inquiry into the intersections of these fields requires it. To answer why human extinction is a negative thing and peace is a positive one sets forth the motivation of this book.

Building on this foundation, I will explore five research lines at this intersection between PCS and ERS. These lines are: (1) Great Powers Conflicts; (2) Peace, Pandemic, and Conflict; (3) Climate Change, Peace, and Survival; (4) Peace, Conflict, and Emerging Technologies; and (5) Totalitarianism. These five were chosen because there are fertile points of departure for discussions on the relationship between survival and peace. They are also areas of investigation where the connections between concerns for peace and concerns for survival are linked.

When it comes to the possibility of a Great Powers conflict, it is clear that a perspective that brings together ERS and PCS is warranted. Both fields were shaped, at least partly by World War II, the dropping of the atomic bomb, the subsequent Cold War, and the threat of nuclear annihilation. At the dawn of the twenty-first century, we will likely see large-scale shifts in the geopolitical order. Just as the close of the twentieth century saw a shift from a bipolar to a unipolar world, new movements toward a multipolar one will likely bring tensions. In a competition among Great Powers, heightened tensions, war, and weapons of mass destruction are always topics of concern.

Human history has been shaped by disease and the pandemics it has survived. This book was written amidst the COVID-19 pandemic, which made our vulnerability to pandemic diseases apparent to the world and the host of compounding issues related to the disease outbreak. The effects of violent conflicts on pandemic diseases have been previously researched under the health for peace framework. One of the many lessons of the COVID-19 pandemic was that pandemics' effects on conflict are less understood. The interplay of pandemic disease, global cooperation, and peace and conflict issues is likely to be an important topic in the future.

It is no doubt that climate change is already one of the most pressing issues of our time and that given current trends having to address it is unavoidable. It is also becoming increasingly apparent that there are multiple ways in which conflict and climate change may feed into each other. There have already been large-scale migrations resulting from climate change, and in many cases, these migrations can contribute to increased tensions with host communities. Additionally, the often predicted but not yet fully realized possibility of waters wars remains an issue of concern. We have seen people fight over profitable resources such as oil or minerals. The level of conflict a violent struggle over water could entail is concerning.

Human history, and in many ways, even human evolution, is tied to its technological advancements. Several technologies exist in rudimentary forms (compared to the possible level of their actualization) that stand to be disruptive and potentially fundamentally transformative. Emerging technologies such as artificial intelligence, biotechnology, and nanotechnology stand poised to have far-reaching effects on almost any aspect of life. Further, their potential to directly or indirectly be used in or contribute to violent conflict is already a possibility that must be considered.

Finally, issues of peace and conflict and those necessary to reduce existent risks need to be acted upon by groups of organized people, the polis. There are already concerns about how the rise of totalitarian political powers may dramatically increase the level of structural and cultural violence in the world and contribute directly or indirectly to existential risks.

These five lines of inquiry were chosen on how they could synergize with each other. To significantly magnify the problem, one risk may interact with the other directly or indirectly. The pathway from highly escalated political tensions among Great Powers to nuclear war is already frighteningly imaginable. For example, competition between Great Powers over an emerging technology such as artificial intelligence could significantly increase the possibility of AI being an existential risk. An "AI arms race" could lead to corner-cutting regarding safety and a lack of the overall patience necessary to most beneficially develop such a powerful technology.

Regarding compounding risks and pandemics, the COVID-19 pandemic has shown how pandemics could become pathways to the rise of and solidification of authoritarian power. When AI augments high levels of surveillance, the overall level of concern could rise dramatically. This book will explore some possible interplays between different existential risks and factors contributing to peace and conflict.

My intention with this book is to introduce these research lines and highlight why they are important and why a perspective that brings together PCS and ERS is needed to understand and address them. For each research line, I discuss the central problems that lie at the intersection between PCS and ERS and then assess the nature and level of the types of risks presented.

The core problem for each topic will be discussed, and the relevant trends in the literature will be examined. I will take up the topic from the perspective of PCS. I will begin by summarizing the trends in PCS literature on the topic, followed by exploring how the topic could be considered a driving force for conflict as well as a force for peace. I will then conclude each section by reflecting on what a perspective at the intersection of PCS and ERS on the topic would look like, what questions arise at this intersection, and why they are important.

REFERENCES

80,000 Hours. 2021. "Our Current List of Pressing World Problems." *80000hours*. Accessed May 24, 2022. https://80000hours.org/problem-profiles/.

Alger, Chadwick F. 2014. *Peace Research and Peacebuilding*. London: Springer.

Anderson, Mary B., and Laura Olson. 2003. *Confronting War: Critical Lessons for Peace Practitioners*. Cambridge: The Collaborative for Development Action.

Baum, Seth D., Stuart Armstrong, Timoteus Ekenstedt, Olle Häggström, Robin Hanson, Karin Kuhlemann, Matthijs M. Maas, et al. 2019. "Long-Term Trajectories of Human Civilization." *Foresight* 21 (1): 53–83.

Berghof Foundation. 2020. *Dialogues*. https://www.berghof-foundation.org/en/publications/handbook/handbook-dialogues/.

Boulding, Kenneth, Bernard Feld, Arthur Larson, Charles Osgood, Ithiel Pool, and Richard Snider. 1963. "Peace Research Priorities." *American Behavioral Scientist* 6 (10): 25–28.
Brown, Michael E., and Richard N. Rosencrance. 1999. *The Costs of Conflict: Prevention and Cure in the Global Arena (Carnegie Commission on Preventing Deadly Conflict)*. Edited by Michael E. Brown and Richard N. Rosencrance. Rowman & Littlefield Publishers.
Collingridge, David. 1980. *The Social Control of Technology*. New York. St. Martin's Press.
Dietrich, Wolfgang. 2012. *Interpretations of Peace in History and Culture*. New York: Palgrave Macmillan.
Dietrich, Wolfgang. 2017. *Elicitive Conflict Mapping*. New York. Palgrave Macmillan.
Dietrich, Wolfgang. 2019. "Conviviality, Ego, Team and Theme Behavior in Transrational Peace Education." *Journal of Peace Education* 16 (3): 252–273.
Finneron-Burns, Elizabeth. 2017. "What's Wrong With Human Extinction?" *Canadian Journal of Philosophy*.
Galtung, Johan. 1960. "Violence, Peace, and Peace Research." *Journal of Peace Research* 6 (3): 167–191.
Galtung, Johan. 1990. "Cultural Violence." *Journal of Peace Research*. 291–305.
Gibbs, Matt. 2020. "See the Most Active Investors Behind the $14.92 Billion Invested into Life Science Companies since 2019." *Cipherbio News*, April 08. https://www.cipherbio.com/blog/see-the-top-life-science-investors-in-2019-2020/.
Global Priorities Institute. 2020. *A Research Agenda for the Global Priorities Institute*. Version 2.1. Oxford: Global Priorities Institute.
IEP. 2017. *Measuring Peace Building Cost-Effectiveness*. Sydney: Institute for Economics and Peace (IEP). http://visionofhumanity.org/app/uploads/2017/03/Measuring-Peacebuilding_WEB-1.pdf.
IEP. 2020. *Global Peace Index 2020: Measuring Peace in a Complex World*. Sydney: Institute for Economics and Peace.
Keown, Damien. 2003. *Oxford Dictionary of Buddhism*. New York: Oxford University Press.
Lederach, John Paul. 2005. *The Moral Imagination: The Art and Soul of Building Peace*. Oxford: Oxford University Press.
OECD. 2010. *Peacebuilding and Statebuilding—Priorities and Challenges: A Synthesis of Findings from Seven Multi-Stakeholder Consultations, Secretariat of the International Dialogue on Peacebuilding and Statebuilding*. Paris: Organisation for Economic Cooperation and Development (OECD).
Open Philanthropy. n.d. "Focus Areas- Global Catastrophic Risks." *Open Philanthropy*. Accessed May 23, 2022. https://www.openphilanthropy.org/focus/global-catastrophic-risks#Focus_areas.

Ord, Toby. 2020. *The Precipice: Existential Risk and the Future of Humanity.* New York: Hachette Books.

Schubert, Stefan, Lucius Caviola, and Nadira S. Faber. 2019. "The Psychology of Existential Risk: Moral Judgments about Human Extinction." *Sci Rep* 9.

SIPRI. 2020. *Stockholm International Peace Research Institute Military Expenditure Database.* Accessed August 21, 2020. https://www.sipri.org/databases/milex.

Snyder, Susi. 2019. *Shorting our Security: Financing the Companies that Make Nuclear Weapons.* Utrecht: International Campaign to Abolish Nuclear Weapons.

Taylor, Noah B. 2021. "Polishing Brass on the Titanic: Reflections on Humanity's Long-term Future." *Many Peaces Magazine.* Accessed May 31, 2022. https://magazine.manypeaces.org/2021/04/11/polishing-brass-on-the-titanic/.

Thee, Marek. 1979. "On Priorities in Peace Research." *Bulletin of Peace Proposals* 7 (1): 69–74.

Thee, Marek. 1983. "Scope and Priorities in Peace Research." *Bulletin of Peace Proposals* 14 (2): 69–74.

UNESCO. 2017. *Facts and figures: R&D expenditure.* https://web.archive.org/web/20171020233546/https://en.unesco.org/node/252279.

United Nations. 2020. "New Peacebuilding Commission Chair Outlines Priorities for 2020 Session, as Delegates Discuss Work Plan, Importance of Expanding Partnerships." *United Nations.* January 29. https://www.un.org/press/en/2020/pbc136.doc.htm.

Webb, Stephen. 2015. *If the Universe Is Teeming with Aliens...WHERE IS EVERYBODY? Seventy-Five Solutions to the Fermi Paradox and the Problem of Extraterrestrial Life.* 2nd ed. Heidelberg: Springer International Publishing.

CHAPTER 4

Great Powers Conflict

The possibility that a Great Power Conflict could pose an existential risk is a natural starting point for discussing the intersections between Existential Risk Studies (ERS) and Peace and Conflict Studies (PCS). Great Power Conflicts have been a primary concern for PCS, given that the development of the field is inexorably tied to the history of two world wars. The potential for catastrophe was made evident in 1945 over Hiroshima and Nagasaki and persists until today. A future Great Power Conflict may be the easiest to imagine, not that it is necessarily the most likely, but rather that it has happened many times before. The shift from a multipolar to a bipolar to a unipolar geopolitical order was a presumed trajectory of the twentieth century. This order is likely in the process of changing again, perhaps into a different kind of multipolar system. These shifts will bring a host of tensions within and between countries.

While it is the nature of countries to compete by looking out for their self-interests, the possibility of competition resulting in escalations of tensions is very real. The destruction wrought by World War I stood in stark contrast to previous Great Power Conflicts due to the industrial revolution changing the scale and scope of what wars could be. This trend continued through World War II and the critical juncture of nuclear war, where the scale and scope increased exponentially. The possibility of a nuclear war has never gone away. By their very existence, such technology always puts global conflicts on the list of global catastrophic risks and

© The Author(s), under exclusive license to Springer Nature Switzerland AG 2023
N. B. Taylor, *Existential Risks in Peace and Conflict Studies*, Rethinking Peace and Conflict Studies,
https://doi.org/10.1007/978-3-031-24315-8_4

possible existential risks. Just as the destruction of war has shaped human history, so has it been shaped by the termination of hostilities and peace. Because Great Power Conflicts have happened before, more is known about how they work while other more seemingly theoretical risks such as artificial super intelligence. The oversimplified process by which a Great Powers Conflict occurs is that normal competition between countries becomes a conflict that continues to escalate until hostilities break out.

Based on this overly simplified model, interventions to prevent or mitigate a Great Power Conflict as an Existential Risk would focus on reducing tensions between Great Powers and decreasing the likelihood of those tensions leading to war and the long-term potential of that war destroying the human species. Beginning with what is known, while keeping in mind what has been learned from the past, can guide humanity into the future.

What Is a "Great Power"?

The designation of "Great Power" and what constitutes a "Great Power Conflict" are not precisely technical terms. The questions of how a Great Power is defined, who gets to make that definition, and what results from that definition are all contentious issues. Definitions have ranged from developed countries, the first world, the wealthiest states, and states with a minimum standard of living or industrial societies (Fettweis 2006).

As Great Power Conflicts invoke the frame of realpolitik, military strength is often thought to be, at least in part, a defining characteristic. Measuring a country's military power is complex and debated. Factors often used are overall military expenditure, military expenditure as related to Gross Domestic Product (GDP), industrial capacity, population size, number of troops, quantity and quality of weapons, and location of military facilities. Definitions from International Relations often build on the importance of measuring military capacity in combination with the overall population, the size of the territory, the amount of natural and economic resources, and the stability of their political system relative to other countries (Waltz 1979). Further power is always a unit of relative measure, so these factors must be considered in relation to other countries. Many ranking systems of the most powerful militaries in 2022 seem to agree on placing the USA, the People's Republic of China (PRC), and Russia in the top three slots. These same systems rank a combination of Germany, Japan, India, Israel, and South Korea for the fourth and fifth positions (GFP 2022; Edudwar 2022; US News 2022).

Possession of nuclear weapons can contribute to status as a Great Power as they are an additional measure of a country's military strength and a bargaining chip. There are nine countries currently thought to have nuclear weapons: the USA, Russia, the PRC, the UK, France, the Democratic People's Republic of Korea (DPRK), India, Pakistan, and Israel[1] (FAS 2022). Of these nuclear-armed countries, only the USA, Russia, and the PRC are usually considered to have the status of Great Powers.

International institutions have also defined Great Powers through formal recognition. For example, the Congress of Vienna brought Austria, Prussia, Russia, Great Britain, and France together. This congress determined the "great powers" to be those that helped to overthrow Napoleon. The United Nations Security Council recognizes five permanent members: the PRC, France, Russia, the UK, and the USA, the victors of World War II. The Group of Seven (G7) is an inter-governmental forum that comprises Canada, France, Germany, Italy, Japan, the UK, and the USA. Membership was determined by various factors, including economic development and liberal democratic institutions and practices.

The Hague Centre for Strategic Studies defines Great Powers based on two main criteria. First, Great Powers can pursue their interests through military, economic, political, and diplomatic means. Secondly, they must be able to impact the global security environment through involvement in wars and alliances and have diplomatic influence bolstered through their strong roles in international institutions. Their list of current Great Powers includes the USA, Russia, the PRC, and the European Union (Sweijs et al. 2014). In addition to all these factors, the American political scientist John Muller adds their behavior, their "actual bellicosity," as one of the key elements distinguishing a Great Power from the others (Muller 1995). In a less sharply defined sense, it may be possible to define Great Powers as those with a more significant possibility of determining the world's fate through their actions or inactions.

For this chapter, two sets of Great Powers will be considered. The first set is the USA and the PRC, and the second set includes the first along with Russia and India. This distinction is helpful because the USA and the PRC can be considered Great Powers in relatively similar ways. The status of the USA as a Great Power since the end of the Cold War has rarely been

---

[1] Israel has never publicly disclosed possession of nuclear weapons; estimates are taken from the Federation of American Scientists.

questioned. Given its economic power and military strength, it has extended its influence worldwide for the past seven decades.

The PRC, which already has the second-largest economy in terms of Gross Domestic Product (GDP), with current economic growth rates will likely continue to be one of the most economically powerful countries. Their military size and possession of nuclear weapons further their overall power. These two countries have a history of economic competition, ideological differences, and multiple possible trigger points (e.g., the South China Sea and Taiwan).

Russia and India are unique cases. The overall economic power of Russia is dwarfed by the USA, the PRC, and India, as well as by many other countries not often considered on the list of contenders for Great Power status. Despite its relatively smaller economy, it is based on oil and gas, resources that will likely remain in high demand for the foreseeable future. Additionally, Russia's military spending is often much higher than in other countries. These military resources, the large number of nuclear weapons, their demonstrated willingness to aggressively violate international norms, and their capacity to destabilize the international order are all reasons for placing it in the Great Powers category. India is also a possible contender for consideration as a Great Power in the near future. It has a large military, possesses nuclear weapons, and most importantly, has exceptionally high levels of economic growth. Additionally, it sits on several potential geopolitical trigger points with contentious border disputes with China and Pakistan, both of which have nuclear weapons.

What Is a Great Power Conflict?

In the global system, countries navigate complex balances of competition and cooperation. A Great Powers Conflict occurs when competition between two or more countries falling in the category of Great Powers escalates to a level that results in violent conflict. Often this level is defined as 1000 battle deaths per year (Levy 1982; Small and Singer 1979). In the past, the types of violence entailed were large-scale ground warfare, aerial bombardments, forced occupation, concentration camps, and nuclear weapons. The nature of a future conflict is unknown. Large-scale ground attacks indeed remain a possibility. The history of the Cold War indicates that proxy warfare is likely. The "War on Terror" could suggest that Great Powers engage with each other by supporting insurgency and counter-insurgency warfare in other countries. It is also likely that the Great Powers would use forms of economic warfare. Further, drone and cyber warfare advancements could contribute to a conflict on that scale.

Why Is It a Problem?

The notion that another Great Power Conflict would be terrible is hard to dispute. Each of the previous two world wars caused the deaths of tens of millions, if not more, and wreaked havoc and suffering on a global scale. A new conflict on this level stands to be particularly disastrous for a variety of reasons. Nuclear weapons only came into existence at the end of World War II; if World War III were to break out, an estimated 13,080 nuclear weapons could be deployed (Arms Control Association 2022a). A Great Powers Conflict will likely lead to the breakdown of the global cooperation needed to address many other potential existential threats that may lie on our horizon—the existential risk potential of nuclear war and the dynamics by which a Great Powers Conflict represents a significant *indirect* risk. In ERS, indirect risks are those that "threaten extinction without killing everyone [and] reduce our long-term ability to survive as a species" (Cotton-Barrat et al. 2020, 272). They are often subdivided into *habitat risks*, those threats that make the future impossible by destroying the environment so they cannot support human life, and capability risks that threaten to remove a fundamental aspect of society, thereby making survival impossible (Cotton-Barrat et al. 2020).

A Great Powers Conflict also represents a philosophical challenge to liberal understandings of world order. The global political system is made up of states. These states may belong to regional organizations such as the Organization of American States, the African Union, or the Association of Southeast Asian Nations. They also may be a part of international institutions such as the United Nations, the World Economic Forum, or the World Trade Organization. Each of these represents efforts to establish platforms for cooperation; however, in most cases, the sovereignty of the nation-state remains *almost* the highest principle and final authority. The status of sovereignty is qualified here because it is arguable that the sovereignty of a Great Power is more secure than that of a less powerful country due to their ability to resist, through the threat of force, violations of their sovereignty. This dilemma frames a crucial political question facing the world regarding how we will organize ourselves going into the future.

Great Power Conflict in Existential Risk Studies

Likelihood and Type of Risk

In order to understand how dangerous a Great Power Conflict could be requires examining the likelihood that it could occur, the type of risk it could pose, and the level of destruction it is likely to bring. For several reasons, calculating the likelihood that a Great Power Conflict will happen is difficult. First of all, the causes of war are complex and multifaceted. They are also time-dependent; there is no assurance that the causal factors that led to the first two world wars and the Cold War would function in the same way now or in the near future. Further, the overall sample size is quite small to make accurate predictions. Jack Levy (1982) calculated that there were only 64 Great Power Conflicts from 1495 to 1975, with only 25% occurring in the last 287 years. His calculations do not count the Cold War (since it ended in 1991). There have only been six Great Power Conflicts (counting the Cold War) in the last 108 years. Further, there are currently only 195 countries in the world. Assuming that there are five Great Powers would mean that Great Powers constitute only 2.5% of the total number of countries.

Toby Ord estimates that the risk of a Great Power Conflict is more than 1% over the next 100 years. In his rough estimation, this would mean that before 2021 one-tenth of the total existential risk was due to Great Powers Conflict. These odds make it one of the most significant contributors, indirectly, to humanity's overall level of existential risks (Ord 2020). The nonprofit organization, 80,000 Hours, has placed it on its list of current issues of concern (80,000 Hours 2021). In a report for the Founders Pledge, *Great Power Conflict* (2021), Stephen Claire estimated, based on a collection of studies, that there is approximately a 33% chance of a Great Power Conflict occurring in the next 100 years at or exceeding the scale of World War II. He points out that this estimate falls in the middle range, below the historical trend of two Great Power Conflicts every hundred years and above the current trend of zero (Clare 2021). These estimates were made before Russia invaded Ukraine in February 2022. I wrote this book during the early days of this conflict. The full scale of this war is yet to be seen. It has likely increased the risk of a Great Power Conflict and perhaps other existential threats.

The literature on Great Power Conflicts frames it as an indirect or a compounding risk. Unlike a cataclysmic asteroid, it is difficult to imagine how such a conflict would directly lead to human extinction. The indirect pathways are easier to imagine. A Great Powers Conflict could result in an intentional or unintended nuclear strike, likely resulting in retaliation and nuclear war. In an even less direct manner, a Great Power Conflict would likely result in a breakdown of trust at the global level, making cooperation on other possible existential risks like climate change difficult. War, especially at this scale, significantly directs resources and attention toward it and away from other issues. This decrease in the overall global resilience to deal with threats to existence could feasibly happen at levels of extreme geopolitical tension without necessarily requiring the outbreak of a violent conflict. Thus, it is imaginable that the overall amount of conflict, directly violent or not, between Great Powers increases the potential for other threats to rise to the level of threatening our existence.

How Bad Could It Be?

In the Founders Pledge report on Great Powers Conflicts, Clare (2021) describes three possible existential risk scenarios that could result from such conflicts. The first is a Great Power Conflict increasing other potential existential risks. A foreseeable pathway to this scenario is where heightened tensions or outright conflict between Great Powers breakdown international cooperation and coordination that would have otherwise mitigated that risk. An example of this scenario would be tensions or conflicts between Great Powers Conflict inhibiting cooperation from addressing extreme climate change, which becomes an existential threat (the likelihood of climate change resulting in an existential risk will be addressed in Chap. 5). Similarly, the state of insecurity created by this breakdown of trust could direct more investment into technological research that could be used for military purposes, increasing the likelihood that an unexpected "black ball technology" is created. These technologies are those that, once invented, destroy their creators. Possible examples of this kind of emerging technologies would be massively more powerful nuclear weapons or unaligned artificial intelligence (the possibility of emerging technologies resulting in an existential risk will be discussed in Chap. 6) (Clare 2021).

A second possible outcome would be the Great Power Conflict directly causing an existential catastrophe. A pathway to this scenario is the ever-present possibility of a nuclear war erupting from a Great Powers Conflict (Clare 2021). As long as nuclear weapons exist, nuclear war is always possible. The doomsday clock of the Bulletin of the Atomic Scientists places the world at 100 seconds to midnight, a symbolic representation of their analysis that we are currently closer to a nuclear catastrophe than at any point since it was created at the outset of the Cold War in 1947 (Bulletin of the Atomic Scientists 2020). There are currently 13,410 nuclear weapons possessed by nine countries (Russia 6370, USA 5800, PRC 320, France 290, UK 195, Pakistan 160, India 150, Israel 90, and DPRK 35[2]) (Korda and Kristensen 2020).

There are four main areas of concern on this nuclear pathway to catastrophe: (1) the escalation of tensions between Great Powers leads to a nuclear conflict; (2) escalating tensions between a nuclear-armed Great Power and a non-nuclear non-Great Power leads to a multiparty nuclear exchange; (3) a nuclear provocation from a Rogue State (a nation or state considered to be breaking international law and posing a security threat) or subnational actors provoke a nuclear response from a Great Power, and (4) an accident or misunderstanding with a nuclear system leads to war.

The escalation dynamics that would likely be the precursor to a nuclear conflict may be further compounded by the influences of emerging technologies such as artificial intelligence, which may undermine the balance of nuclear security (Horowitz 2018). Further, social media has already shown to be a disruptive technology and to escalate tensions during times of crisis between Great Powers and could be a factor pushing the escalation of such a conflict (Williams and Drew 2020). The combination of these technologies, for example, distributing sophisticated deepfake videos across social media, is likely to be a concern for conflict escalation in the near future.

The next step in the chain of logic of determining how severe a Great Power Conflict could be if it leads to nuclear war is to assess the possible scope and magnitude of a nuclear conflict. A nuclear conflict's overall effects would be determined by the interactions between a wide range of factors, from the number and type of weapons used, where they were detonated, at what altitude, the weather, how much smoke is produced, the immediate and subsequent reactions of affected populations and countries. The initial blasts would cause death and destruction. This magnitude would be determined by the number of nuclear weapons deployed and their targets. Next would come radioactive fallout that would likely kill

---

[2] These are estimates from the Federation of American Scientists. The exact number of nuclear weapons often has to be estimated and countries such as Israel have never publicly disclosed having nuclear weapons.

many more than the blasts as the acute and chronic effects would be widespread and enduring.

Likely, the radiation itself would not constitute an existential risk. It is estimated that nuclear exchanges involving most of the world's nuclear arsenal would not irradiate the entire earth (Feld 1979). The next level of effects would come from the nuclear fallout causing a temporary but severe global temperature drop and blocking out the sun. This lack of sunlight would dramatically shorten growing seasons worldwide, disrupt food chains, and lead to food insecurity (Robock et al. 2007). Even dramatic food shortages are not likely to cause an existential risk as some food production would be possible. No current researchers argue that a nuclear winter would lead to our extinction (Ord 2020).

Another possible step in this chain of logic is that the reduction in food security could lead to a subsequent conflict through decreasing food security and increasing desperation, which leads to increased conflict. There is little evidence in scholarly research that shows a short-term reduction in food access increases the likelihood of conflict. This assumption is likely because initiating a violent conflict requires both means and will; hunger inhibits both (Vestby et al. 2018). Nonetheless, since a food shortage on this scale due to nuclear winter has not occurred before, it is prudent to consider the combined effect of these variables on further conflicts and existential risk.

Similarly, there is also the question of how governments and people are likely to react to a nuclear conflict. It remains unknown if the history of World War II is sufficient guidance for modeling a future nuclear-weapon deployment. Would the shock of such a horror dramatically change the frame, public opinion, and political will and move toward a de-escalation, or would a nuclear strike and its after-effects lead to further conflict escalation between Great Powers and other nuclear-armed states? With the potential for large-scale harm possible through Great Powers Conflict, it will be important for research to explore which factors are most likely to increase the chances of a Great Powers Conflict. How could these factors lead to a nuclear conflict, and to what degree does this constitute an existential risk?

The third possible scenario is where a Great Power Conflict combines with another risk to cause an existential catastrophe. In this scenario, the risk that the conflict combines with is not directly due to the conflict itself. There are at least two possible pathways that could result in this outcome. The first of these could occur when, in the aftermath of a Great Power

Conflict, the winner(s) can impose their political order and governance system on others, resulting in a totalitarian lock-in. A series of events would need to occur for this pathway to find its way to becoming an existential risk. First, there would have to be a Great Power War that is highly destructive. A totalitarian regime would need to either be the victor or survive the conflict less scathed than others. This regime would need to want to leverage this position to become a global empire. This new Great, or perhaps "Greatest" power, would then need to achieve a level of hegemony to impose its values on the rest of the world while simultaneously being able to successfully quell any competition to its status while suppressing revolt worldwide. This new geopolitical system would then need to be able to persist indefinitely. For most of these final steps to occur, the new regime would likely have to have technology that does not yet exist to achieve surveillance and control on this scale (2021). The likelihood of totalitarianism becoming an existential risk will be discussed in Chap. 8.

A second possible pathway for a Great Power Conflict to become an existential threat is through its synergy with another existential threat, where a disaster that would typically be survivable occurs in the aftermath of a global war. A world at relative peace may be able to mitigate the risk that something like an asteroid impact would destroy our existence. A world still reeling from the destruction that such a war could create may not have that ability. Another worrying example would be the spread of a pandemic disease in the aftermath of a Great Power Conflict. The COVID-19 pandemic has already made apparent that a world not in the throes of a Great Power Conflict was largely unprepared to deal with such a threat (Clare 2021). The connections among pandemic diseases, conflicts, and existential risks will be discussed in Chap. 5.

So, how dangerous is a Great Powers Conflict? Estimates vary in the likelihood of its occurrence, but all estimates are above zero, and if they have happened before, they can happen again. The particular constellations a future Great Powers Conflict could take are diverse. The players are unknown—which countries may be considered "Great Powers" in the future depends on a complex set of economic, political, and military variables and how history unfolds. The undetermined set of actors is given the tools of interstate, proxy, hybrid, economic, and cyber warfare to be deployed in combination with each other. There are many ways in which these conflicts could result in an existential catastrophe. Breakdowns in international cooperation may leave humanity in a vulnerable position with regard to other threats. As cooperation breaks down, distrust rises, making a rapid and reckless investment into dangerous technology more likely. Added to these dangerous dynamics is the ever-present specter of nuclear arms. The concern is warranted.

Great Powers Conflict in Peace and Conflict Studies

Since humanity has experienced many Great Power Conflicts in its history, observations have been made on causative factors. The way humanity has understood these dynamics led to the development of theories, structures, and institutions to understand and address these problems. These understandings must be continually reassessed for their current relevance and potential value while keeping a critical eye. While the past is a good place to start when understanding the present and can serve as a cautious guide to the future, the ways of understanding Great Power Conflicts may apply more to the past than to the future.

Conflict Escalation and De-escalation

Conflict escalation is the primary dynamic that transforms competition between states into conflict. These escalatory dynamics have, in the past, resulted in arms races and the buildup of military capacity. These types of relationships can often trigger a security/insecurity dilemma where the buildup of military might in one country results in the perception of insecurity in another country, motivating them to build up their military, and the loop continues to spiral.

A somewhat caricaturized model of escalation dynamics follows a bell curve tracking conflict intensity over time. Latent conflict exists between the parties, and some triggering events or developments push the conflict to emerge and escalate to the point of stalemate. Neither party can afford to escalate the conflict further and is more likely to be open to negotiation. Through these negotiations, a settlement to the dispute is found, and efforts are made to rebuild the damaged relationships (Brahm 2003). Parties escalate the conflict to win, not lose, cover investments, gain support, seize an advantage, punish, or reward. Zartman and Faure identify nine ways a conflict can be escalated[3] (2005, 7–9). The body of research

---

[3] Escalation of means, ends, space, price, parties, images, risk, costs, and commitment (Zartman and Faure 2005, 7–9).

on conflict escalation dynamics is vast, and it is likely the exact pathway by which escalation would occur in a specific conflict would not fit neatly into any model. Nonetheless, reassessment of these models in light of current and future geopolitical dynamics is likely to prove valuable. These new models would also need to account for developments in technology, the influences of climate change, social media, and other existential risks. Further bilateral tensions between two countries can spill over into the international arena.

Attention to the models or heuristics that guide analysis regarding Great Powers Conflicts is important. Thucydides Trap is a model in International Relations. The term refers to the dynamics between Athens and Sparta during the Peloponnesian War. It is often summarized as "it was the rise of the Athens and the fear this instilled in Sparta that made war inevitable" (Thucydides 1972, 51). The term describes a situation where "a rising power threatens to displace a ruling power" and sets the stage for a dangerous situation (Allison 2017, 8). More than a single event that sparks the war, it is a complex set of social and cultural factors that lay the foundation for war and allow manageable conflicts to escalate into a war. In his book *Destined for War*, Graham Allison points out that the USA and the PRC facing Thucydides' Trap is "the natural, inevitable discombobulation that occurs when a rising power threatens to displace a ruling power" (2017, 27).

Given the attention this perspective has received, it warrants the consideration of researchers concerned with existential risks and peace to assess its validity and predictive power. Conflict transformation strategies must be developed in this context if the model holds. However, the accuracy and relevance of this model need to be critically assessed. Thucydides' Trap is most commonly used to characterize relations between the PRC and the USA, lending credence to the perspective that conflict between these two powers is likely. The model may be less valid if conflicts between the USA and rising countries such as Brazil, India, or the PRC are considered as these conflicts are rarely discussed (Holmes 2013). Many Chinese scholars hold that this model does not accurately describe Sino-US relations and, instead, that the rise of China needs to be understood from a holistic perspective and not as a zero-sum game (Shengli and Huiyi 2018). Others warn that Thucydides' Trap may be a self-fulfilling prophecy and that framing US-China relations in such a manner may predispose us to think that conflict is inevitable (Kissinger 2011). Care needs to be taken by researchers so that the lessons learned from history and the models developed for analyzing Great Power Conflicts illuminate more than they obscure.

A Great Power Conflict likely becomes an existential risk by escalating one or more conflicts. Further, given the possible stakes of a future world war, extra impetus may be put on efforts to mitigate tensions before hostilities intensify through diplomacy and other structures. Efforts to reduce conflict escalation between Great Powers have been and will continue to be a key facet of working on Great Powers Conflicts.

Zartman and Faure (2005) identify many variables that can influence the escalation of conflict—fear, fatigue, and mutually hurting stalemates;[4] changes in stakes, changes in parties, changes in attitudes, disengagement, confidence- and security-building measures, learning, reaffirming relationships, mutually enticing opportunities, and cultural values (12–13)—all of these stand to be important variables in methods of intervening in conflict escalation between Great Powers. Further, large-scale shocks, either natural or anthropogenic, may provide opportunities for ending rivalries between Great Powers (Goertz and Diehl 1995).

Approaches to Prevention and Mitigation of Great Power Conflicts

Since Great Power Conflicts occur between nations, approaches to addressing them have tended to come from statecraft, diplomacy, and international relations. These approaches have focused mainly on preventing or diffusing tensions between states, stopping the escalation of conflict once it starts to develop, and efforts to develop sets of international norms to make it less likely that such a war would become an existential catastrophe.

The first leverage point in preventing a Great Powers Conflict from becoming an existential catastrophe is efforts to prevent tensions between countries from arising or being exacerbated into war. Intervening at either of these points requires interventions focusing on how countries relate; diplomacy is a natural starting point. The role and function of a diplomat long predates the invention of the state. Likely, the need for an individual to represent the needs and interests of a group stretches back into prehistory. Today, professional diplomats appointed by the state play out their roles in protocols established by the Vienna Convention. Ostensibly, they

---

[4] A mutually hurting stalemate is a ripe moment for negotiation due to escalation on all sides to the point where no further escalation is considered worthwhile (Zartman and Faure 2005).

are charged with building and maintaining the connections necessary to facilitate bilateral relations between the host country and the home country, which also implies that the diplomat is involved in preventing or mitigating bilateral tensions.

While important, traditional diplomacy is inadequate as a sole means of diffusing international tensions. There have been diplomats in every Great Powers Conflict. Just as PCS emerged when World War II showed that previous approaches to conflict prevention were insufficient to stop the outbreak of a world war, so too have there been calls to challenge and expand the understanding of what diplomacy is and who can do it. The designations of track 1.5 and track 2 approaches are now commonplace examples of this expansion. Track 1.5 expanded the understanding of diplomacy to understand officials working in an unofficial capacity with the addition of nongovernmental experts. Track 1.5 approaches have also expanded into track 2, which takes place outside the frame of the government and refers to all those less-than-official efforts focused on reducing conflict, lowering tensions, building trust, and improving cooperation. This categorization is a recognition of the role of professional peace work beyond the scope of the government. Because it is outside the official channels, track 2 diplomatic efforts are often easier because less pressure is put on them, and less press coverage can reduce the need for hardline posturing.

The nature of diplomatic work has changed over time. In the past, far from the countries they represented, diplomats largely had to rely on their capacities to navigate territories of power. They had to skillfully deploy their charisma and communication skills within the narrow confines of protocols. Dietrich (2013) notes that the information technology revolution has contributed most significantly to the changing nature of diplomatic work. What was once done by diplomats can now be done directly through the centers of power with the result that "traditional diplomacy has been downgraded from an art to an administrative tool" (161).

While these two approaches to diplomatically managing tensions fall more in the realm of International Relations, an example of what could be considered a PCS approach to diplomacy is the role the Esalen Institute played between the USA and the Soviet Union during the Cold War. Esalen was established in 1962 in Big Sur, California, by Michael Murphy and Dick Price. The institute aimed to assist humanity in the realization of its highest potential. It was responsible for many advancements in psychology, psychotherapy, and the development of humanistic and transpersonal psychology. The works of Abraham Maslow, Carl Rogers, Virginia Satir,

Frederick Perls, Ruth Cohn, Gregory Bateson, Paul Goodman, and Ludwig von Bertalanffy all came out of the fields of psychology that developed in Esalen. These same advancements became essential foundations of Elicitive Conflict Transformation (Dietrich 2013).

In the 1960s and 1970s, Esalen played an important role at the end of the Cold War. Through their "Russian American Center," which later became "Track Two: An Institute for Citizen Diplomacy," Esalen engaged in what would now be called multitrack diplomacy. They facilitated the creation of the space for scientists to come to the USA from the Union of Soviet Socialist Republic and vice versa. They also participated in novel programs such as the US-Soviet Space Bridge. This program began in the 1980s and utilized satellite communication technology to facilitate teleconferences between citizens on both sides of the iron curtain. These communications aimed to work on issues of mutual mistrust between the two countries. Keyssar (1994) evaluated the effectiveness of these programs and found that they changed the perceptions of ordinary citizens, particularly in the Soviet Union. The impact could also be seen at the governmental level. Kripal builds on these claims stating, "Esalen played its own part in the collapse of Soviet Communism, the softening of American militarism, and the ending of the Cold War" (2007, 316).

The work of the Esalen Institute went well beyond the understanding of track 2 diplomacy at the time. Their work can be understood in the frame of multitrack diplomacy, which classifies the diplomatic role and modes of action into nine sectors: (1) Government, (2) Professional Conflict Resolution, (3) Business, (4) Private Citizens, (5) Research, Training, and Education, (6) Peace Activism, (7) Religion, (8) Funding, and (9) Media and Public Opinion (Diamond and McDonald 1996). This way of understanding diplomacy sees the sector as integrally important and interconnected in supporting the overall goal of peace, rather than being a support system for official track 1 approaches.

A critical question for Peace Research is how diplomacy can be used to prevent another world war. The expansion of diplomatic efforts to include additional types of actors and modes of working has helped to "put diplomacy back into the hands of society without excluding or abolishing traditional diplomacy" (Dietrich 2013, 163). This expansion of diplomacy is an obvious foundation for addressing the problem of Great Power Conflicts given the possible stakes increasing who is involved and how will be necessary. Suppose this diplomatic expansion is brought together with an overarching concern for the survival of the human species. In that case, this transpersonal orientation may serve as a powerful impetus for more trust in diplomatic solutions.

The second leverage point in preventing a Great Powers Conflict from becoming an existential catastrophe is efforts aimed at preventing the destruction of humanity—identifying ways to discourage nuclear-armed states from using those weapons. Nuclear states have previously and are amassing staggering nuclear stockpiles, and despite this literal minefield, humanity has not extinguished itself. This remarkable feat is often attributed to the international nonproliferation regime. The Treaty on the Non-Proliferation of Nuclear Weapons (NPT) is regarded as one of the most important international efforts to address the problem of nuclear weapons. The NPT entered into force in 1970. It identifies the nuclear-weapon states as the USA, Russia, the UK, France, and the PRC. In its core agreements, non-nuclear-weapons countries will not pursue the development of nuclear-weapons programs, the nuclear-weapons countries agree to share the benefits of peaceful nuclear technology, and all agree to work toward the total elimination of nuclear weapons. More countries are part of the NPT than any other arms limitation treaty, pointing to the importance of these efforts (UN n.d.).

In many ways, the NPT can be seen as having achieved many of its important objectives. Due to the NPT and subsequent treaties, the total number of long-range nuclear weapons in the world was cut in half between 1968 and 2007, and the total size of the nuclear stockpile has continued to decrease since then (Cirincione 2008). The Federation of American Scientists has measured that over the last 30 years, the total global nuclear inventory has been on a steady decline (FAS 2022). With the addition of the Comprehensive Test Ban Treaty in 1996, there have been no nuclear tests until North Korea's test in 2007. Much of the world has established nuclear-weapon-free zones (NWFZ). These zones span much of the global south, including Latin America, the South Pacific, Southeast Asia, Africa, and Central Asia (Arms Control Association 2022b).

The overarching objective of the NPT, a world free of nuclear weapons, remains elusive. Russia and the USA still possess 90% of the global nuclear warheads and delivery systems stock. The collapse in 2019 of the 1987 Intermediate-range Nuclear Forces Treaty (INF) was a setback in arms control efforts. Further arms control negotiations have been deadlocked between Russia and the USA since 2010 while working on the New Strategic Arms Reduction Treaty (New START). In the past few years, there has been an increase in the number of nuclear warheads in stockpiles, including those for operational forces (FAS 2022). In many ways, the arms control architecture developed during the Cold War has eroded (SIPRI 2022).

The Cold War-era posture has continued with thousands of nuclear missiles ready to launch with short notice. Some of these weapons are set up for launch-on-warning, meaning that the reality of an attack would not need to be confirmed before launching a counter-attack. Such postures dramatically increase the chance of an accidental nuclear strike. US presidents Regan, George W. Bush, and Obama have all expressed concern about the short time window a US president would have to decide to launch a nuclear counter-attack. Bush complained that he would not even have enough time to "get off the crapper" (Blair 2020). The concern is warranted. The history of nuclear security is full of examples of close calls. In 1996 a Norwegian weather rocket was mistaken for a US ballistic missile by the Russian military. Boris Yeltsin had the nuclear suitcase open, but luckily for humanity, he decided that the radar was mistaken (Cirincione 2008).

Despite the hurdles that nuclear nonproliferation regimes have encountered and that they have not yet achieved the ambitious goal of a world free from nuclear weapons, their successes point toward their utility. If the NPT could be negotiated and implemented amidst the tensions of the Cold War, then it is likely that similar efforts will prove useful in the future (Bernstein 2018). Such agreements can be understood as orienting global vision and action from the present to the future. In a joint statement on the NPT in 2018 signed by Sergey Lavrov (Russian Minister of Foreign Affairs), Boris Johnson (Foreign Secretary of the UK), and Michael Pompeo (US Security of State), leaders agreed that the success of the NPT was never a sure thing and its future success is not inevitable, but rather the efforts that founded it represent an investment in the shared future of humanity to ensure our security and prosperity. These efforts require continued commitment and responsiveness to a changing world and emerging proliferation challenges (US Department of State 2018).

Questions for the Future

How could the dynamics that lead to a Great Powers Conflict increase existential risks?

Which diplomacy, conflict transformation, or peacebuilding strategies are likely to be most effective in mitigating these risks?

To what degree can previous models of Great Power Conflicts accurately guide preventing them in the future?

The experiences of Great Powers Conflicts, particularly World Wars I and II, lead to the development of both PCS and ERS. The specter of another, even more destructive war has haunted humanity since the dropping of the first nuclear bomb. This critical juncture in human history revealed many truths to humanity. For the first time, humanity had a clear image of how it could contribute to its own destruction. Humanity also learned that our understanding was not great enough and we could not trust it enough to ensure that we would not start another world war and use these weapons again. Since World War II the possibility that a Great Power Conflict could lead to human extinction has increased. The total number and power of the world's nuclear arsenal has grown since then.

Further, we can now imagine the possible compounding interactions between risks like climate change, which existed during World War II, but we were not aware of it as well as risks we could not have imagined, such as artificial intelligence. There is a need for more and diverse research on the dynamics that could lead to a Great Power Conflict and how that could increase the likelihood of an existential threat. When conceptualizing ways of stopping or preventing a Great Power Conflict with its known potential to contribute to existential risk, it will be important to explore which strategies are most likely to be effective in mitigating these risks. Since Great Power Conflicts are one of the few possible existential risks that humanity has historically experienced, there are existing theories, models, and best practices, and it will be prudent for peace researchers to assess how much what has been learned from the past can accurately guide humanity in the future.

References

80,000 Hours. 2021. "Our Current List of Pressing World Problems." *80000hours*. Accessed May 24, 2022. https://80000hours.org/problem-profiles/.

Allison, Graham T. 2017. *Destined for War: Can America and China Escape Thucydides's Trap?* Houghton Mifflin Harcourt.

Arms Control Association. 2022a. "Nuclear Weapons: Who Has What at a Glance." *Arms Control Association*. Accessed June 12, 2022. https://www.armscontrol.org/factsheets/Nuclearweaponswhohaswhat.

Arms Control Association. 2022b. "Nuclear-Weapon-Free Zones (NWFZ) At a Glance." *Arms Control Association*. Accessed May 14, 2022. https://www.armscontrol.org/factsheets/nwfz#:~:text=A%20nuclear%2Dweapon%2Dfree%20zone%20(NWFZ)%20is%20a,spanning%20the%20entire%20Southern%20Hemisphere.

Bernstein, Jackie O'Halloran. 2018. "Successes, Challenges, and Steps Forward for Nonproliferation." *Arms Control Today* 48 (5): 12–15.

Blair, Bruce G. 2020. "Loose Cannons: The President and US Nuclear Posture." *The Bulletin of Atomic Scientists*. January 1. Accessed September 1, 2022. https://thebulletin.org/premium/2020-01/loose-cannons-the-president-and-us-nuclear-posture/.

Brahm, Eric. 2003. "Conflict Stages." *Beyond Intractability*. edited by Guy Burgess and Heidi Burgess. Conflict Information Consortium, University of Colorado, Boulder. September. http://www.beyondintractability.org/essay/conflict-stages.

Bulletin of the Atomic Scientists. 2020. "Current Time." *Bulletin of the Atomic Scientists*. January 23. https://thebulletin.org/doomsday-clock/current-time.

Cirincione, Joseph. 2008. "The Continuing Threat of Nuclear War." In *Global Catastrophic Risks*, edited by Nick Bostrom and Milan M. Ćirković. New York: Oxford University Press.

Clare, Stephen. 2021. *Great Power Conflict*. Founders Pledge.

Cotton-Barrat, Owen, Max Daniel, and Andres Sandberg. 2020. "Defence in Depth Against Human Extinction: Prevention, Response, Resilience, and Why they All Matter." *Global Policy* 11 (3): 271–282.

Diamond, Louise, and John McDonald. 1996. *Multi-Track Diplomacy: A Systems Approach to Peace*. 3rd ed. Boulder, CO: Kumarian Press.

Dietrich, Wolfgang. 2013. *Elicitive Conflict Transformation and the Transrational Shift in Peace Politics*. New York: Palgrave Macmillan.

Edudwar. 2022. "Strongest Militaries in the World." *Edudwar*, August 26. Accessed September 1, 2022. https://www.edudwar.com/strongest-militaries-in-the-world/.

FAS. 2022. "Status of World Nuclear Forces." *Federation of American Scientists*. Accessed June 09, 2022. https://fas.org/issues/nuclear-weapons/status-world-nuclear-forces/.

Feld, Bernard T. 1979. "The Consequences of Nuclear War." *Bulletin of the Atomic Scientists* 32 (6): 10–13.

Fettweis, Christopher J. 2006. "A Revolution in International Relations Theory: Or, What If Muller is Right." *International Studies Review* 8 (4): 677–697.

GFP. 2022. "Countries Listing." *Global Fire Power*. Accessed July 21, 2022. https://www.globalfirepower.com/countries-listing.php.

Goertz, Gary, and Paul F. Diehl. 1995. "The Initiation and Termination of Enduring Rivalries: The Impact of Political Shocks." *American Journal of Political Science* 39 (1): 30–52.

Holmes, James. 2013. "Beware the 'Thucydides Trap' Trap: What the U.S. and China aren't necessarily Athens and Sparta or Britain and Germany Before WWI." *The Diplomat*, June 13. https://thediplomat.com/2013/06/beware-the-thucydides-trap-trap/.

Horowitz, Michael C. 2018. "Artificial Intelligence, International Competition, and the Balance of Power." *Texas Security Review* 1 (3): 36–57.

Keyssar, Helene. 1994. "Space Bridges: The U. S.-Soviet Space Bridge Resource Center." *PS: Political Science and Politics* 27 (2): 247–253.

Kissinger, Henry A. 2011. "Avoiding a U.S.—China Cold War." *The Washington Post*, January 14. https://www.washingtonpost.com/wp-dyn/content/article/2011/01/13/AR2011011304832.html.

Korda, Matt, and Hans M. Kristensen. 2020. "Status of World Nuclear Forces." *Federation of American Scientists.* September. https://fas.org/issues/nuclear-weapons/status-world-nuclear-forces/.

Kripal, Jeffrey. 2007. *Esalen: America and the Religion of no Religion*. Chicago: University of Chicago Press.

Levy, Jack S. 1982. "Historical Trends in Great Power War, 1495–1975." *International Studies Quarterly* 26 (2): 278–300.

Muller, John. 1995. *Quiet Cataclysm: Reflections on the Recent Transformation of World Politics*. New York: HarperCollins.

Ord, Toby. 2020. *The Precipice: Existential Risk and the Future of Humanity*. New York: Hachette Books.

Robock, Alan, Luke Oman, and Georgiy L. Stenchikov. 2007. "Nuclear Winter Revisited With a Modern Climate Model and Current Nuclear Arsenals: Still Catastrophic Consequences." *Journal of Geophysical Research* 112.

Shengli, Ling, and Lv Huiyi. 2018. "Why Are China and the U.S. Not Destined to Fall into the 'Thucydides' Trap'?" *China Quarterly of International Strategic Studies* 4 (4): 494–514.

SIPRI. 2022. "Nuclear Arms Control." *Stockholm International Peace Research Institute.* Accessed June 15, 2022. https://www.sipri.org/research/armament-and-disarmament/weapons-mass-destruction/nuclear-arms-control.

Small, Melvin, and David Singer. 1979. "Conflict in the International System, 1816–1977: Historical Trends and Policy Futures." In *Challenges to America: United States Foreign Policy in the 1980s*, edited by Charles W. Kegley and Patrick J. McGowan, 57–82. Beverly Hills, CA: Sage Publishing.

Sweijs, Tim, Willem Theo Oosterveld, Emily Knowles, and Menno Schellekens. 2014. *Why are Pivot States so Pivotal? The Role of Pivot States in Regional and Global Security.* The Hague: The Hague Centre for Strategic Studies.

Thucydides. 1972. *History of the Peloponnesian War.* Edited by Moses I. Finley. Translated by Rex Warner. London: Penguin Books.

UN. n.d. "Treaty on the Non-Proliferation of Nuclear Weapons (NPT)." *United Nations Office for Disarmament Affairs.* Accessed June 12, 2022. https://www.un.org/disarmament/wmd/nuclear/npt/.

US Department of State. 2018. "Joint Statement by the Foreign Ministers of the Depositary Governments for the Treaty on the Non-Proliferation of Nuclear Weapons." *United States of America Department of State.* Accessed June 22,

2022. https://www.state.gov/wp-content/uploads/2019/03/NPT-Joint-Statement.pdf.

US News. 2022. "These Countries Have the Strongest Militaries." *US News.* Accessed September 1, 2022. https://www.usnews.com/news/best-countries/rankings/strong-military.

Vestby, Jonas, Ida Rudolfsen, and Halvard Buhaug. 2018. "Does Hunger Cause Conflict?" *Peace Research Institute Oslo Climate and Conflict.* May 18. https://blogs.prio.org/ClimateAndConflict/2018/05/does-hunger-cause-conflict/.

Waltz, Kenneth N. 1979. *Theory of International Politics.* New York: Random House.

Williams, Heather, and Alexi Drew. 2020. "Escalation by Tweet: Managing the New Nuclear Diplomacy." *Centre for Science and Security Studies-Kings College London.* July. https://www.kcl.ac.uk/csss/assets/10957%E2%80%A2twitterconflictreport-15july.pdf.

Zartman, William, and Guy Oliver Faure. 2005. "The Dynamics of Escalation and Negotiation." In *Escalation and Negotiation in International Conflicts*, edited by William Zartman and Guy Oliver Faure, 3–21. Cambridge: Cambridge University Press.

CHAPTER 5

Peace, Pandemics, and Conflict

The second area of necessary inquiry at the intersection of Peace and Conflict Studies (PCS) and Existential Risk Studies (ERS) is the nexus between peace, pandemics, and conflict. Pandemics and conflicts are particularly timely topics as the world is still coming to grips with the impacts of the COVID-19 pandemic. This chapter focuses on naturally occurring pandemics; Chap. 6 will consider engineered pathogens. The *Oxford Dictionary of Epidemiology* (2014) defines pandemics as epidemics that cover a wide area, cross international borders, and affect many people, and epidemics as the occurrence of an illness in a community that would generally be expected.

Diseases have inexorably shaped human history. Our genetics and history have been altered by the sheer number of humans who have died of pandemics (Crosby 1978; Kilbourne 1983; McNeill 1978). Half of all humans who have ever lived may have died of Malaria (Whitfield 2002), with 150–300 million in the last century alone (Carter and Mendis 2002). When the Black Death spread across the planet from 1346 to 1352, it is estimated to have killed between 5% and 14% of the world's population (Benedictow 2004). Europeans came to the Americas in 1492 and brought measles, influenza, and smallpox. This host of diseases, along with the invasion, is estimated to have killed upwards of 95% of the indigenous population within 100 years. However, the actual number may never be known (Nunn and Qian 2010; Newson 2001). When the 1918 flu spread

© The Author(s), under exclusive license to Springer Nature Switzerland AG 2023
N. B. Taylor, *Existential Risks in Peace and Conflict Studies*,
Rethinking Peace and Conflict Studies,
https://doi.org/10.1007/978-3-031-24315-8_5

worldwide, it is estimated to have killed between 3% and 6% of the global population. The 1918 flu, whose estimated death rate was between 3% and 6%, killed more people than in World War I (Taubenberger and Morens 2006) (Ord 2020, 124–125). At the time of writing this book, there have been 562 million cases of COVID-19, with an estimated 6.37 million deaths worldwide (Ritchie et al. 2022).

Risk Potentials of Pandemics

Pandemics alone may not be an actual existential risk. A pandemic alone is unlikely to bring about the extinction of the human species. Humanity has survived many plagues in the past. There are many reasons to believe that, as a species, humanity would likely survive most global pandemics (Snyder-Beattie et al. 2019; Ord 2020). Humans are spread out across the planet, with some groups primarily isolated from the rest of the world, making it possible that some groups would remain unaffected. Given the scale of the global population, it is likely that some groups of people will have greater resistance to a particular disease than others. Modern sanitation practices and advancements in preventative and curative medicine have significantly reduced the transmission of communicable diseases in many parts of the world. Though sometimes not operated in the most efficient manner, medical systems worldwide have significant capacity to mitigate the terminal spread of a pandemic disease.

When reviewing fossil records, the Global Challenges Foundation calculated that the risk of a pandemic becoming an existential risk was approximately 0.0005% per century. For a pandemic in the future to exceed estimates of the total natural existential risk of 0.1% per century, there would need to increase by a factor of at least 20. The factors that contribute to the destructive potential of a pandemic are the capacity of national and international health systems to respond, the speed at which medical research can be done, the mobility of the response, and the development of effective anti-pandemic measures (Global Challenges Foundation 2015). That being said, the Global Challenges Foundation also found when studying historical epidemics that epidemics, in general, have "a power law with a small exponent: many plagues have been found to follow a power law with an exponent of 0.26" and that "if this law holds for future pandemics as well, then the majority of people who will die from epidemics will likely die from the single largest pandemic" (Pamlin and Armstrong 2015, 85, Hanson 2001).

The immediate risk of a pandemic becoming an existential threat seems unlikely; rather, the more concerning threat would be the role a pandemic might play in contributing to a permanent collapse of civilization globally and its potential to compound with other existential threats (Ord 2020). A pandemic may become an existential risk if it either results or coincides as the overall fragmentation of human society decreases the overall resilience and inhibits possibilities of recovery (Maher Jr and Baum 2013).

Pandemics should instead be understood as falling between a natural and an anthropogenic risk. Non-engineered pathogens that emerge from nature do not represent the same type of direct natural risk as an event such as an asteroid strike. Understanding a pandemic in terms of a global catastrophic risk is more practical, meaning that it could threaten permanent civilizational collapse (Bostrom and Ćirković 2011). The John Hopkins Center for Health Security has followed this idea in defining pandemics as possible "Global Catastrophic Biological Risks" (GCBRs). Which they define as

> biological events—deliberate, accidental, or emerging—that could lead to sudden, extraordinary, widespread disaster beyond the collective capability of national and international governments and the private sector to control [that] if unchecked […] would lead to great suffering, loss of life, and sustained damage to national governments, international relationships, economies, societal stability, or global security. (Schoch-Spana et al. 2017, 323)

Though humanity has lived with diseases since its earliest history, the contemporary possibility of such a risk has increased. The global population recently climbed to over 8 billion, and the overall population density continues to increase (Roser et al. 2013). With more individuals, there are more possible origins of new pandemic diseases. As of 2018, 55% of the world's population lived in urban areas (UN DESA 2018), and an estimated 65% by 2050 (UN DESA 2019). People living closer to one another will likely increase the transmission rates.

Many facets of modern life further increase a pandemic's possible severity, scope, and scale (Jones et al. 2008; Morse 1995). Deforestation, industrial farming, and meat production practices combined with climate change increase the likelihood of zoonotic transmission of pathogens from animals to humans. The melting permafrost, increased ultraviolet immunosuppression, changing weather patterns, and arctic thawing that comes with global warming may unleash pathogens frozen long ago (Hofmeister et al. 2021). Alternatively, trigger pathogenic mutations in previously non-pathogenic organisms. The ease of global transportation also dramatically increases the risk of future pandemics (Ord 2020). In addition to these variables, war is a significant factor that results in the spread of pandemic disease, both unintentionally as troops move into foreign lands and intentionally and potentially when used as a weapon (A. T. Price-Smith 2009).

Another often singled but under-recognized future pandemic risk is so-called super bugs, antimicrobial resistant bacteria. Superbugs fall into three categories defined by their susceptibility to antimicrobial agents. Multidrug-resistant pathogens are not susceptible to at least one agent in three or more categories, extensively drug-resistant are not susceptible to at least one agent in all but two or fewer categories, and the most concerning the pandrug-resistant which have no known susceptibility to any antimicrobial agents (Magiorakos et al. 2012).

The potential risk from superbugs is grave. The general director of the WHO described it as being a "fundamental threat to human health, development and security" (Fox 2016). In the USA alone, in 2019 the rate of superbug infections was 2.8 million each year with more than 35,000 deaths (CDC 2019). This rate has likely risen by 15% between 2019 and 2020 (Mishra 2022). Globally the situation is worse. In 2019 an estimated 1.27 million deaths were directly tied to these superbugs, with another 4.95 million associated with such infections. The global burden of these infections is likely higher than HIV or Malaria. Like many other pandemic-related topics, the global burden of these diseases unequally spread with much higher concentrations in Sub-Saharan Africa and South Asia (Antimicrobial Resistance Collaborators 2022).

Biomedical researcher Dr. Brian K. Coombes described the severity of the situation, "antibiotics are the foundation on which all modern medicine rests. Cancer chemotherapy, organ transplants, surgeries, and childbirth all rely on antibiotics to prevent infections. If you can't treat those, then we lose the medical advances we have made in the last 50 years" (Miller 2015).

Even if bio risks, such as pandemics, are not technically defined as a genuine existential threat and are instead understood as a global catastrophic risk, there is a consensus that they should be an issue of global priority (Connell 2017; Palmer et al. 2017). These evaluations of the destructive potential of pandemics focus on it being the direct cause of an existential or global catastrophic threat. The possibility of pandemics following similar pathways as discussed regarding Great Power Conflicts makes a pandemic's indirect or compounding risk a topic of concern. Global cooperation is needed to address another existential risk a pandemic could hinder. A pandemic could occur alongside another existential threat, such as a Great Power Conflict or runaway global warming overtaxing the systems that might otherwise make us resilient to such a risk.

PEACE, PANDEMICS, AND CONFLICT

Two relationships are essential when considering a PCS perspective on pandemics: (1) What effects do violent conflict have on pandemic diseases? (2) How do pandemics affect violent conflict? The former is currently better understood than the latter. This second relationship reflects an essential priority for the field of Peace Research that will remain so for the foreseeable future. Generally, the relationship between the overall health of a population and peace is well understood. Societies with a higher level of positive peace also tend to be healthier overall. Violent conflicts are also usually correlated with most measures of ill-health (IEP 2022).

Armed conflict between warring states and groups within states has been a significant cause of ill-health and mortality for most of human history. Estimates vary, but it is likely that armed conflict has directly killed somewhere between 100 million and 1 billion lives throughout human history (Roser et al. 2016; Eckhardt 1991). Most estimates do not account for deaths due indirectly to war, so the death toll could be much higher. At the most direct level, large-scale violence results in deaths, with an estimated 90% of causalities being civilians (UNSC 2022). On the topic of disease and conflict, Kaniewski and Marriner (2020) write that "historically, wars disrupted the human-microbe balance, resulting in devastating outbreaks of microbial diseases and high rates of mortality and morbidity all over the world" (2). In addition to the deaths directly due to conflicts, there are also health consequences due to the conflict, what Sartin (1993) refers to as the "third army," owing to how diseases, directly and indirectly, related to violent conflict often kill as many or more people than die directly on the battlefield. Deaths from these diseases are tied to the movements of troops, the displacement of populations, the breakdown of health and social services, the destruction of safe waste treatment capacity, reductions in food security, and access to clean drinking water (Murray et al. 2002). In low-income countries with a reduced public health capacity, armed conflict exacerbates the effects of diseases, making respiratory infections, diarrheal illnesses, tuberculosis, malaria, and HIV rise into the top ten causes of death. It seems clear that even though more is to be understood, the link between infectious disease and violent conflict is indisputable (Goniewicz et al. 2021; McMichael 2015). Violent conflict has the effect of spreading infectious diseases (Bousquet and Fernandez-Taranco n.d.). Recently an analysis conducted by Mohamed Daw (2021) demonstrated that in Libya, Syria, and Yemen that armed conflict increased the spread of COVID-19 and that this synergistic interaction between the pandemic and violence is likely to be ongoing.

The relationships between violence and disease spread are complex and reciprocal in the Democratic Republic of Congo, with many small-scale attacks against government and health workers in 2019 (Paquette and Sun 2019). These episodes can be understood as a violent backlash resulting from heavy-handed top-down approaches used in communities where there was already long-standing mistrust between local communities during the August–November outbreak of 2014 (Cohn and Kutalek 2016). During the Ebola outbreak from August 2018 to June 2020, there were eruptions of violence and the aura of suspicion and distrust were further exacerbated by rumors that international organizations and the local government were conspiring to intentionally spread the outbreak to sell the dead's organs (Hayden 2019).

It is also clear that conflicts, particularly large-scale direct violence and prolonged cultural and structural violence, make populations more susceptible to disease and disease transmission. This linkage is due to the destruction of physical infrastructures (food supply lines, access to medicine, sanitation) and political structures (the inability of certain groups to access these physical infrastructures) (Ghobarah et al. 2004). Troops, refugees, and prisoners of war are often "housed" in close quarters with makeshift sanitation promoting rapid spread of contagions. Further violent conflicts contribute to the emergence and proliferation of pathogens in the following ways: increasing population density as individuals flee from conflict areas and into displacement or refugee camps, compromising immune systems through famine, increasing poverty, reducing the effectiveness of public health surveillance systems, and generally creating situations of prolonged physical and psychological stress (A. T. Price-Smith 2009).

The effects of pandemic diseases on the emergence or exacerbation of violent conflicts are less straightforward. New and emerging infectious diseases have already been considered a threat to national security in addition to a threat to global health (National Intelligence Council 2000). Their threat is through directly challenging the state's power, compromising economic resources, undermining the legitimacy and effectiveness of the state, paralyzing institutions, and stoking intrastate violence (A. T. Price-Smith 2009). Beyond understanding pandemics as security threats to the state, PCS needs to develop a more complex and nuanced perspective on how pandemics can drive conflict and peace.

COVID-19 has highlighted the importance of understanding the relationships between peace, conflict, and pandemics. The COVID-19 outbreak was declared a public health emergency of international concern on January 30th and a pandemic on March 11th, 2020, by the World Health Organization (WHO 2020a, 2020b). Less than a month later, the pandemic became a concern for the United Nations. The UN Security General Antonio Guterres delivered remarks to the Security Council regarding the consequences the COVID-19 pandemic could have on global peace and security. Amongst his concerns, Guterres highlighted that the pandemic had already eroded trust in public institutions in many countries. It had resulted in the postponement of elections resulting in political tensions and undermining the legitimacy of governments. He worried that the economic fallout in fragile societies could threaten their stability and resilience. Further, the uncertainty created in the pandemic's wake could incentivize malicious actors to sow division or provide windows of opportunity for terrorism (Guterres 2020).

Already at this point in the pandemic, it has been clear that COVID-19 revealed the global lack of pandemic preparedness. For many, this came as a shock, given outbreaks of Ebola, H1N1, Zika Avian Flu (H5N1), SARS, and MERS in recent memory. There were earlier warnings from the scientific community about the reservoir of SARS-COVID-type viruses in China (Cheng et al. 2007). The threat of emerging diseases was even a topic of many popular nonfiction best sellers such as Robin Marantz Heing's (1994) *Dancing Matrix*, Richard Preston's (1999) *The Hot Zone*, and Laurie Garrett's books *The Coming Plague* (1995) and *Betrayal of Trust* (2003). Even Wolfgang Petersen's film *Outbreak* (1995) begins with Nobel laureate Joshua Lederberg's now haunting line, "The single biggest threat to man's continued dominance on the planet is the virus." Lederberg wrote that though humanity has, through its technology, dominated the plant and animal kingdoms, it is the "microbes that remain our competitors of last resort" (1988, 684). Like the twist ending in H.G. Wells' *War of the Worlds* (1898), when predatory megafauna has been subdued, humanity's smallest enemies could be their undoing.

In his book The *Causes of War* (Blainey 1988), Geoffrey Blainey writes that wars often start when the belligerents are optimistic. When elites who make decisions are confident and, therefore, willing to take risks, they tend to be less likely to negotiate. Following his logic, peace may best be served by pessimism. Building on this point, Posen (2020) argues that, at least in the short-term, the pessimism and overall contraction resulting from a pandemic may function as a *Pax Epidemica*. According to him, contagious diseases are not conducive to war. Funding is often directed away from the military, and national economies are a primary source of military power. Diseases do not take sides, and soldiers and sailors may be more vulnerable to infection (Posen 2020).

This type of thinking, alongside the general atmosphere of uncertainty, may have led to a temporary downturn in the global level of violent conflicts and military spending shortly after the United Nations Secretary General's call for a global ceasefire in March 2020. A similar call for the ending of all wars to pool efforts to fight the pandemic was made by the Pope (Bordoni 2020). At this moment in history, there was a fleeting hope for a kind of *Pax Epidemica*, that the common enemy of a global pandemic may be a driving force for peace. There have been past precedents for a large-scale disaster having a positive effect on peacebuilding, such as the influence of the 2004 tsunami in catalyzing the peace agreement in Ache, Indonesia (Berghof Foundation 2020). The UNSG's call received the backing of more than 180 UN member states, several armed movements, and many civil society organizations (Yazgi et al. 2020).

There were promising signs. Israel and Hamas began negotiating a prisoner swap in April 2020 (Harel 2020). In Yemen, the Coalition to Restore Legitimacy in Yemen announced a two-week pause in fighting to allow discussions to take steps to a permanent ceasefire (WAM 2020; Chmaytelli 2020). The *Ejército de Liberación Nacional* (ELN) in Colombia called for a 90-day ceasefire to create an environment to restart the peace dialogue (Télam 2020). The Philippines saw dual unilateral ceasefires declared by the New People's Army and the Government of the Philippines (CPP 2020; Santos 2020). In some cases, armed groups such as the United Wa State Army in Myanmar or drug cartels in Mexico were working to deliver pandemic assistance (Burke 2020; Felbab-Brown 2020). As of July 2022, there were 40 unilateral and 16 bi-/multilateral ceasefires during the COVID-19 pandemic (University of Edinburgh n.d.).

Many hoped the pandemic would serve as a common enemy that would bring forth a common future leading to global cooperation and a more peaceful world. As of 2022, this has not been the case. The opportunity for peace out of the disaster of the pandemic may have been squandered (Brattberg 2020).

Before focusing more on effects directly attributable to the pandemic, an overall picture of the changes during the Global Peace Index (GPI) for 2022 provides an overall picture of the state of peace in 2022. The GPI is calculated by the Institute for Economics and Peace (IEP) and measures 23 qualitative and quantitative indicators from three main domains: (1) ongoing conflicts, (2) safety and security, and (3) militarization. From 2021 to 2022 the IEP found that global peacefulness deteriorated by 0.3%, the 11th year of deterioration over the last 14 years. This timeframe saw a deterioration of 9.3% in the domain of ongoing conflicts and a 3.6% deterioration in safety and security. There was some improvement with decreasing levels of militarization. While it is impossible to delineate which of these effects were causally related to the COVID-19 pandemic, a general inference can be drawn. During this time of the global pandemic, there has been a general increase in the number and intensity of internal and external conflicts fought and the total number of refugees and Internally Displaced Persons (IDPs). One of the most significant changes observed was the number of violent demonstrations, which saw a 50% deterioration, with 77 out of 126 nations recorded as having increased in the total number. Additionally, the economic impact of violence increased by 12.4% from the previous year to $16.5 trillion in purchasing power parity (IEP 2022).

At the outset of the pandemic, it was feared that it would negatively impact peacebuilding efforts. This has primarily turned out to be true. The Carnegie Endowment for International Peace conducted a study early in the pandemic into its effects on 12 conflict-affected areas: Afghanistan, Eastern Ukraine, Iran, Iraq, Israel-Palestine, Kashmir-India-Pakistan, Libya, North Korea, Somalia, Syria, Venezuela, and Yemen. Their preliminary findings were that "the pandemic and efforts to contain it are much more likely to aggravate and multiply conflicts than reducing or end them" (Blanc and Brown 2020). They observed that nation-states and nonstate actors often instrumentalized the pandemic for their own gain. These same observations were found by Sara Polo in a study at the beginning of the pandemic using data from the Armed Conflict Location and Data Project (ACELD) (Polo 2020). The pandemic also tested the legitimacy of all actors claiming authority. It tended to compound existing economic, health, and conflict problems. The pandemic also caused a widespread reorganization of peace processes (Blanc and Brown 2020).

The pandemic has also contributed to conflict by exacerbating many of the underlying root causes (Polo 2020). It has accelerated deep-seated socioeconomic inequality, thus increasing the risk of conflict worldwide (Blattman and Miguel 2010; Cederman et al. 2011). The impact pandemics have on social and economic inequality is essential to consider when understanding the relationships between pandemics and conflict. Poverty and inequality are principal variables in the spread of pathogens (Farmer 2003). Further, both are also factors that can exacerbate violent conflict. In his book *The Great Leveller* (2017), Walter Scheidel argued that events such as wars and pandemics generally have a leveling effect on economic inequality. In his observations, social-economic systems generally unequally distribute wealth. Because it is often advantageous to those in power to keep the status quo, the system reaches a kind of homeostasis. It is a function of complex systems in balance to be resistant to change. A large-scale and sustained shock to the system allows systems to be reorganized. He argued that this had been the historical trend; economic inequality is reduced following a pandemic.

Two years into the COVID-19 pandemic, this historic observation does not seem to hold. The pandemic has made evident and further exacerbated the levels and scope of socioeconomic inequality. Though measuring inequality within and between countries at the global level is complex, the pandemic is still far from over, and the data is not fully available. However, it does seem that generally speaking, social, political, and economic inequality has increased during the COVID-19 pandemic (IMF 2021; Stiglitz 2020; UNDP 2020; Goldin and Muggah 2020).

The negative impacts are more acutely felt by those at lower socioeconomic levels and less by those who are more affluent. Generally, the death rates are greater among minorities and the poor compared to those who can afford health care and whose living and working circumstances make them less likely to contract COVID-19. Similarly, the effects of unemployment resulting from the pandemic have been spread unevenly across societies, significantly affecting the poor, working class, and marginalized (Stiglitz 2022).

At the outset of the pandemic, there were well-founded fears that uncertainty and economic contractions in OECD (Organisation for Economic Co-operation and Development) countries would have a knock-down effect of decreasing global investment in overseas aid and international peacekeeping efforts (IEP 2020). Luckily, this was not the case, with OECD spending rising to record levels in 2020 and 2021 (OECD 2022).

In their first update to their textbook *Peace and Conflict Studies* (2022) since the COVID-19 pandemic began, David Barash and Charles Webel wrote,

> This pandemic made it clear that we are not all in the same boat: The rich and powerful continue, for the most part, to sail through these heavy seas on their yachts (sometimes literally) while the rest of humanity had to paddle their rowboats through a superstorm. (926)

The economist Joseph Stiglitz confirms this observation. He writes that the pandemic's most significant impact "will be a worsening of inequality, both within the U.S. and between developed and developing countries" (Stiglitz 2022). The world's billionaires got about $1.9 trillion richer in 2020 and $1.6 trillion richer in 2021 (Peterson-Withorn 2020). The trend seems likely to continue. At the same time, it is estimated that 75–95 million more people than pre-pandemic projections are likely to be living in extreme poverty by the end of 2022 (Mahler et al. 2022). This increase in extreme poverty has a corresponding effect on acute food insecurity, putting millions of children at risk of famine, and placing additional pressure on social and health systems already at their limits (UNICEF 2020).

The COVID-19 pandemic has brought many long-standing shadow problems into the light. On the material level, food security has been a long-standing concern in many countries and regions worldwide (FAO 2019). The pandemic has already had dramatic effects on food insecurity (McDermott and Swinnen 2022), which is being further exacerbated by the 2022 war in Ukraine (WFP 2022). Tensions and long-standing sanctions on countries like Iran and Cuba have hindered the pandemic response (IEP 2020). The neoliberal structures in the geopolitical system compounded by the pandemic have resulted in many countries with poor credit being unable to borrow or repay debt, likely leading to increases in poverty, political instability, and violence. All of which can be further compounding factors for conflict and contributors to existential risks.

The pandemic has also exposed structural and cultural violence systems, bringing many long-standing sociopolitical issues to the surface, revealing fault lines, prejudices, and discrimination that have been made worse through the pandemic and made visible. The scapegoating of minorities and pandemics have gone hand in hand throughout history (Nelkin and Gilman 1988). Studies of past and present epidemics have shown that this mixture makes social conflicts more likely (Jedwab et al. 2021). Already at the beginning of the COVID-19 pandemic, these relationships were evident. In the USA, the news was full of stories of people of Asian descent being intimidated, attacked, and scapegoated for having "caused" the pandemic (Tavernise and Oppel Jr 2020; Abdulllah and Hughes 2021; NPR 2021). Anti-Chinese sentiments and discrimination against Asian peoples grew across Africa (DW 2020; Solomon 2020). At the same time, in China, people of African origin were forcibly tested, evicted, and quarantined (Vincent 2020; Al Jazeera 2020). In the Gulf countries, there was an increase in xenophobia against people from Asia living and working in countries like Kuwait and Bahrain (Migrant Rights 2020).

What is perhaps unique about pandemics as a global catastrophic risk are their effects on humanity's ability to work together. As Yuval Noah Harari argues, people's ability to collaborate is one of the fundamental reasons we have survived and thrived as a species (2015, 2018). Social distancing, quarantines, and lockdown brought forth the challenge of working together and developing a sense of community when the very act of being physically together could be a hazard. This, it seems, will prove to be an essential lesson for the future. Coordination and collaboration are critical elements in responding to a pandemic and are essential for addressing most, if not all, existential risks. This ability becomes a concern when considering the nexus of infectious disease, existential risks, and conflict. Similar to the dynamics discussed in the chapter on Great Powers Conflicts, international trust and cooperation tend to fall as tensions rise and are further diminished through conflicts. From the experiences of the COVID-19 pandemic, it is possible to imagine how responses to pandemics can be hindered through the collapse of trust. In situations of high uncertainty and fear, mistrust of government officials can be extended to health and aid workers. At the same time, governments can become reluctant to provide aid to populations affected by ongoing conflicts. These dynamics can make it difficult for vulnerable populations to receive assistance during a pandemic. Authoritarian governments can also use the opportunities presented by a pandemic to use the closure of borders, the adaptation of high-tech surveillance systems, and new legal frames to restrict collaboration they see as threatening to their power (Burke 2020).

Peacebuilding in Pandemics

Given the relationships between pandemics and conflicts, it is clear that there need to be ways of building peace during pandemics. "Peace through health" has already been an established framework for thinking about this task. This approach is based on the idea that health care is interdependent in a causal fashion. Health is affected by conflict, and peace can be fostered through health initiatives (Abuelaish et al. 2020). This global perspective on the interrelationship between peace and health is reflected in the frame of "global health," which emerged in the 1970s and emphasized a focus on considering the global population's health needs over the concerns of specific nation-states (Brown et al. 2006).

There is precedent for pandemics to be moments of cooperation, even between rivals. During the Cold War, scientists from the USA and the Soviet Union collaborated to develop and improve the polio vaccine. During times of conflict and political instability, there have been examples of regional cooperation among belligerent groups in disease surveillance, detection, and response in the Mekong Basin, Middle East, and East Africa (Long 2020).

It is clear that violent conflict hinders effective response to a pandemic and that garnering the political will to even temporarily stop fighting would improve the global health crisis (Berghof Foundation 2020). Global considerations on health have further developed into an approach of "global health diplomacy" that focuses on improving health and relations, particularly in conflict-affected areas (Adams et al. 2008). Global health diplomacy reflects a multileveled and multi-actor perspective on global health policy (Kickbusch and Buss 2011). It remains an open question as to the overall effectiveness of such frames in coordinating efforts at the intersection of peace and health, and care will need to be taken so these frames do not replicate the violence of their historical precursors in early missionary work colonialism and health development aid.

At the outset of the pandemic, the International Crisis Group (ICG), concerned about the potential for COVID-19 in fragile states to lead to widespread unrest and straining the international crisis management systems, released a special briefing, "COVID-19 and Conflicts: Seven Trends to Watch" (2020). They stressed warranted concerns for the vulnerability to disease outbreaks of people in conflict-affected areas, damage to the International Crisis Management and Conflict Resolution Mechanisms, the risk to the overall social order, and the possibility of political exploitation of the crisis. In addition to these concerns that in these moments of disruption, there may be glimmers of hope, room for humanitarian gestures between rivals, and ways of developing crisis mitigation measures that enhance cooperation.

The oft-cited adage that there are opportunities in crisis should not be ignored with this topic. The global disruption, trauma, and threat of the COVID-19 pandemic have created moments for imagining ways of thinking about the future and about what survival beyond the day could mean. Systems are resilient to change, but disruptions to systems allow for the establishment of new relational patterns. In addition to the remarkable feats of resilience seen around the world, many once "unthinkable" ideas quickly found their way to reality. The speed at which a vaccine could be created and rolled out is now different than it was before. For example, it took less than a year from the identification of SARS-CoV-2, the virus that causes COVID-19, to the emergence use authorization Pfizer vaccine from the Food and Drug Administration (FDA). The previous fastest vaccine developed was for mumps and took four years (S. Cohen 2020).

The ability to move to hybrid and remote forms of work, once thought impractical, was quickly made the norm. The threshold between the impossible and the practical with regard to political decisions has been called the Overton Window, which is a concept that refers to the limited range of sociopolitical approaches that are acceptable to the public in a given moment (Mackinac 2019). The bounds of this window have changed in the past. In the USA, the experience of the Great Depression made policy actions such as Social Security, Roosevelt's New Deal, the 40-hour work week, minimum wage, workers' compensation, and unemployment benefits become the norm (Barash and Webel 2022). It remains to be seen as the world emerges from the pandemic if ideas such as expanding the social safety net, universal basic income, tuition-free college, and universal health care may also become a feasible social expectation in more countries.

Questions for the Future

How to develop a deeper understanding of how pandemics and conflicts interact and how these dynamics may contribute to existential risks?

What opportunities do pandemic responses provide for peacebuilding and conflict transformation?

There are opportunities to intervene and respond in the nightmare causal chain that leads from pandemic and conflict, to civilizational collapse, to an existential threat leading to a catastrophe resulting in humanity's extinction. History will decide if the COVID-19 pandemic will be another critical juncture point in the field of Peace Research. The inadequacy of ways of understanding and approaches to preventing war were made apparent by World War II. A similar disillusionment may come from the experience of the pandemic. Faith may have been shaken in the ability of many institutions, structures, and practices to protect our species from a global threat effectively.

"Getting back to normal" in these regards would be inadvisable. The global public health infrastructure and its integration with systems of conflict resolution and peacebuilding need reimagining. Ali Khan wrote in his book *The Next Pandemic* (Khan and Patrick 2016), "the time has come for us to move beyond seeing public health as the ax in the display case, where the sign says in case of emergency, break glass" (259). Humanity will need to find ways to build pandemic prevention into the very communities and infrastructures that are the foundation of its resiliency. It will be important for peace researchers to focus on the interactions between pandemics and conflicts and how they may contribute to larger existential risks. Further, since future pandemics are likely, it will be important to explore ways in which pandemic responses may be made with a peace lens.

Part of what is needed is yet another turn in the wheel of the understanding of peace. Solon Simmons, Professor of Conflict Analysis and Resolution at George Mason University, reflected on this need in his "An Agenda for Peace and Conflict Studies After the Coronavirus Catastrophe" (2021). Within PCS, the previous turns to peace with a lowercase "p" have been important, and this turn to "the local" and "every day" understandings of peace has been an important contribution to the field. The pandemic, having exposed many structural and cultural problems worldwide, calls for rethinking the understanding of peace within this new context. Solon Simmons (2021) writes that these moments of crisis

> will touch on every aspect of peace and conflict studies, from the boundaries and duties of the nation and state to the scope of human rights and the reach of the rule of law and from systems of business and economic disruption to definitions of personhood and the dynamics of identity formation. (9)

He calls for a conception of a "big peace" to be explored in addition to the previous trend of more narrowing definitions. In this way, he is harkening back to the impetus of why the early PCS researcher sought to nuance and expand their understanding of the peace in the wake of World War II and the tensions of the Cold War when there was a palpable sense that all life was at stake. This call joins the notion of "Peace Writ Large," originally coined by the NGO Collaborative Learning Projects (CDA) to describe one of the major conclusions of their Reflecting on Peace Practice Program (Chigas and Woodrow 2009). One of their chief conclusions from their research was that for peace work to be effective, individual efforts needed to have a clear connection to peace on a broader societal or global level (Anderson and Olson 2003). This notion of peace will be important for the development of research at the intersection of PCS and ERS to counteract the negative effects of increasing constriction in the understanding of peace. An overemphasized focus on drivers of war is this larger notion of peace which calls for bringing together peacebuilding work with addressing the major threats to human survival (Chigas and Woodrow 2009).

References

Abdulllah, Tami, and Trevor Hughes. 2021. "Hate Crimes Against Asian Americans are on the Rise. Here's What Activists, Lawmakers and Police are Doing to Stop the Violence." *USA TODAY*, February 27.

Abuelaish, Izzeldin, Michael S. Goodstadt, and Rim Mouhaffel. 2020. "Interdependence Between Health and Peace: A Call for a New Paradigm." *Health Promotion International* 1-11.

Adams, Vincanne, Thomas E. Novotny, and Hannah Leslie. 2008. "Global Health Diplomacy." *Medication Anthropology* 27 (4): 315-323.

Al Jazeera. 2020. "African Nationals 'mistreated, evicted' in China Over Coronavirus." *Al Jazeera*. April 12. Accessed July 21, 2022. https://www.aljazeera.com/news/2020/4/12/african-nationals-mistreated-evicted-in-china-over-coronavirus.

Anderson, Mary B., and Laura Olson. 2003. *Confronting War: Critical Lessons for Peace Practitioners*. Cambridge: The Collaborative for Development Action.

Antimicrobial Resistance Collaborators. 2022. "Global Burden of Bacterial Antimicrobial Resistance in 2019: a Systematic Analysis." *Lancet* 399 (10325): 629-655.

Barash, David P., and Charles P. Webel. 2022. *Peace and Conflict Studies*. 5th Edition. London: Sage.

Benedictow, Ole J. 2004. *The Black Death, 1346–1353: The Complete History.* Woodbridge: Boydell Press.

Berghof Foundation. 2020. "Prospects for Peace Amid a Global Pandemic." *Berghof Foundation.* June 16. https://www.berghof-foundation.org/en/news-article/prospects-for-peace-amid-a-global-pandemic/.

Blainey, Geoffrey. 1988. *The Causes of War.* Free Press.

Blanc, Jarrett, and Frances Z. Brown. 2020. "Conflict Zones in the Time of Coronavirus: War and War by Other Means." *Carnegie Endowment for International Peace.* December 17. https://carnegieendowment.org/2020/12/17/conflict-zones-in-time-of-coronavirus-war-and-war-by-other-means-pub-83462.

Blattman, Christopher, and Edward Miguel. 2010. "Civil War." *Journal of Economic Literature* 48 (a): 3-57.

Bordoni, Linda. 2020. "Pope Reiterates Appeal for Global Ceasefire, Calls for Peace in the Caucasus." *Vatican News.* July 19. https://www.vaticannews.va/en/pope/news/2020-07/pope-appeal-global-ceasefire-pandemic-violence-caucasus.html.

Bostrom, Nick, and Milan M. Ćirković. 2011. *Global Catastrophic Risks.* Edited by Nick Bostrom and Milan M. Ćirković. Oxford: Oxford University Press.

Bousquet, Franck, and Oscar Fernandez-Taranco, n.d. "COVID-19 in Fragile Settings: Ensuring a Conflict-Sensitive Response." *United Nations.* Accessed July 17, 2022. https://www.un.org/en/un-coronavirus-communications-team/covid-19-fragile-settings-ensuring-conflict-sensitive-response.

Brattberg, Erik. 2020. "The Pandemic is Making Transatlantic Relations More Toxic." *Carnegie Endowment for International Peace.* April 29. Accessed 15 July, 2020. https://carnegieendowment.org/2020/04/29/pandemic-is-making-transatlantic-relations-more-toxic-pub-81675.

Brown, Theodore M., Marcos Cueto, and Elizabeth Fee. 2006. "The World Health Organization and the Transition from International to Global Public Health." *American Journal of Public Health* 96 (1): 62-72.

Burke, Adam. 2020. "Peace and the Pandemic: the Impact of COVID-19 on Conflict in Asia." *DevPolicy.* April 14. Accessed 15 July, 2020. https://devpolicy.org/peace-and-the-pandemic-the-impact-of-covid-19-on-conflict-in-asia-20200414/.

Carter, Richard, and Kamini N Mendis. 2002. "Evolutionary and Historical Aspects of the Burden of Malaria." *Clinical Microbiology Reviews* 15 (4): 564-94.

CDC. 2019. "2019 AR Threats Report." *Center for Disease Control.* December. Accessed July 25, 2022. https://www.cdc.gov/drugresistance/biggest-threats.html.

Cederman, Lars-Erik, Nils B. Weidmann, and Kristian Skrede Gleditsch. 2011. "Horizontal Inequalities and Ethno-nationalist Civil War: A Global Comparison." *American Political Science Review* 105 (3): 478-795.

Cheng, Vincent C.C., Susanna K. P. Lau, Patrick C. Y. Woo, and Kwok Yung Yuen. 2007. "Severe Acute Respiratory Syndrome Coronavirus as an Agent of Emerging and Reemerging Infection." *Clinical Microbiology Reviews* 20 (4): 660–694.

Chigas, Diana, and Peter Woodrow. 2009. "Envisioning and Pursuing Peace Writ Large." In *Peacebuilding at a Crossroads? Dilemmas and Paths for Another Generation*, edited by Beatrix Schmelzle and Martina Fischer, 47-58. Berlin: Berghof Research Center for Constructive Conflict Management.

Chmaytelli, Maher. 2020. "Saudi-led Coalition Announces One-month Extension of Yemen Ceasefire." *Reuters*. April 24. https://www.reuters.com/article/us-yemen-security-saudi/saudi-led-coalition-announces-one-month-extension-of-yemen-ceasefire-idUSKCN2261GS.

Cohen, Sandy. 2020. "The Fastest Vaccine in History." *UCLA Health*. December 10. Accessed September 12, 2022. https://connect.uclahealth.org/2020/12/10/the-fastest-vaccine-in-history/.

Cohn, Samuel, and Ruth Kutalek. 2016. "Ebola Virus Disease and Cholera: Understanding Community Distrust and Social Violence with Epidemics." *PLOS Currents*.

Connell, Nancy D. 2017. "The Challenge of Global Catastrophic Biological Risks." *Health Security* 15 (4): 345-346.

CPP. 2020. "Ceasefire Order: 00.00H of 26 March 2020 to 23.59H of 15 April 2020." *Central Committee Communist Party of the Philippines*. March 24. Accessed July 21, 2022. https://cpp.ph/statements/ceasefire-order-00-00h-of-26-march-2020-to-23-59h-of-15-april-2020/.

Crosby, Alfred W. 1978. *Epidemic and Peace*. Westport: Greenwood.

Daw, Mohamed A. 2021. "The Impact of Armed Conflict on the Epidemiological Situation of COVID-19 in Libya, Syria and Yemen." *Public Health* 9 (667364).

DW. 2020. "Coronavirus Fuels anti-Chinese Discrimination in Africa." *Deutsche Welle*. February 19. Accessed July 21, 2022. https://www.dw.com/en/coronavirus-fuels-anti-chinese-discrimination-in-africa/av-52428454.

Eckhardt, William. 1991. "War-related Deaths Since 300 BC." *Bulletin of Peace Proposals* 22 (4): 437-443.

FAO. 2019. *2019 The State of Food Security and Nutrition in the World: Safeguarding Against Economic Slowdowns and Downturns*. Rome: Food and Agriculture Organization of the United Nations.

Farmer, Paul. 2003. *Pathologies of Power: Health, Human Rights, and the New War on the Poor*. Berkeley and Los Angles: University of California Press.

Felbab-Brown, Vanda. 2020. "Mexican Cartels and the COVID-19 Pandemic." *Mexico Today*. March 24. Accessed July 21, 2022. https://mexicotoday.com/2020/04/24/opinion-mexican-cartels-and-the-covid-19-pandemic/.

Fox, Maggie. 2016. "NBC News." *Drug-Resistant Superbugs Are a 'Fundamental Threat', WHO Says*. September 21. Accessed July 28, 2022. https://www.nbcnews.com/health/health-news/who-labels-drug-resistant-superbugs-fundamental-threat-humans-n651981.

Garrett, Laurie. 2003. *Betrayal of Trust: The Collapse of Global Public Health.* Oxford: Oxford University Press.

Garrett, Laurie. 1995. *The Coming Plague: Newly Emerging Diseases in a World Out of Balance.* New York: Penguin.

Ghobarah, Hazem Adam, Paul Huth, and Bruce Russett. 2004. "The Post-war Public Health Effects of Civil Conflict." *Social Science and Medicine* 59 (4): 869-884.

Global Challenges Foundation. 2015. *Global Challenges: 12 Risks That Threaten Human Civilization.* Global Challenges Foundation.

Goldin, Ian, and Robert Muggah. 2020. "COVID-19 is Increasing Multiple Kinds of Inequality: Here's What We Can Do About It." *World Economic Forum.* October 9. Accessed July 21, 2022. https://www.weforum.org/agenda/2020/10/covid-19-is-increasing-multiple-kinds-of-inequality-here-s-what-we-can-do-about-it/.

Goniewicz, Krzysztof, Frederick M. Burkle, Simon Horne, Marta Borowska-Stefanska, Szymon Wisniewski, and Amir Khorram-Manesh. 2021. "The Influence of War and Conflict on Infectious Disease: A Rapid Review of Historical Lessons We Have Yet to Learn." *Sustainability* 13.

Guterres, António. 2020. "Secretary-General's Remarks to the Security Council on the COVID-19 Pandemic [as delivered]." *United Nations.* April 09. Accessed July 17, 2020. https://www.un.org/sg/en/content/sg/statement/2020-04-09/secretary-generals-remarks-the-security-council-the-covid-19-pandemic-delivered.

Hanson, Robin. 2001. "Catastrophe, Social Collapse, and Human Extinction." In *Global Catastrophic Risks*, edited by Nick Bostrom and Milan M. Cirkovic, 363-378. Oxford: Oxford University Press.

Harel, Amos. 2020. "Coronavirus Brings Israel and Hamas Closer to a Long-delayed Prisoner Swap." *Haaretz.* March 16. https://www.haaretz.com/israel-news/.premium-coronavirus-brings-israel-and-gaza-closer-to-a-long-delayed-prisoner-swap-1.8769553.

Hayden, Sally. 2019. "How Misinformation is Making it almost impossible to contain the Ebola outbreak in DRC." *TIME.* June 20. Accessed 07 17, 2022. https://time.com/5609718/rumors-spread-ebola-drc/.

Heing, Robin Marantz. 1994. *Dancing Matrix: How Science Confronts Emerging Viruses.* New York: Vintage.

Hofmeister, Anne M, James M Seckler, and Genevieve M Criss. 2021. "Possible Roles of Permafrost Melting, Atmospheric Transport, and Solar Irradiance in the Development of Major Coronavirus and Influenza Pandemics." *International Journal of Environmental Research and Public Health* 8 (16): 3055.

ICG. 2020. "COVID-19 and Conflict: Seven Trends to Watch." Vers. Special Briefing No 4. *International Crisis Group.* March 24. Accessed July 17, 2022. https://www.crisisgroup.org/global/sb4-covid-19-and-conflict-seven-trends-watch.

IEP. 2020. *COVID-19 and Peace.* Sydney: The Institute for Economics and Peace.

IEP. 2022. "Global Peace Index 2022: Measuring Peace in a Complex World." *Vision of Humanity.* Accessed 07 19, 2022. https://www.visionofhumanity.org/wp-content/uploads/2022/06/GPI-2022-web.pdf.

IMF. 2021. "Inequality in the Time of COVID-10." *International Monetary Fund.* Accessed July 21, 2022. https://www.imf.org/external/pubs/ft/fandd/2021/06/inequality-and-covid-19-ferreira.htm#:~:text=The%20severe%20impact%20of%20the,extreme%3A%20the%20wealth%20of%20billionaires.

Jedwab, Remi, Amjad M Khan, Jason Russ, and Esha D. Zaveri. 2021. "Epidemics, pandemics, and social conflict: Lessons from the past and possible scenarios for COVID-19." *World Development* 147.

Jones, Kate E, Nikkita G Patel, Marc A Levy, Adam Storeygard, Deborah Balk, John L Gittleman, and Peter Daszak. 2008. "Global Trends in Emerging Infectious Diseases." *Nature* 451 (21): 990–993.

Kaniewski, David, and Nick Marriner. 2020. "Conflicts and the Spread of Plagues in Pre-industrial Europe." *Humanities and Social Sciences Communications Volume* 7 (162).

Khan, Ali S, and William Patrick. 2016. *The Next Pandemic: On the Front Lines Against Humankind's Gravest Dangers.* New York: PublicAffairs.

Kickbusch, Ilona, and Paulo Marchiori Buss. 2011. "Global Health Diplomacy and Peace." *Infectious Disease Clinics of North America* 25 (3): 601-610.

Kilbourne, Edwin D. 1983. "Are New Diseases Really New?" *Natural History* 92: 28–32.

Lederberg, Joshua. 1988. "Medical Science, Infectious Disease, and the Unity of Humankind." *JAMA The Journal of the American Medical Association* 260 (5): 684-685.

Long, William J. 2020. "Coronavirus Puts System for International Cooperation to the Test." *United States Institute for Peace.* March 30. Accessed July 15, 2020. https://www.usip.org/publications/2020/03/coronavirus-puts-systems-international-cooperation-test.

Mackinac. 2019. "A Brief Explanation of the Overton Window." *Mackinac Center for Public Policy.* Accessed July 21, 2022. https://www.mackinac.org/OvertonWindow#overview.

Magiorakos, AP, A Srinivasan, RB Carey, Y Carmeli, ME Falagas, CG Giske, S Harbarth, et al. 2012. "Multidrug-resistant, Extensively Drug-resistant and Pandrug-resistant Bacteria: an International Expert Proposal for Interim

Standard Definitions for Acquired Resistance." *Clinical Microbiology and Infection* 3: 268-81.

Maher Jr, Timothy M, and Seth D. Baum. 2013. "Adaptation to and Recovery from Global Catastrophe." *Sustainability* 5: 1461-1479.

Mahler, Daniel Gerszon, Nishant Yonzan, Ruth Hill, Christoph Lakner, Yaoyu Wu, and Nobuo Yoshida. 2022. "Pandemic, Prices, and Poverty." *World Bank Blogs*. April 13. Accessed July 21, 2022. https://blogs.worldbank.org/opendata/pandemic-prices-and-poverty.

McDermott, John, and Johan Swinnen. 2022. *COVID-19 and Global Food Security: Two Years Later*. International Food Policy Research Institute.

McMichael, Celia. 2015. "Climate Change-related Migration and Infectious Disease." *Virulence* 6 (6): 1-6.

McNeill, William H. 1978. *Plagues and Peoples*. New York: Doubleday.

Migrant Rights. 2020. "The COVID-19 Crisis is Fueling More Racist Discourse Towards Migrant Workers in the Gulf." *Migrant Rights*. April 5. Accessed July 21, 2022. https://www.migrant-rights.org/2020/04/the-covid-19-crisis-is-fueling-more-racist-discourse-towards-migrant-workers-in-the-gulf/.

Miller, Kelli. 2015. "Superbugs: What They Are and How You Get Them." *Web MD*. April 17. Accessed July 22, 2022. https://www.webmd.com/a-to-z-guides/news/20150417/superbugs-what-they-are.

Mishra, Manas. 2022. "U.S. Deaths from Antibiotic Resistant 'Superbugs' Rose 15% in 2020." *Reuters*, July 12.

Morse, Stephen S. 1995. "Factors in the Emergence of Infectious Diseases." *Emerging Infectious Diseases* 1: 7-15.

Murray, Christopher JL, Gary King, Alan D Lopez, Niels Tomijima, and Etienne G Krug. 2002. "Armed Conflict as a Public Health Problem." *British Medical Journal* 324 (7333): 346-349.

National Intelligence Council. 2000. "National Intelligence Estimate: The Global Infectious Disease Threat and Its Implications for the United States." *Office of the Director of National Intelligence*. January. Accessed 07 16, 2022. https://www.dni.gov/files/documents/infectiousdiseases_2000.pdf.

Nelkin, Dorothy, and Sander L. Gilman. 1988. "Placing Blame for Devastating Disease." *Social Research* 55 (2): 361–378.

Newson, Linda. 2001. "Pathogens, Places and Peoples." In *Technology, Disease and Colonial Conquests, Sixteenth to Eighteenth Centuries*, edited by George Raudzens, 167-210. Boston: Brill.

NPR. 2021. "More Than 9,000 Anti-Asian Incidents Have Been Reported Science the Pandemic Began." *National Public Radio*. August 12. Accessed July 22, 2022. https://www.npr.org/2021/08/12/1027236499/anti-asian-hate-crimes-assaults-pandemic-incidents-aapi?t=1658428267500.

Nunn, Nathan, and Nancy Qian. 2010. "The Columbian Exchange: A History of Disease, Food, and Ideas." *Journal of Economic Perspectives* 24 (2): 163-188.

OECD. 2022. "Preliminary ODA Levels in 2021." *Organization for Economic Cooperation and Development*. April 12. Accessed July 22, 2022. https://www.oecd.org/dac/financing-sustainable-development/development-finance-standards/ODA-2021-summary.pdf.

Ord, Toby. 2020. *The Precipice: Existential Risk and the Future of Humanity*. New York: Hachette Books.

Palmer, Megan J, Bruce C Tiu, Amy S Weissenbach, and David A. Relman. 2017. "On Defining Global Catastrophic Biological Risks." *Health Security* 15 (4): 347-348.

Pamlin, Dennis, and Stuart Armstrong. 2015. "12 Risks That Threaten Human Civilisation: The Case for a New Risk Category." *Global Challenges Foundation*.

Paquette, Danielle, and Lena H. Sun. 2019. "With more than 1,100 dead, Congo's Ebola Outbreak is Only Getting Worse. Now Doctors are Forced to go Undercover." *The Washington Post*. May 16. Accessed 07 17, 2022. https://www.washingtonpost.com/world/africa/with-more-than-1100-dead-congos-ebola-outbreak-is-only-getting-worse-now-doctors-are-forced-to-go-undercover/2019/05/16/b7e15d80-7712-11e9-a7bf-c8a43b84ee31_story.html.

Petersen, Wolfgang, director. 1995. *Outbreak*. Warner Bros.

Peterson-Withorn, Chase. 2020. "The World's Billionaires Have Gotten $1.9 Trillion Richer in 2020." *Forbes*. December 16. Accessed July 22, 2022. https://www.forbes.com/sites/chasewithorn/2020/12/16/the-worlds-billionaires-have-gotten-19-trillion-richer-in-2020/?sh=8c3d8de7386f.

Polo, Sara M.T. 2020. "A Pandemic of Violence? The Impact of COVID-19 on Conflict." *Peace Economics, Peace Science and Public Policy* 1-13.

Posen, Barry R. 2020. "Do Pandemics Promote Peace? Why Sickness Slows the March to War." *Foreign Affairs*. April 23. Accessed July 15, 2020. https://www.foreignaffairs.com/articles/china/2020-04-23/do-pandemics-promote-peace.

Preston, Richard. 1999. *The Hot Zone: A Terrifying True Story of the Origins of the Ebola Virus*. New York: Random House.

Price-Smith, Andrew T. 2009. *Contagion and Chaos: Disease Ecology and National Security in the Era of Globalization*. Cambridge, MA: MIT Press.

Ritchie, Hannah, Edouard Mathieu, Lucas Rodés-Guirao, Cameron Appel, Charlie Giattino, Esteban Ortiz-Ospina, Joe Hasell, Bobbie Macdonald, Diana Beltekian, and Max Roser. 2022. "Coronavirus Pandemic (COVID-19)." *Our World in Data*. 07 18. Accessed 07 18, 2022. https://ourworldindata.org/coronaviru.

Roser, Max, Hannah Ritchie, and Esteban Ortiz-Ospina. 2013. "World Population Growth." *Our World in Data*. Accessed 07 20, 2022. https://ourworldindata.org/world-population-growth.

Roser, Max, Joe Hasell, Bastian Herre, and Bobbie Macdonald. 2016. "Global Deaths in Conflict Since the Year 1400." *Our World in Data*. Accessed 09 09, 2022. https://ourworldindata.org/war-and-peace.

Santos, Elmor. 2020. "Duterte Declares Unilateral Ceasefire with CPP-NPA to Focus on COVID-19 Fight." *CNN Philippines*. March 18. Accessed July 21, 2022. https://www.cnnphilippines.com/news/2020/3/18/duterte-cpp-npa-ceasefire-covid-19.html?fbclid.

Sartin, J S. 1993. "Infectious diseases during the Civil War: the Triumph of the 'Third Army'". *Clinical Infectious Diseases* 16 (4): 580-584.

Scheidel, Walter. 2017. *The Great Leveler: Violence and the History of Inequality from the Stone Age to the Twenty-First Century.* Princeton: Princeton University Press.

Schoch-Spana, Monica, Anita Cicero, Amesh Adalja, Gigi Gronvall, Tara Kirk Sell, Diane Meyer, Jennifer B Nuzzo, et al. 2017. "Global Catastrophic Biological Risks: Toward a Working Definition." *Health Security* 15 (4): 323-328.

Simmons, Solon. 2021. "Big Peace: An Agenda for Peace and Conflict Studies After the Coronavirus Catastrophe." In *Conflict Resolution After the Pandemic: Building Peace, Pursuing Justice*, edited by Richard E Rubenstein and Solon Simmons, 9-17. London and New York: Routledge.

Snyder-Beattie, Andrew E, Toby Ord, and Michael B Bonsall. 2019. "An Upper Bound for the Background Rate of Human Extinction." *Scientific Reports* 9 (11054).

Solomon, Salem. 2020. "Coronavirus Brings 'Sinophobia' to Africa." *VOA News*. March 04. Accessed July 21, 2022. https://www.voanews.com/a/science-health_coronavirus-outbreak_coronavirus-brings-sinophobia-africa/6185249.html.

Stiglitz, Joseph R. 2022. "COVID Has Made Global Inequality Much Worse" *Scientific American*. March 01. Accessed July 22, 2022. https://www.scientificamerican.com/article/covid-has-made-global-inequality-much-worse/.

Stiglitz, Joseph. 2020. "The Pandemic Has Laid Bare Deep Divisions, But it's Not Too Late to Change Course." *International Monetary Fund*. September. Accessed July 21, 2022. https://www.imf.org/en/Publications/fandd/issues/2020/09/COVID19-and-global-inequality-joseph-stiglitz.

Taubenberger, Jeffery K, and David M Morens. 2006. "1918 Influenza: the Mother of All Pandemics." *Emerging Infectious Diseases* 12 (1): 69-79.

Tavernise, Sabrina, and Richard A. Oppel Jr. 2020. "Spit On, Yelled At, Attacked: Chinese-Americans Fear for their Safety." *The New York Times*, March 23.

Télam. 2020. "El ELN le propuso al Gobierno Colombiano un Cese al Cuego Bilateral por 90 días." *Télam Digital*. July 8. Accessed July 21, 2022. https://www.telam.com.ar/notas/202007/486861-colombia-eln-ivan-duque.html.

UNDESA. 2018. "Population Facts: The Speed of Urbanization Around the World." *United Nations Department of Economic and Social Affairs Population*

Division. December. Accessed July 21, 2022. https://population.un.org/wup/Publications/Files/WUP2018-PopFacts_2018-1.pdf.

UNDESA. 2019. *World Urbanization Prospects: The 2018 Revision (ST/ESA/SER.A/420)*. New York: United Nations, Department of Economic and Social Affairs Population Division.

UNDP. 2020. "Coronavirus vs. Inequality." *United Nations Development Project*. Accessed July 21, 2022. https://feature.undp.org/coronavirus-vs-inequality/.

UNICEF. 2020. "COVID-19 and Conflict: A Deadly Combination." *UNICEF*. December 30. Accessed July 20, 2022. https://www.unicef.org/coronavirus/covid-19-and-conflict-deadly-combination.

University of Edinburgh. n.d. "Ceasefires in a Time of COVID-19." *The University of Edinburgh*. Accessed July 21, 2022. https://pax.peaceagreements.org/static/covid19ceasefires/.

UNSC. 2022. "Ninety Per Cent of War-Time Casualties Are Civilians, Speakers Stress, Pressing Security Council to Fulfil Responsibility, Protect Innocent People in Conflicts." *United Nations Meetings Coverage and Press Releases*, May 25: SC/14904.

Vincent, Danny. 2020. "Africans in China: We Face Coronavirus Discrimination." *BBC*. April 17. Accessed July 21, 2022. https://www.bbc.com/news/world-africa-52309414.

WAM. 2020. "Coalition to Restore Legitimacy in Yemen Announces One-month Extension of Comprehensive Ceasefire." *Emirates News Agency*. April 24. Accessed July 21, 2022. https://www.wam.ae/en/details/1395302838796.

Wells, H.G. 1898. *The War of the Worlds*. London: William Heinemann.

WFP. 2022. "War in Ukraine Dries Global Food Crisis." *World Food Program*. June 24. Accessed July 33, 2022. https://www.wfp.org/publications/war-ukraine-drives-global-food-crisis.

Whitfield, John. 2002. "Portrait of a Serial Killer." *Nature*.

WHO. 2020a. "Statement on the second meeting of the International Health Regulations (2005) Emergency Committee regarding the outbreak of novel coronavirus (2019-nCoV)." *World Health Organization*. January 30. Accessed 0716,2022.https://www.who.int/news-room/detail/30-01-2020-statement-on-the-second-meeting-of-the-international-health-regulations-(2005)-emergency-committee-regarding-the-outbreak-of-novel-coronavirus-(2019-ncov).

WHO. 2020b. "WHO Director-General's Opening Remarks at the Media Briefing on COVID-19 - 11 March 2020." *World Health Organization*. March 11. Accessed 07 16, 2022. https://www.who.int/director-general/speeches/detail/who-director-general-s-opening-remarks-at-the-media-briefing-on-covid-19%2D%2D-11-march-2020.

Yazgi, Simon, Hardy Giezendanner, and Himayu Shiotani. 2020. "Ceasefires and Conventional Arms Control in the COVID-19 Pandemic." *Arms Control Today* 50 (7): 17-23.

CHAPTER 6

Climate Change Peace and Conflict

Climate change may be the penultimate example of a "risk from unintended consequences," and nevertheless it is one of humanity's most significant challenges and will likely remain so for the foreseeable future. There is overwhelming evidence that climate change is occurring and human activity is contributing to it. This consensus is shared by 90–100% of publishing climate scientists (Cook et al. 2016; AAAS 2014). The effects of climate change are complex and multifaceted. Research into the nexus between climate change, existential risk, peace, and conflict will be necessary for many years.

The earth's climate has warmed by approximately 1 °C above preindustrial levels in 2017 (IPCC 2018). The Intergovernmental Panel on Climate Change (IPCC) estimates a 1.39–5.5 °C increase in the next 100 years (NASA 2020). The amount of greenhouse gasses that have already been put into the atmosphere will have effects lasting upwards of 10,000 years (Clark et al. 2016). If humanity survives another 10,000 years, it may turn out that human-influenced climate change will affect more people than existed, from our origins to the industrial revolution (Torres 2017b). Increases in global temperature will affect growing seasons, weather patterns, droughts, severe weather events, sea levels, and the arctic ice (USGCRP 2017). The direct effects of climate change are likely to significantly impact social and environmental determinants of health, such as access to and quality of drinking water, food production, economic development, natural disasters, air pollution, and vector-, food, and water-borne diseases (WHO 2020).

This chapter will focus on three areas to assess the relationships between climate change and peace and conflict. First, it will consider the type and scale of risk that climate change poses. Secondly, the current understanding of the effects climate change has on conflict and peacebuilding will be examined. Finally, the connections that current and near-future interventions to mitigate climate change may have with issues of peace and conflict will be discussed.

Risk Potentials of Climate Change

The specific scale, scope, timeline, and implications of climate change are debated by experts. The possible threat and the need to address it are much less contentious. The Intergovernmental Panel on Climate Change (IPCC) is "the scientific group assembled by the United Nations to monitor and assess all global science related to climate change" (Nature 2022). They periodically release reports that focus on different dimensions of climate change. The 1.5 °C mark is considered to be the threshold to avoid catastrophic climate effects. The sixth IPCC report shows that current efforts to limit warming to 1.5 °C above preindustrial levels through limiting greenhouse gas emissions are unlikely to succeed. It is worth mentioning that some of the effects of a 1.5 °C warmer world are an increase in heatwaves, an increase in droughts and floods, rising sea levels, 90% die-off of the coral reefs resulting in less productive fisheries, the thawing of arctic ice (40% is expected to be gone by the end of the century), and large-scale species loss (IPCC 2018, Maizland 2021). Warming greater than 1.5 °C stands to have worse effects.

One of the main drivers of climate change is the release of large amounts of carbon dioxide into the environment. Light from the sun passes through carbon dioxide to the earth's surface as visible light. After warming the surface, it radiates back out as infrared light (infrared radiation). The carbon dioxide does not allow this radiation to pass through, trapping the heat within the earth's atmosphere and producing the greenhouse effect.

The most dangerous climate change situation is thought to be the runaway greenhouse effect. Water vapor is a potent greenhouse gas. When the atmosphere warms, it can hold more moisture, and more vapor in the atmosphere makes it warmer, creating an amplifying feedback loop. Carbon dioxide also contributes to the greenhouse effect. As the ecosystem changes and forests die off, stored carbon is released and warms the atmosphere. The earth's warming will release large amounts of methane, an even more potent greenhouse gas, from the ocean's depths and the melting permafrost (Ord 2020). The warmer climate causes the melting of the glacial and polar ice, which is very effective at reflecting sunlight without converting it into heat. With these reflective surfaces gone, there is even more surface area to absorb heat. If these feedback loops accelerate to the point where the earth is absorbing more light than it can radiate out as heat, humanity runs the risk of being trapped in an amplifying spiral similar to the fate of the planet Venus, which likely underwent a similar process (Torres 2017a).

Climate change is already a topic of discussion in Existential Risk Studies (ERS). Given the wide range of its effects, the speed of change, and reach of influence, nothing is likely to be spared from its consequences. Ord estimates that the existential risk posed by climate change within the next 100 years is 1 in 1000 (Ord 2020, 167). Others estimate the risk that climate change will lead to a global catastrophe as below 1% and 3% (Halstead 2018). Given the timescale and the dynamics of the risks posed, while it is less likely that humanity will face extinction from climate change in the near future, it is highly likely that it is the decisions made now and the systems and structures created that will determine the degree of existential risk in the medium- to long-term future. Climate change has also risen to a topic of concern in ERS due to its synergetic effects, making many of the other threats more likely (Ord 2020).

One of the overarching concerns when assessing the dangers of climate change is that the threat involves the interactions of highly complex and often chaotic systems. Trying to understand these types of systems and make predictions about them leads to uncertainty. And humans in general and science, in particular, have a hard time with uncertainty. The economist Robert Pindyck (2014) has pointed out that many ways of assessing the full impact of climate change, particularly Integrated Assessment Models, underemphasize uncertainty. Following an analysis by another economist, Nicholas Stern (2013) warns that many climate models do not adequately capture the full scale of what climate change may bring. He specifically warns that economic models do not focus on the effects climate change might have on individual lives, livelihoods, migration, and conflict. Further, he notes that these models often underestimate the total risk potential because they fail to consider "the possibility of catastrophic outcomes" (838).

Not considering the role of uncertainty in models tends to limit considerations of more extreme scenarios. A warming of 4 °C would be exponentially more catastrophic than 2 °C (World Bank 2012), leading to, among a host of disasters, a rise in sea levels of 0.5 meters which by 2050 is expected to cause billions of dollars in damage and displace 1.5 million people (Lynas 2008). At 6 °C, the climate system may enter into feedback loops, resulting in the near total destruction of the oceans, coral, the rainforests, worldwide desertification making vast areas of the earth uninhabitable, extreme reduction of available water and food, and the potential migration of billions of people. These effects would make the earth look similar to what it did during the Eocene, 33.9–55.8 million years ago. In this world, there would be no ice at either of the poles. There would likely be mass extinctions. The potential for large stores of methane stored in the deep ocean as methane hydrates are only stable at low temperatures may emerge, sparking an even higher surge in global temperatures (Schneider, 2009, Lynas 2007, 2008). At the far end of the 2–5 °C threshold are global catastrophic levels of death, famine, societal collapse, and mass migration (Pamlin and Armstrong 2015).

The effects of climate change are already unequally distributed, with the areas of the world least responsible for the current amount of greenhouse gasses in the atmosphere bearing the brunt of the damage (World Bank 2020; Singh 2015; Dehghan 2020). UN Secretary-General António Guterres recently referenced the connection between climate change and conflict, calling it a "perfect storm," warning, "Inequalities are still growing inside countries, but they are now growing in a morally unacceptable way between north and south, and this is creating a divide which can be very dangerous from the point of view of peace and security" (McVeigh 2022). The poorest areas are likely to be hit first and hardest by the effects of climate change, resulting in large areas of the tropics and sub-tropics becoming uninhabitable (Lynas 2008). This effect is further exacerbated by the fact that adaptation to significant climate change is likely expensive (World Bank 2011).

Efforts to address global inequalities sometimes worsen inequality by contributing to climate change. Using fossil fuels to power industrialization and economic expansion allowed today's prosperous economies to develop their great wealth. Now that the world stands on such a precarious threshold, today's poorer nations are discouraged by those same wealthy countries from following that same path toward economic strength and prosperity.

Just as the effects of climate change have been unequally distributed worldwide, so has the current climate crisis exacerbated inequality. The ratio of the Gross Domestic Product (GDP) between rich and developing countries may be as much as 25% larger than it would have been without global warming. There is also high likelihood that global per capita GDP is currently lower than it would be otherwise (Diffenbaugh and Burke 2019). Climate change can diminish the effectiveness of efforts to reduce poverty through extreme weather events, which most damagingly affect the most climate-sensitive regions, which often overlap with areas of high poverty. As climate change worsens and extreme weather events become increasingly common, this may be a significant hurdle to poverty reduction programs.

The World Bank has linked climate change to the increase in extreme poverty from 2019 to 2020, the first time in 25 years that the level of extreme poverty increased worldwide. They estimate that climate change may push 68–135 million people into poverty by 2030. This effect will likely be most severe in Sub-Saharan Africa and South Asia (World Bank 2020). The influence of climate on inequality has also been found within countries, though both levels tend to follow similar pathways. Disadvantaged groups are more susceptible to the effects of climate change, more susceptible to its damages, and at the same time, their ability to cope with and recover from these damages is also decreased (Islam and Winkel 2017).

When looking at the overall picture of climate change, the Global Challenges Foundation found that the most important factors influencing its impact are: (1) the uncertainties in climate change models, (2) the likelihood of global coordination for controlling emissions being effective, (3) the speed at which low-carbon economies are implemented in the future, (4) whether future advancements in technology have a positive or negative effect on the climate, and (5) the overall long-term impact of the change on the climate (Pamlin and Armstrong 2015). These factors are likely also important when assessing the overall influence climate change and conflict will have on each other.

Even though risk estimates of climate change-induced human extinction are relatively low for the near future, they are not zero. Historical evidence shows that a change of 6 °C may have resulted in mass extinction (Benton and Twitchett 2003). A large and rapid enough climate shock runs the risk of being a global catastrophic risk resulting in conflict and civilizational collapse (Lynas 2008, Pamlin and Armstrong). While the collapse of past civilizations has often been attributed to combinations of social, political, and economic forces, there is increasing evidence that climate change may play a significant or even leading role in the future (Bradley 2001).

While the alarm bells ring, it may serve humanity well that humans tend to be an intelligent species, especially when backed up against a wall. Unlike other species that have gone extinct during climate upheavals, technological and organizational capacities may make humans more resilient (Pamlin and Armstrong 2015; Pörtner et al. 2022).

Climate Change, Peace, and Conflict

Climate change has been recognized as a national security concern since the 1980s (Liberman 2019). It is a current topic of concern in the field of Security Studies and was mentioned in the 2019 *Worldwide Threat Assessment of the US Intelligence Community*, which states that "the effects of climate change and global environmental degradation are likely to fuel competition for resources, economic distress, and social discontent" (Coats 2019, 23). The connection between climate change with security threats shaped much of the early thinking on the relationship between peace, conflict, and climate. It is tempting to quickly draw causal links between the fact that the last decade has been the warmest on record, and the same time period saw the severity of armed conflicts rise to levels reminiscent of the Cold War (Buhaug and von Uexkull 2021). Despite the wealth of research on climate change in policy development, it has only been in the past two decades that significant research has taken place on the relationships between peace, conflict, and climate change (Bowles et al. 2015; Harrison 2005). Much of the early research has found connections, correlations, and to some limited extent, causation among these three (Buhaug 2015; Buhuang et al. 2014; Burke et al. 2009; Burke et al. 2009; Hsiang and Meng 2014; Hsiang et al. 2013; Miguel et al. 2004).

Clear-cut answers to the causal nature of these relationships are challenging to extract from the research, with one researcher referring to the task as resulting in a "cacophony of different findings" (Salehyan 2014, 1). Long-term historical data has not revealed direct connections between climate change and violence (Scheffran et al. 2012). This lack of connection could be due to the complex nature of conflict and the influence of other social, economic, and political developments. An essential question at this nexus between climate change and conflict is: to what extent can previous trends in climate change and conflict inform our predictions, given the drastic increase in the rate of climate change. The most recent IPCC report found that "compared to other socioeconomic factors, the influence of climate on conflict is assessed as relatively weak" (Pörtner et al. 2022, 17). However, it has also been shown that many of the same causal factors influence both the adverse effects of climate change and the potential for experiencing violent conflict (Gartzke and Böhmelt 2015).

Much of the initial peace research on climate change focused on understanding how climate variability increased the probability of conflict onset. Some studies suggested that environmental changes may weaken some governments, causing them to lose their monopoly on violence and increasing the likelihood of subnational conflicts (Bowles et al. 2015). Other studies found that international conflict might likely be aggravated when tensions are intensified by climate-fueled interstate migration, increased demands for natural resources, and water boundary disputes (Harrison 2005).

Peace researchers caution that it is not accurate to infer from the ambiguity of these initial research findings that there is no influence of climate on armed conflict but rather "research has failed to converge on a specific and direct association between climate and violent conflict" (Buhuang et al. 2014). There are several lessons learned from this research. First is a call for caution when discussing the security dimensions of climate change to avoid strong claims until a "larger body of nuanced and context-sensitive analyses is available" (Buhaug 2015, 269). Second, another interpretation of these initial findings could be that the complexities of the relationships between conflict and climate require more sophisticated research designs that are context-dependent and that difficult-to-quantify concepts such as "climate" and "conflict" need to be handled with care (Salehyan 2014).

Subsequent research on the climate-conflict relationship has tended to focus more on the indirect influence of climate change on conflict risk. This systems approach focuses on understanding this relationship where dynamics such as rapid climate change, resource depletion, political tensions, and migration are studied in tandem with each other (Buhaug 2016). Future research on linkages between vulnerability, conflict, and climate impacts is likely to be fruitful (Buhaug and von Uexkull 2021). An approach focused on these linkages is likely to more accurately capture notions of resiliency and vulnerability found in third-wave ERS perspectives.

Climate Change as a Risk Multiplier

There is a trend to consider climate change as a threat, crisis, or risk "multiplier," which worsens the current potential for conflict (Bowles et al. 2015). The argument goes that through the effects of climate change on agricultural production, access to drinking water, and economic activity, there will be increases in resource scarcity and decreases in the stability and viability of livelihoods (Salehyan 2008). Resource scarcity, food insecurity, and migration could lead to competition and violence (Conciliation Resources 2022). It has been shown that environmental changes and poor political response can increase food prices and decrease food security, contributing to the likelihood of violence (Scheffran et al. 2012; Messer 2009). While this pathway may well be true, the systems of relations are much more complex. It has also been shown that abundant natural resources can contribute to civil conflict (de Soysa 2002; Collier and Hoeffler 2004; Le Billon 2001; Salehyan 2008; Ross 2004).

The unequal distribution of climate change effects may also influence the impact of climate change on conflict. The worst environmental impacts of climate change will likely be experienced in equatorial countries. These countries, which are often more dependent on agriculture and have less robust social, political, and economic systems, have less resilience to mitigate the effects of climate change. Following this same logic, western countries stand a better chance of enduring environmental changes (Chin 2019). Though a popular belief, it may not be accurate. A global temperature rise above 2 °C is likely to cause catastrophic harm through increased severe weather events and damage to food production. The global harm caused by environmental change would interact with other political and economic trends and weaken internal stability across the globe (Laybourn-Langton et al. 2019).

The nexus between climate change-related migration and conflict is another substantial topic of discussion on the influence of environmental changes on conflict. In almost all models, this influence is one of the mechanisms by which climate change becomes a multiplier. It is predicted that as climate change increases, the number of displaced peoples will increase (O. Brown 2008, Brzoska and Fröhlich 2016). The causal chain through this lens follows the same logic as described above. As the climate changes, people whose livelihoods depend on access to natural resources will face a narrow set of options. They can stay where they are and try to mitigate the environmental changes, or they can try to go elsewhere.

Whether the migration is internal or international, there will be competition over natural resources between the host communities and those newly arriving. Such a view on the effects of conflict through the pathway of migration influenced by climate change may be overly simplistic. There is a need for complexifying the understanding of these relationships to understand the deeper mechanisms and design more effective interventions (Raleigh and Urdal 2007; Brzoska and Fröhlich 2016).

There are more pathways connecting climate change and conflict and more options than this logic suggests. Migration is not the only response to environmental changes, and there are possible ways in which political, social, and international systems could respond to reduce the need for migration. The vulnerability of communities related to dependence on natural resources could be addressed. The degree to which climate change will fuel migration is also likely related to the rate at which it occurs, and responses will need to be tailored to current understandings of climate change models.

Likely, the primary way migration could increase the likelihood of conflict is as an exacerbating factor whereby migration brings to the surface or destabilizes existing tensions. In the case of migration across international borders, if the moving people are received by communities close to the border, this may influence existing center-periphery dynamics between the central government and those at its edges (Hugo 2013). Additionally, migrations through pass-through countries (e.g., migrants coming to the USA through Mexico) often become a source of tension between the intermediary country and the receiving country.

There is also concern that as much as climate change may be a conflict multiplier, it could also be a "peace inhibiter" (Bowles et al. 2015), making current peacebuilding efforts less effective as attention and resources are reallocated to mitigating environmental damage, possibly leading to a downturn in the current trends toward peace (Gleditsch 2012). The extent to which this is true and the dynamics involved are areas for further research.

Of primary importance when examining the interactions between climate change and conflict are the ways in which climate change can function as a risk multiplier (Schubert et al. 2007). It can be argued with a high degree of certainty that a global environmental crisis could run parallel with an economic one (Chin 2019). It is then easy to imagine how issues such as migration and competition over resources or resentment over unequal responsibility for the crisis could exacerbate a Great Powers

Conflict. Further, the framing of climate change and migration as a security issue could make the use of military solutions more likely. Thinking of migration in terms of security could contribute to a feedback loop in a Great Powers Conflict and become a self-fulfilling prophecy (Scheffran et al. 2012; Gleditsch 2012).

Compounding Effects of Climate Change

Climate change has been recognized as a threat to global health (Watts et al. 2015). Access to medical care, nutrition, sanitation, and shelter effect conflict and climate change (Connolly et al. 2004). The compounding risk of these different factors is difficult to calculate, and the potential for a self-reinforcing system to develop is high. Global coordination is required to address climate change. Anything inhibiting international trust and cooperation threatens to increase climate change's existential and global catastrophic risk potential. This problem has been evident in decreased climate change funding during the COVID-19 pandemic (Alayza and Caldwell 2021). The effects of climate change and conflict can be even more significant when combined and indirectly increase the spread of pandemic diseases, especially when paired with inhibited coordination and implementation of disease eradication efforts (Patz et al. 1996). A Great Powers Conflict would be another threat to global cooperation. A world at war is unlikely to be able to devote resources and attention to the mitigation of climate change and also unlikely to work together effectively. These inabilities may create catastrophes that would otherwise have been mitigated. However, the threat of compounding risks related to climate change may incentivize countries to collaborate on energy and climate issues while still allowing for confrontations in different domains (Jones 2020).

Despite the overwhelming bleak picture presented when considering the compounding risks of climate change and conflict and how they relate to other existential risks, their interconnected nature provides additional possibilities to address them. Climate change and peace are quickly becoming essential research areas, as are the relationships between issues such as migration and conflict. A peace-oriented framing of this nexus of issues may be a departure point for large-scale efforts approaching the problems from many angles. This same frame may help prevent problems caused by an overemphasis on the security framing of these issues.

Peacebuilding and Climate Change

A recent report from Conciliation Resources, an NGO that works for peacebuilding and the prevention of violence, reflects this dual-potential brought by climate change, writing that "the climate crisis will put pressure on peace and prosperity, and complicate efforts to build peace in areas already affected by, and vulnerable to conflict," while going to write that "the common threat of extreme weather events and environmental change, can also be used as a bridge to bring divided communities together, working collaboratively towards a common goal" (Conciliation Resources 2022). The recognition of the importance of combining initiatives that focus on conflict, peacebuilding, and the environment has been increasing (Stockholm+50 2022).

Tegan Blain with the United States Institute of Peace (USIP) writes that in light of the most recent IPCC report, peacebuilders need to be aware that they now occupy a precarious position where climate change soon will likely increasingly correlate with increases in conflict many times in the same places where a rapid transition to a low-carbon or net-zero carbon system may contribute to future tensions (Blaine 2022). In her reading of the IPCC report, she describes several factors that will be important in peacebuilding. The first is that climate change is likely to expose long-standing grievances and create new ones; this is one of the reasons that climate sensitivity will be increasingly crucial in peacebuilding. The second factor is that climate change threatens many aspects of human security: access to food, water, and adequate health care. Thirdly, climate change has and will likely continue to contribute to migration. Migration on its own, especially in fragile and conflict-affected areas, can become a force fueled by conflict and a driver of conflict. Finally, she stresses that the tendency for climate change to exacerbate inequality means that not everyone will suffer the effects of climate change equally. Already marginalized communities, minorities, and indigenous people are especially vulnerable to climate change (Blaine 2022).

The connection between peacebuilding and climate work has several implications. The first is a call to ensure that existing and future peacebuilding and conflict transformation programs are "climate-sensitive," meaning that they are aware of the effects that climate adaptation and mitigation would have on their intended outcomes (Läderach et al. 2021), and conversely that climate change initiatives are both context and conflict sensitive, meaning that they are attuned to the potential conflict dynamics of their programming (Sitati et al. 2021).

Current, actionable research is critical to working on climate change and peacebuilding. The Climate-related Peace and Security Risks program is a new example of such a program, created by a collaboration between the Stockholm International Peace Research Institute (SIPRI) and the Norwegian Institute of International Affairs (NUPI). The program aims to create and disseminate information on the nexus between climate, peace, development, and security. In some of their recent reports, they have looked at the current and near-term future impacts of climate change on conflict-affected areas in Ethiopia, Sudan, and Afghanistan. In Ethiopia, their report found that the long-standing problems the country has faced due to drought, famine, and locusts are further exacerbated by climate change. Access to land and water has already been a driver of conflicts between agriculturalists and pastoralists, threatening to further spill across the border into South Sudan and Kenya. These conflicts, alongside other communal and armed conflicts, particularly in the Tigray region, have increased food insecurity. With current climate projections, this situation is likely to worsen, and the country's capacity and resilience to cope with climate change are further diminished (SIPRI 2022b).

Sudan is in a similar situation but made more challenging by being one of the least developed countries that have already had problems with extreme weather, floods, and droughts. These environmental factors and unsustainable land use have led to large-scale ecosystem degradation. The capacity for this climate change-sensitive country to adapt to predicted climate changes has been further decreased due to the political instability after the 2021 military coup. There are further concerns that gender-based disparities in access to resources and the overall security risks for women and girls will be further exacerbated through climate change (SIPRI 2022c).

Afghanistan shares similarities with Ethiopia and Sudan in being both vulnerable to the effects of climate change and being a conflict-affected area. Amidst the worst drought in three decades, the current political turmoil after the takeover of the Taliban has increased the overall humanitarian emergency. Climate change will likely exacerbate many of the conditions contributing to this insecurity. There is a worry that climate change may increase the risk of local conflicts over access to resources. This increase in conflict will further diminish the resilience of communities to adapt to a changing climate while facing a prolonged humanitarian crisis (SIPRI 2022a).

Methods of Mitigating the Risks of Climate Change

All approaches to addressing climate change require levels of global cooperation that have not yet been seen and that are difficult to imagine. The current climate emergency has occurred, in part, because modern political and economic perspectives have put a high value on economic growth through the production of cheap energy and goods. Addressing this issue will require massive changes in almost all facets of life—changes in how farming is done, how land is used, the means of energy production, the structure of the power grid, and the preservation of natural habitats, to name a few. Countries and businesses will have to value nature beyond economic gains or, more likely, value survival enough to find ways of working that are both profitable and protective of nature and the climate.

One of the challenges in addressing climate change is that many of the economic and political forces that directly or indirectly contribute to climate change are difficult to change, often because it is not in the economic or political interest of those in power. Innovative approaches that do not directly fight against these forces but instead change the frame of the situation are likely to be necessary. The current movement for plant-based and cultured meat provides an interesting example. Current industrial practices of animal protein production are a significant driver of climate change. Two ways industrial meat production contributes to climate change are emission production (Xu et al. 2021) and deforestation (Weisse and Goldman 2021). Climate change effects driven by agriculture create feedback loops that increase droughts, and extreme weather events, reduce the amount of arable land, and threaten water supplies (Cohen et al. 2022). Studies have shown that even if fossil fuel emissions were immediately halted, global protein production alone would make meeting the Paris Agreement's 1.5 °C target impossible (Clark et al. 2020). This fact alone is alarming and made even more so given that global meat production and consumption are expected to double by 2050 as populations increase alongside the demand for meat (FAO 2018). Further, the vast majority of antibiotics consumed worldwide are given to animals and contribute to the overall problem of antibiotic-resistant microorganisms (CDC 2021; Wallinga and Kar 2020).

Plant-based and cultivated meats may provide a viable alternative to current practices. These approaches to creating protein at the industrial level require much less land, energy, and water and emit significantly fewer greenhouse gasses (Searchinger et al. 2019). The recent IPCC report on climate change identified plant-based and cultivated meats as transformative solutions that may help address climate change (Pörtner et al. 2022). Organizations such as the Good Food Institute (GFI) have made significant progress in advocacy and support with policymakers, business leaders, and researchers on this issue. Plant-based and cultivated meats along with the approach of organizations such as GFI are interesting because it takes a low-friction approach to addressing the problem of protein production and climate change. Convincing individuals to change behaviors is difficult, as is convincing businesses to operate in ways that are not maximally profitable. This new approach takes out the friction. Instead, GFI acknowledges that many people like to and want to eat meat and that this trend is likely to increase. If it is possible to find ways to produce meat that are significantly better for the climate, that taste as good as animal-based meats, and, importantly, costs the same or is cheaper. Then approaches like this may stand a chance of helping to reduce global warming (GFI 2021).

Emissions Reduction

Emission reductions are a logical place for addressing climate change since emissions are a known cause of global warming. Recent interesting proposals focus on the potential effectiveness of city-level emission reduction programs (O'Shaughnessy et al. 2016; Shan et al. 2018). The World Bank's 2021–2025 action plan identified the city-level focus as one of their priority systems of interest (World Bank 2021). Despite this, emission reduction efforts continue to be coordinated internationally.

International agreements, usually in the form of treaties, have been one of the primary avenues of garnering global cooperation on climate change. The United Nations Framework Convention on Climate Change (UNFCCC) was the first global treaty to explicitly address climate change. This convention established the basic legal framework for cooperation on climate change to stabilize the concentrations of greenhouse gases and find ways to mitigate the dangers of anthropogenic interference with the climate. It had been the precursor for treaties on climate change (United Nations 1992).

The subsequent Kyoto Protocol was agreed upon in 1992 and implemented in February 2005, operationalizing the United Nations Framework Convention on Climate Change. The main focus of the Kyoto Protocol was the establishment of five courses of action for addressing climate change: (1) control the emission of carbon dioxide and five other greenhouse gasses, (2) assign percentage targets for reducing or limiting emissions, (3) allow for the trading of emissions, (4) create incentives for implementation reduction projects among countries required to cut their emissions, and (5) establish incentives for countries that are required to cut their emissions to assist other countries in their emission reduction programs (United Nations 1998).

The more expansive Paris Agreement, adopted in 2015, addresses the interrelated issues of climate change, mitigation, adaptation, and finance. It entered into force in November 2016. The long-term aim of the agreement is to reduce global greenhouse gas emissions so that the total level of global warming stays below 2 °C above preindustrial levels and aims to lower that cap to 1.5 °C further. Countries are required to review their commitments every five years. The agreement also seeks to provide financing for developing countries to mitigate climate change and increase resilience and the ability to adapt to its impacts (United Nations 2015).

The most recent treaty addressing climate change, the Glasgow Climate Pact, was signed at the November 2021 United Nations Climate Change Conference (COP26). The pact reaffirms the goals of the Paris Agreement and commits to reducing global carbon dioxide emissions by 45% by 2030 and to net zero by the middle of the century. The agreement also commits to reducing other greenhouse gases and is the first to mention the "phasing down" of coal usage explicitly. It also includes a commitment to climate financing for developing countries (United Nations 2021).

Valid criticism is leveled against these climate change agreements. The Kyoto Protocol may overemphasize a focus on short-term perspectives, focus too heavily on carbon and did not address other greenhouse gases, and pay more attention to the emission of greenhouse gases and not the overall concentration in the atmosphere (Böringer 2003). The Paris Agreement may still be too new to assess accurately. When asked about his evaluation of the agreement, Michael Oppenheimer, a climate scientist at Princeton, said, "based on whether we have any prospect of meeting a 2°C target, from that point of view, it's probably a D or an F" (Cornwall 2020). The rise in carbon dioxide emissions two years after the agreement was not a promising sign (Dimitrov et al. 2019). There is some consensus among experts that the agreement is not enough to prevent warming to 1.5 °C (Maizland 2021). The overall success of the agreement may be tied to the domestic politics of its signatories. The departure of the USA from the agreement under the Trump administration with few repercussions is evidence of that potential weakness (McGrath 2020).

The most recent international climate change agreement, COP26, has been criticized for lacking sufficiently strong commitments to addressing rising climate change adequately. By one estimate, even though the treaty aims at reducing emissions by 45% of 2010 levels to maintain a warming level under 1.5 °C by 2030, under current pledges, total emissions may be 14% higher by then (Tollefson 2021). Even if countries meet their 2030 targets, global temperatures are estimated to rise by 2.4 °C (Climate Action Tracker 2021). Further, it failed to include other needed measures, such as establishing "loss and damage" financing for countries vulnerable to climate change and not major emitters of greenhouse gasses (Schalatek and Roberts 2021).

Even if they have not fully addressed climate change, these agreements have had some important achievements nonetheless. The Kyoto Protocol was an ambitious project resulting from a decade of negotiations. Ratifying countries may have already reduced their emissions by as much as 7% by 2019. For the first time, nations addressed the fact that emissions are a global problem that requires a cooperative solution (Maamoun 2019). The burden-sharing mechanisms it proposed showed that, to some extent, the countries were willing to work together (Böringer 2003). It also established international consensus on the science of climate change and the need to set emission standards. There is consensus among experts that the Paris Agreement may still be able to deliver on its goals (Dimitrov et al. 2019). One of its major achievements has been to help to make climate change a continued topic of concern globally (Cornwall 2020).

A treaties-based approach to reducing emissions has only been mildly effective. Many scholars point to the fact that even legally binding mechanisms lack effective enforcement mechanisms (Allen et al. 2009). Others argue that the problem of climate change is not an issue that can adequately be addressed through a tool such as a treaty (Barrett 2013). It is likely that international treaties alone are not effective enough to address the climate problem but should be seen as part of a complex intervention. The most popular low-carbon means of producing energy, hydroelectric, nuclear, and sustainable biomass are insufficient to bring the world to net-zero emissions and will require additional investment in solar and wind energy as well as carbon capture in order to possibly achieve that goal (Halsted 2018). International climate treaties in conjunction with the emerging efforts at subnational emission reduction, particularly at the city level, will be required to even begin to meet emission reduction goals (Markolf et al. 2020). Further, these approaches need to hold-to-account large corporations such as Starbucks and Amazon which have pledged to reduce emissions (Nguyen 2020).

Geoengineering

What is perhaps unique about climate change is that a newly emerging technological field aimed it the scale at which it operates exists (Shepherd 2009). Geoengineering is the "deliberate large-scale manipulation of the planetary environment to counteract anthropogenic climate change" (The Royal Society 2009, 1). As a potential tool for addressing the problem of climate change, it has garnered increasing attention, especially since the latest IPCC report has shown that cutting our emissions would no longer be enough; it will also be needed to remove carbon already in the atmosphere (Nature 2022).

The host of approaches under the banner of geoengineering span from low-cost, easily implementable interventions that can be done with existing technologies to those proposals that border on science fiction. Solutions aim to reduce climate change in two different ways. The first is decreasing the amount of carbon in the atmosphere, and the second is managing the incoming solar radiation. It is important for those working at the intersection between climate change, peace, and conflict to pay attention to these approaches. Technological solutions, once available, will seem increasingly viable. Certainly, as the climate worsens these solutions may become more appealing, and they have important considerations for Peace and Conflict due to the scale and scope of their impact, potential to be weaponized, to contribute to global inequality, and the multitude of governance concerns which would come with such technologies.

An analysis done by the Founders Pledge, using Neglectedness, Importance, and Tractability described in Chap. 3, found that carbon capture and storage are among the most likely investments to impact the future climate (Halsted 2018). Direct carbon capture goes beyond carbon sequestration, which refers to the techniques to capture and store carbon dioxide from the gases released by power stations (Torres 2017a). Direct carbon capture extracts carbon dioxide from the atmosphere, directly addressing one of the primary mechanisms responsible for global warming.

Massive reforestation programs that drastically increase the planting of trees are two methods of direct carbon capture that use current technologies and are likely to have few harmful effects on the climate. New technologies have been invented to remove carbon from the atmosphere, such as Iceland's Carbfix, which developed technology that dissolves carbon dioxide in water and injects it underground where it undergoes a reaction and forms a stable natural mineral (Snæbjörnsdóttir et al. 2020). Global Thermostat has developed large banks of honeycomb-like fans that take carbon from the atmosphere and concentrate it so it can later be sold for industrial use (Gambhir and Tavoni 2019). Recent advancements in artificial tree technology have been made, such as Carbon Collect Inc.'s "mechanical tree" that uses coated discs to collect CO_2 from the wind for storage or other possible uses (Carbon Collect Inc. 2021).

More radical ideas have also been proposed, such as seeding iron into parts of the ocean's surface to stimulate phytoplankton growth. These algal blooms would absorb carbon dioxide from the atmosphere into their biomass, sinking into the deep ocean. Preliminary experiments have been done using this methodology, though not specifically designed to test the feasibility of this method as a carbon removal strategy (de Baar et al. 2005). The overall effectiveness of this method in sequestering atmospheric carbon and its long-term effects on ecosystems are still not understood (Buesseler et al. 2008).

However, these types of carbon capture can be thought of as treating the symptom, not the disease, since they do not address the amount of carbon dioxide currently being released. These approaches are usually conceptualized as being implemented alongside efforts to achieve a net-zero carbon world while acknowledging that even if all emissions were stopped soon, there is enough carbon in the atmosphere to cause widespread damage and suffering for years.

The second major geoengineering approach to addressing climate change is developing ways to limit the amount of sunlight absorbed by the earth by blocking or reflecting it before it hits the earth's surface and is radiated back as heat. These approaches are appealing because they are quicker and cheaper than carbon removal (Torres 2017a).

One technique for managing incoming solar radiation is surface albedo modification (SAM). Albedo here refers to "the percentage of solar radiation reflected by an object" (Oliver 2008, 33). The higher the level of albedo the more solar radiation is reflected. For example, polar ice is much more reflective than the dark ocean surface. The ice has a much higher albedo and thus reflects more light, and the dark oceans have a low albedo, absorbing more light. The SAM attempts to increase the amount of light reflected off the earth's surface. Some approaches are likely to have a few downsides, such as Urban SAM, which uses light-colored or reflective surfaces for rooftops and pavements (Akbar et al. 2012).

Similarly, there are proposals to increase the albedo of the ocean by making the wakes created by ships "bright and foamy" (Hand 2016), which might be able to reduce global temperatures by 0.5 °C (Crook et al. 2016). Other approaches would need further research into their possible side effects, such as engineering agricultural crops to have a higher albedo since crop albedo is already often higher than that of surrounding vegetation (Matthews et al. 2002) or more extensive projects such as placing reflective materials across large areas of the desert (Gaskill 2004). The effectiveness of SAM approaches is still uncertain, and some findings suggest that they may be only locally effective, seasonal, and may disrupt weather patterns, particularly in the case of desert SAM.

Some scientists have suggested using space-based reflectors (Irvine et al. 2012). Though the technology does not currently exist, there have been ideas to place a large mirror at the inner Lagrangian point (L1), the point between the earth and the sun where the gravitational forces between the two cancel each other out, allowing an object to essentially hover in place (The European Space Agency n.d.). Such a mirror could positively reflect solar radiation before it gets to the earth's surface without the risk of disrupting weather patterns on earth.

Currently, a more popular approach to managing solar radiation is the injection of sulfate aerosols (hydrogen sulfide, sulfur dioxide, or sulfuric acid) into the stratosphere using airborne probes, balloons, or aircraft (Falk 2017, Torres 2017a). Once these particulates are in the atmosphere, they reflect solar radiation into space, producing an effect called "global dimming" (Wild 2008). Similar to the effect of a large volcanic eruption, this could be an approach to counteracting global warming. These have been the most scientifically explored methods of reducing solar radiation (Caldeira and Wood 2008; Reach et al. 2009). Some modeling suggests that such a method would result in surface temperatures returning to their preindustrial levels in a few years (Matthews and Caldeira 2007). This speed could make such an approach an appealing emergency intervention.

A significant potential drawback of using sulfur aerosols or any other solar radiation management technique is that once it is started, it would need to be continued indefinitely; this is even more so the case if they are not used with effective emissions reduction and carbon removal measures

(Brovkin et al. 2009). This is because the total amount of carbon in the atmosphere would still increase. Once the method of reducing the incoming radiation is halted, there would likely be a rebound shock where global warming would resume at an even faster pace (Keller et al. 2014).

There are many unknowns with this type of technology, including the issue of political control, which would put a direct peace and security threat. Given the possibly increasingly dire situation and the potential appeal of a technological fix, governments or even sufficiently motivated billionaires could decide to implement any of these technologies unilaterally. Current global governance institutions do not have a framework for coordinating the implementation of such technologies, and their status under international law is uncertain. With sufficiently advanced geoengineering technologies, the weather itself could become politicized. Frameworks would need to be put in place to ensure that some countries would not benefit nor suffer disproportionally from others (Robock et al. 2009). There are also security risks to consider as some of these techniques, particularly sulfur injections, could be weaponized (Halsted 2018).

The greatest challenge with geoengineering is that some elements of it will likely become necessary to forestall climate catastrophes, yet there are many unknowns, and there is always the risk that it might backfire (Keller et al. 2014). Despite these uncertainties, there is agreement that geoengineering should not be discounted outright. All major reports have found enough evidence to warrant further research into such technologies (Shepherd 2009; National Academy of Sciences 2015; Schäfer et al. 2015). This research should proceed while not letting efforts toward its development affect commitments to global emissions reduction (Shepherd 2009). Given the range and scale of its possible effects research into geoengineering will also benefit from a peace and conflict lens.

Questions for the Future

How does climate change affect the likelihood of a conflict occurring and the type, duration, and scale of conflicts?

Which approaches to working on climate change alongside peacebuilding would be mutually beneficial?

Climate change is already an issue of significant importance. Given all current estimates, it will likely continue to be a vital issue for the foreseeable future. By its very nature, it affects everyone everywhere, albeit to different degrees. Even if climate change does not yet alone cross the threshold into an extinction-level event, from what is currently known, there will be increasing challenges to sustaining human life. Climate change is already an indirect factor in causing and prolonging violent conflicts, and it exacerbates most existing root causes of conflicts. As the climate continues to change, peace researchers will need to develop increasingly nuanced models to understand the relationships between conflicts and climate change. This research will have to contend with how climate change and conflict may compound each other and other existential risks to magnify them all. Finally, peace researchers will have to explore peacebuilding and climate initiatives as interrelated projects with a focus on how working on climate change and peacebuilding may be paired together.

References

AAAS. 2014. "What We Know: The Reality, Risks, and Response to Climate Change." American Association for the Advancement of Science. https://whatweknow.aaas.org/wp-content/uploads/2014/07/whatweknow_website.pdf.

Akbar, Hashem, H. Damon Matthews, and Donny Seto. 2012. "The Long-term Effect of Increasing the Albedo of Urban Areas." Environmental Research Letters 7 (024004).

Alayza, Natalia, and Molly Caldwell. 2021. Financing Climate Action and the COVID-19 Pandemic: An Analysis of 17 Developing Countries. Washington, DC: World Resource Institute.

Allen, Myles R., J. David Frame, Chris Huntingford, Chris D. Jones, Jason A. Lowe, Malte Meinshausen, and Nicolai Meinshausen. 2009. "Warming Caused by Cumulative Carbon Emissions Towards the Trillionth Tonne." Nature 458 (7242): 1163-1166.

Böringer, Christoph. 2003. "The Kyoto Protocol: A Review and Perspectives." Oxford Review of Economic Policy 19 (3): 451-466.

Barrett, Scott. 2013. "Climate Treaties and Approaching Catastrophes." Journal of Environmental Economics and Management 66: 235-250.

Benton, Michael J., and Richard J. Twitchett. 2003. "How to Kill (almost) All Life: the End-Permian Extinction Event." Trends in Ecology and Evolution 18 (7): 358-365.

Blaine, Tegan. 2022. "The Peacebuilding Implications of the Latest U.N. Climate Report to Stay Ahead of Climate Curve, a Transition to Green Energy Must be

Coupled with Informed Peacebuilding." United States Institute of Peace. March 3. Accessed August 8, 2022. https://www.usip.org/publications/2022/03/peacebuilding-implications-latest-un-climate-report.

Bowles, Devin C., Colin D. Butler, and Neil Morisetti. 2015. "Climate Change, Conflict and Health." Journal of the Royal Society of Medicine 1-6.

Bradley, Raymond S. 2001. "What Drives Societal Collapse?" Science 291 (5504): 609-610.

Brovkin, Victor, Vladimir Petoukhov, Martin Claussen, Eva Bauer, David Archer, and Carlo Jaeger. 2009. "Geoengineering Climate by Stratospheric Sulfur Injections: Earth System Vulnerability to Technological Failure." Climatic Change 92: 243–259.

Brown, Oli. 2008. Migration and Climate Change. Geneva: International Organization for Migration.

Brzoska, Michael, and Christiane Fröhlich. 2016. "Climate Change, Migration and Violent Conflict: Vulnerabilities, Pathways and Adaptation Strategies." Migration and Development 5 (2): 190-210.

Buesseler, Ken O, Scott C. Doney, David M. Karl, Philip W. Boyd, Ken Caldeira, Fei Chai, Kenneth H. Coale, et al. 2008. "Ocean Iron Fertilization-Moving Forward in a Sea of Uncertainty." Science (319): 162.

Buhaug, Halvard. 2015. "Climate–conflict Research: Some Reflections on the Way Forward." WIREs Climate Change 6 (3): 269–275.

Buhaug, Halvard. 2016. "Climate Change and Conflict: Taking Stock." Peace Economics, Peace Science and Public Policy 22 (4): 331–338.

Buhaug, Halvard, and Nina von Uexkull. 2021. "Vicious Circles: Violence, Vulnerability, and Climate Change." Annual Review of Environment and Resources 46: 545–68.

Buhaug, Halvard and Nina von Uexkull. 2021. "Climate-Conflict Research: A Decade of Scientific Progress." New Security Beat. February 23. Accessed July 30, 2022. https://www.newsecuritybeat.org/2021/02/climate-conflict-research-decade-scientific-progress/.

Buhuang, H., J. Nordkvelle, T. Bernauer, T. Böhmelt, M. Brzoska, J.W. Busby, A. Ciccone, et al. 2014. "One Effect to Rule Them All? A Comment on Quantifying the Influence of Climate on Human Conflict, Climatic Change." Climate Change 127: 391-397.

Burke, Marshall B., Edward Miguel, Shanker Satyanath, John A. Dykema, and David B. Lobell. 2009. "Warming Increases the Risk of Civil War in Africa." *Proceedings of the National Academy of Sciences* (Proceedings of the National Academy of Sciences of the United States of America) 106 (49): 20671-20674.

Caldeira, Ken, and Lowell Wood. 2008. "Global and Arctic Climate Engineering: Numerical Model Studies." Philosophical Transactions of the Royal Society 366 (1882): 4039-4056.

Carbon Collect Inc. 2021. "Mechanical Trees." Carbon Collect Inc. April. Accessed August 3, 2022. https://mechanicaltrees.com/mechanicaltrees/.

CDC. 2021. "Where Resistance Spreads: Food Supply." Center for Disease Control. November 21. Accessed August 8, 2022. https://www.cdc.gov/drugresistance/food.html.

Chin, Warren. 2019. "Technology, War and the State: Past, Present and Future." International Affairs 95 (4): 765-783.

Clark, Michael A., G.G. Nina Domingo, Kimberly Colgan, Sumil K. Thakrar, David Tilman, John Lynch, Inês L. Azevedo, and Jason D. Hill. 2020. "Global Food System Emissions Could Preclude Achieving the 1.5° and 2°C Climate Change Targets." Science 370 (6517): 705-708.

Clark, Peter U, Jeremy D Shakun, Shaun A Marcott, Alan C Mix, Michael Eby, Scott Kulup, Anders Levermann, et al. 2016. "Consequences of Twenty-first-century Policy for Multi-millennial Climate and Sea-level Change." Nature 6 (4): 360-369.

Climate Action Tracker. 2021. "2100 Warming Projections." Climate Action Tracker. November 9. Accessed July 30, 2022. https://climateactiontracker.org/global/temperatures/.

Coats, Daniel R. 2019. "Worldwide Threat Assessment of the US Intelligence Community." Senate Select Committee on Intelligence.

Cohen, Madeline, Sheila Voss, and Shira Fischer. 2022. "Agriculture is at a Climate Crossroads: Alternative Proteins are a Global Solution." The Good Food Institute. April 22. Accessed August 1, 2022. https://gfi.org/blog/agriculture-is-at-a-climate-crossroads-alternative-proteins-are-a-global-solution/.

Collier, Paul, and Anke Hoeffler. 2004. "Greed and Grievance in Civil War." Oxford Economic Papers 56-4.

Conciliation Resources. 2022. "How is the Climate Crisis Impacting Conflict and Peace?" Conciliation Resources. May 22. Accessed July 29, 2022. https://www.c-r.org/news-and-insight/how-climate-crisis-impacting-conflict-and-peace?utm_source=Conciliation+Resources+newsletter&utm_campaign=adaa150589-EMAIL_CAMPAIGN_2022_03_24_02_44_COPY_01&utm_medium=email&utm_term=0_b348a3d428-adaa150589-56614533&mc.

Connolly, M. A., M. Gayer, MJ Ryan, P Salama, P Spiegel, and D.L Heymann. 2004. "Communicable Diseases in Complex Emergencies: Impact and Challenges." Lancet 364: 1974-1983.

Cook, John, Naomi Oreskes, Peter T Doran, William R.L. Anderegg, Bart Verheggen, Ed W. Mailbach, J. Stuart Carlton, et al. 2016. "Consensus on Consensus: a Synthesis of Consensus Estimates on Human-Caused Global Warming." Environmental Research Letters.

Cornwall, Warren. 2020. "The Paris Climate Pact is 5 Years Old: Is it Working?" Science. December 11. Accessed August 3, 2022. https://www.science.org/content/article/paris-climate-pact-5-years-old-it-working.

Crook, Julia A, Lawrence S Jackson, and Piers M Forster. 2016. "Can Increasing Albedo of Existing Ship Wakes Reduce Climate Change?" Journal of Geophysical Research: Atmospheres 121: 1549-1558.

de Baar, Hein J.W., Philip W. Boyd, Kenneth H. Coale, Michael R. Landry, Atsushi Tsuda, Philipp Assmy, Dorothee C.E. Bakker, et al. 2005. "Synthesis of Iron Fertilization Experiments: From the Iron Age in the Age of Enlightenment." Journal of Geophysical Research 110: C09S16.

de Soysa, Indra. 2002. "Paradise Is a Bazaar? Greed, Creed, and Governance in Civil War, 1989–99." Journal of Peace Research 39 (4): 395–416.

Dehghan, Saeed Kamali. 2020. "World's Poorest Bear Brunt of Climate Crisis: 10 Underreported Emergencies." The Guardian. January 14. Accessed July 30, 2022. https://www.theguardian.com/global-development/2022/jan/14/worlds-poorest-bear-brunt-of-climate-crisis-10-underreported-emergencies#:~:text=The%20world's%20poorest%20are%20bearing,cause%20it%2C%E2%80%9D%20he%20said.

Diffenbaugh, Noah S, and Marshall Burke. 2019. "Global Warming has Increased Global Economic Inequality." Proceedings of the National Academy of Sciences of the United States of America 116 (20): 9808-9813.

Dimitrov, Radoslav, Jon Hovi, Detlef F. Sprinz, Håkon Sælen, and Arild Underdal. 2019. "Institutional and Environmental Effectiveness: Will the Paris Agreement Work?" WIREs Climate Change 10 (583).

Falk, Dan. 2017. "Can Hacking the Planet Stop Climate Change?" NBC News. May 2. Accessed July 29, 2022. https://www.nbcnews.com/mach/environment/%20can-hacking-planet-stop-runaway-climate-change-n752221.

FAO. 2018. The Future of Food and Agriculture: Alternative Pathways to 2050. Food and Agriculture Organization of the United Nations.

Gambhir, Ajay, and Massimo Tavoni. 2019. "Direct Air Carbon Capture and Sequestration: How It Works and How It Could Contribute to Climate-Change Mitigation." One Earth 405-409.

Gartzke, Erik, and Tobias Böhmelt. 2015. "Climate and Conflict: Whence the Weather?" Peace Economics, Peace Science and Public Policy 21 (4): 445–451.

Gaskill, Alvia. 2004. Summary of Meeting with U.S. DOE to Discuss Geoengineering Options to Prevent Abrupt and Long-Term Climate Change. Research Triangle Park, N.C.: Environmental Reference Materials, Inc.

GFI. 2021. Global food Transition is Necessary to Keep Warming Below 1.5C: Opportunities for Alternative Proteins. Good Food Institute/Climate Advisers.

Gleditsch, Nils Petter. 2012. "Whither the Weather? Climate Change and Conflict." Journal of Peace Research 49 (1): 3–9.

Halstead, John. 2018. "Stratospheric Aerosol Injection Research and Existential Risk." Futures 102: 63-77.

Halsted, John. 2018. Climate Change: Cause Area Report. Founders Pledge.

Hand, Eric. 2016. "Could Bright, Foamy Wakes from Ocean Ships Combat Global Warming?" Science. January 29. Accessed July 29, 2022. https://www.science.org/content/article/could-bright-foamy-wakes-ocean-ships-combat-global-warming.

Harrison, Stephan. 2005. "Climate Change, Future Conflict and the Role of Climate Science." The RUSI Journal 150 (6): 18-23.

Hsiang, Solomon M., Marshall Burke, and Edward Miguel. 2013. "Quantifying the Influence of Climate on Human Conflict." *Science* 341 (6151): 1–7.

Hsiang, Solomon M., and Kyle C. Meng. 2014. "Reconciling Disagreement Over Climate–conflict Results in Africa." *Proceedings of the National Academy of Sciences* 111 (6): 2100–2103.

Hugo, G. 2013. "Introduction." In Migration and Climate Change, edited by G. Hugo, xv-xlii. Cheltenham: Edward Elgar Publishing.

IPCC. 2018. "Summary for Policymakers." Edited by Valérie Masson-Delmotte, Hans-Otto Pörtner, Jim Skea, Panmao Zhai, Debra Roberts, Priyadarshi R. Shukla, Anna Pirani, et al. Global Warming of 1.5°C. An IPCC Special Report on the Impacts of Global Warming of 1.5°C Above Pre-Industrial Levels and Related Global Greenhouse Gas Emission Pathways, in the Context of Strengthening the Global Response to the Threat of Climate Change (World Meteorological Organization).

Irvine, Peter J, Andy Ridgwell, and Daniel J Lunt. 2012. "Climatic Effects of Surface Albedo Geoengineering." Journal of Geophysical Research 16 (D2412).

Islam, S. Nazrul, and John Winkel. 2017. "Climate Change and Social Inequality." UN Department of Economic and Social Affairs (DESA) Working Papers No. 152.

Jones, Bruce. 2020. "China and the Return of Great Power Strategic Competition." Global China: Assessing China's Growing Role in the World (The Brookings Institution) 8–9.

Keller, David P., Ellias Y. Feng, and Andreas Oschlies. 2014. "Potential Climate Engineering Effectiveness and Side Effects During a High Carbon Dioxide-emission Scenario." Nature Communications 5 (3304).

Läderach, Peter, Julian Ramirez-Villegas, Giulia Caroli, Claudia Sadoff, and Grazia Pacillo. 2021. "Climate Finance and Peace: Tackling the Climate and Humanitarian Crisis." The Lancet Planetary Health 5 (12): E865-E858.

Laybourn-Langton, Laurie, Lesley Rankin, and Darren Baxter. 2019. "This is a Crisis: Facing up to the Age of Environmental Breakdown." Institute for Public Policy Research.

Le Billon, Philippe. 2001. "The Political Ecology of War: Natural Resources and Armed Conflicts." Political Geography 20 (5): 561-584.

Liberman, Bruce. 2019. "A Brief Introduction to Climate Change and National Security." Yale Climate Connections. July 23. https://yaleclimateconnections.org/2019/07/a-brief-introduction-to-climate-change-and-national-security/.

Lynas, Mark. 2008. Six Degrees: Our Future on a Hotter Planet. New York: HarperCollins

Lynas, Mark 2007. "Six Steps to Hell." *The Guardian.* April 23. Accessed July 29, 2022. https://www.theguardian.com/books/2007/apr/23/scienceandnature.climatechange.

Maamoun, Nada. 2019. "The Kyoto Protocol: Empirical Evidence of a Hidden Success." Journal of Environmental Economics and Management 95: 227-256.

Maizland, Lindsay. 2021. "Global Climate Agreements: Successes and Failures." Council on Foreign Relations. November 17. Accessed July 30, 2022. https://www.cfr.org/backgrounder/paris-global-climate-change-agreements.

Markolf, Samuel A., Inês M.L. Azevedo, Mark Muro, and David G. Victor. 2020. Pledges and Progress Steps Toward Greenhouse Gas Emissions Reductions in the 100 Largest Cities Across the United States. The Brookings Institute.

Matthews, H. Damon, and Ken Caldeira. 2007. "Transient Climate-carbon Simulations of Planetary Geoengineering." Proceedings of the National Academy of Sciences 104 (24): 9949-9954.

Matthews, H. Damon, Andrew J Weaver, Michael Eby, and Katrin J Meissner. 2002. "Radiative Forcing of Climate by Historical Land Cover Change." Journal of Geophysical Research Letters 30 (2): 1055.

McGrath, Matt. 2020. "Climate Change: US Formally Withdraws From Paris Agreement." BBC. November 4. Accessed August 2, 2022. https://www.bbc.com/news/science-environment-54797743.

McVeigh, Karen. 2022. "Perfect Storm Crises: Widening Global Inequality Says UN Chief." The Guardian. July 2. Accessed July 30, 2022. https://www.theguardian.com/environment/2022/jul/02/perfect-storm-crises-widening-global-inequality-says-un-chief.

Messer, Ellen. 2009. "Rising Food Prices, Social Mobilizations, and Violence: Conceptual Issues in Understanding and Responding to the Connections Linking Hunger and Conflict." National Association for the Practice of Anthropology Bulletin 32 (1): 12-22.

Miguel, Edward, Shanker Satyanath, and Ernest Sergenti. 2004. "Economic Shocks and Civil Conflict: An Instrumental Variables Approach." *Journal of Political Economy* 112 (41): 725–753.

National Academy of Sciences. 2015. Climate Intervention: Reflecting Sunlight to Cool Earth. Washington, D.C.: National Academies Press.

Nature. 2022. "The Latest IPCC Report: What is it and Why Does it Matter?" The Nature Conservancy. April 04. Accessed July 25, 2022. https://www.nature.org/en-us/what-we-do/our-insights/perspectives/ipcc-report-climate-change/.

Nguyen, Terry. 2020. "More Companies Want to be "Carbon Neutral." What Does That Mean?" Vox News. June 16. Accessed August 2, 2022. https://www.vox.com/the-goods/2020/3/5/21155020/companies-carbon-neutral-climate-positive.

O'Shaughnessy, Eric, Jenny Heeter, David Keyser, Pieter Gagnon, and Alexandra Aznar. 2016. "Estimating the National Carbon Abatement Potential of City Policies: A Data-Driven Approach." Office of Energy Efficiency and Renewable Energy. October 20. Accessed July 30, 2022. https://www.energy.gov/eere/analysis/downloads/estimating-national-carbon-abatement-potential-city-policies-data-driven.

Oliver, John E. 2008. Encyclopedia of World Climatology. Berlin: Springer Science & Business Media. Accessed August 8, 2022. https://www.geoengineering-monitor.org/2021/04/surface-albedo-modification-technology-factsheet/.

Ord, Toby. 2020. The Precipice: Existential Risk and the Future of Humanity. New York: Hachette Books.

Pörtner, H O, D C Roberts, E. S. Poloczanska, K. Mintenbeck, M. Tigno, A. Alegría, M. Craig, et al. 2022. "Climate Change 2022 Impacts, Adaptation and Vulnerability Summary for Policymakers." In Climate Change 2022: Impacts, Adaptation, and Vulnerability edited by H. O. Pörtner, D.C. Roberts, M. Tignor, E.S. Poloczanska, K. Mintenbeck, A. Alegría, M. Craig, et al. Cambridge University Press. https://www.ipcc.ch/report/ar6/wg2/downloads/report/IPCC_AR6_WGII_SummaryForPolicymakers.pdf.

Pamlin, Dennis, and Stuart Armstrong. 2015. "12 Risks That Threaten Human Civilisation: The Case for a New Risk Category." Global Challenges Foundation.

Patz, Jonathan A, Paul R Epstein, Thomas A Burke, and John M Balbus. 1996. "Global Climate Change and Emerging Infectious Diseases." JAMA The Journal of the American Medical Association 275 (3): 217-223.

Pindyck, Robert S. 2014. "Climate Change Policy: What Do the Models Tell Us?" Journal of Economic Literature 51 (3): 860–872.

Raleigh, Clionadh, and Henrik Urdal. 2007. "Climate Change, Environmental Degradation and Armed Conflict." Political Geography 26: 647-694.

Reach, Philip J., Simone Tilmes, Richard P. Turco, Alan Robock, Luke Oman, Chih-Chieh Chen, Georgiy L Stenchikov, and Rolando R. Garcia. 2009. "An Overview of Geoengineering of Climate Using Stratospheric Sulphate Aerosols." Philosophical Transactions Mathematical Physical & Engineering Sciences 366 (1882): 4007-4037.

Robock, Alan, Allison Marquardt, Ben Kravitz, and Georgiy Stenchikov. 2009. "Benefits, Risks, and Costs of Stratospheric Geoengineering." Geophysical Research Letters 36 (19).

Ross, Michael. 2004. "What Do We Know About Natural Resources and Civil War?" Journal of Peace Research 41 (3): 337–356.

Salehyan, Idean. 2014. "Climate Change and Conflict: Making Sense of Disparate Findings." Political Geography 43: 1-5.

Salehyan, Idean. 2008. "From Climate Change to Conflict? No Consensus Yet." Journal of Peace Research 315-326.

Schäfer, Stefan, Mark Lawrence, Harald Stelzer, Sean Low, Asbjørn Aaheim, Paola Adriázola, Gregor Betz, et al. 2015. The European Transdisciplinary Assessment of Climate Engineering (EuTRACE): Removing Greenhouse Gases from the Atmosphere and Reflecting Sunlight away from Earth.

Schalatek, Liane, and Erin Roberts. 2021. "Deferred not defeated: the outcome on Loss and Damage finance at COP26 and next steps." The Heinrich Böell Foundation. December 16. Accessed July 30, 2022. https://us.boell.org/en/2021/12/16/deferred-not-defeated-outcome-loss-and-damage-finance-cop26-and-next-steps#:~:text=In%20the%20early%20days%20of,funding%20specifically%20for%20that%20purpose.

Scheffran, Jürgen, Michael Brzoska, Jasmin Kominek, P. Michael Link, and Janpeter Schilling. 2012. "Climate Change and Violent Conflict." Science 336 (18): 869-871.

Schubert, R., H. J. Schellnhuber, N. Buchmann, A. Epiney, R. Grießhammer, M. Kulessa, D. Messner, S. Rahmstorf, and J. Schmid. 2007. "Climate Change as a Security Risk." German Advisory Council on Global Change.

Searchinger, Tim, Richard Waite, Craig Hanson, and Janet Ranganathan. 2019. Creating a Sustainable Food Future: A Menu of Solutions to Feed Nearly 10 Billion People by 2050. World Resources Report.

Shan, Yuli, Dabo Guan, Klaus Hubacek, Bo Zheng, Steven J. Davis, Lichao Jia, Jianghua Lio, et al. 2018. "City-level Climate Change Mitigation in China." Science Advances 4 (6).

Shepherd, John. 2009. Geoengineering the Climate: Science, Governance and Uncertainty. The Royal Society.

Singh, Harjeet. 2015. "Solving the Climate Crisis Means Tackling Global Inequality." Thomson Reuters Foundation. May 26. Accessed July 30, 2022. https://news.trust.org/item/20150525141853-ld051/.

SIPRI. 2022a. "Climate, Peace and Security Fact Sheet: Afghanistan." Stockholm International Peace Research Institute. February. Accessed August 8, 2022. https://www.sipri.org/sites/default/files/Fact%20Sheet%20Afghanistan_february2022_FINAL.pdf.

SIPRI. 2022b. 2022. "Climate, Peace and Security Fact Sheet: Ethiopia." Stockholm International Peace Research Institute. June. Accessed August 8, 2022. https://sipri.org/sites/default/files/NUPI%20Fact%20Sheet%20Ethiopia%20June%202022%20LR5%5B12%5D.pdf.

SIPRI. 2022c. 2022. "Climate, Peace and Security Fact Sheet: Sudan." Stockholm International Peace Research Institute. May. Accessed August 8, 2022. https://sipri.org/sites/default/files/NUPI%20SIPRI%20Fact%20Sheet%20Sudan%20May%202022.pdf.

Sitati, A., E. Joe, B Pentz, C. Grayson, C. Jaime, E. Gilmore, E. Galapaththi, et al. 2021. "Climate Change Adaptation in Conflict-affected Countries: A Systematic Assessment of Evidence." Discover Sustainability 2 (42).

Snæbjörnsdóttir, Sandra Ó., Bergur Sigfússon, Chiara Marieni, David Goldberg, Sigurður R. Gislason, and Eric H. Oelkers. 2020. "Carbon Dioxide Storage Through Mineral Carbonation." Nature Reviews Earth & Environment 1: 90-102.

Stern, Nicholas. 2013. "The Structure of Economic Modeling of the Potential Impacts of Climate Change: Grafting Gross Underestimation of Risk onto Already Narrow Science Models." Journal of Economic Literature 51 (3): 838–859.

Stockholm+50. 2022. "Leadership Dialogues." Stockholm+50. June 2-3. Accessed July 29, 2022. https://www.stockholm50.global/processes/leadership-dialogues.

The European Space Agency. n.d. "The European Space Agency." L1, the first Lagrangian Point. Accessed July 29, 2022. https://www.esa.int/Science_Exploration/Space_Science/L1_the_first_Lagrangian_Point.

The Royal Society. 2009. Geoengineering the Climate: Science, Governance and Uncertainty. London: The Royal Society.

Tollefson, Jeff. 2021. "'COP26 Hasn't Solved the Problem': Scientists React to UN Climate Deal." Nature. November 14. Accessed July 30, 2022. https://www.nature.com/articles/d41586-021-03431-4.

Torres, Émile P. 2017a. "Engineering the Atmosphere: Is it Possible? And Would it Prevent Catastrophe, or Cause It?" Salon. May 6. Accessed July 29, 2022. https://www.salon.com/2017/05/06/engineering-the-atmosphere-is-it-possible-and-would-it-prevent-catastrophe-or-cause-it/.

Torres, Phil. 2017b. Morality, Foresight, and Human Flourish: An Introduction to Existential Risk. Durham, NC: Pitchstone Publishing.

United Nations. 2015. Adoption of the Paris Agreement. United Nations / Framework Convention on Climate Change: Paris.

United Nations. 1998. Kyoto Protocol to the United Nations Framework Convention on Climate Change. United Nations Framework Convention on Climate Change. https://unfccc.int/resource/docs/convkp/kpeng.pdf.

United Nations. 2021. "The Glasgow Climate Pact – Key Outcomes from COP26." United Nations Framework Convention on Climate Change. November 13. Accessed July 30, 2022. The Glasgow Climate Pact – Key Outcomes from COP26.

United Nations. 1992. "United Nations Framework Convention on Climate Change." United Nations Framework Convention on Climate Change. Accessed July 30, 2022. https://unfccc.int/files/essential_background/background_publications_htmlpdf/application/pdf/conveng.pdf.

USGCRP. 2017. Climate Science Special Report: Fourth National Climate Assessment, Volume I. Edited by DJ Wuebbles, D. W. Fahey, K.A. Hibbard, D. J. Dokken, B. C. Stewart, and T. K. Maycock. Washington, DC: U.S. Global Change Research Program.

Wallinga, David, and Avinash Kar. 2020. "New Data: Animal vs. Human Antibiotic Use Remains Lopsided." The Natural Resources Defense Council. June 15. Accessed August 8, 2022. https://www.nrdc.org/experts/david-wallinga-md/most-human-antibiotics-still-going-us-meat-production.

Watts, Nick, W. Neil Adger, Paolo Agnolucci, Jason Blackstock, Peter Byass, Wenjai Cai, Sarah Chaytor, et al. 2015. "Health and Climate Change: Policy Responses to Protect Public Health." The Lancet 386: 1861-1914.

Weisse, Mikaela, and Elizabeth Goldman. 2021. "Just 7 Commodities Replaced an Area of Forest Twice the Size of Germany Between 2001 and 2015." World Resource Institute. February 11. Accessed August 1, 2022. https://www.wri.org/insights/just-7-commodities-replaced-area-forest-twice-size-germany-between-2001-and-2015.

WHO. 2020. "Climate Change Data and Statistics." World Health Organization Regional Office for Europe. https://www.euro.who.int/en/health-topics/environment-and-health/Climate-change/data-and-statistics#:~:text=Climate%20change%20affects%20air%20pollution,global%20warming%20and%20cooling%20effects.

Wild, Martin. 2008. "Global Dimming and Brightening: A review." Journal of Geophysical Research D00D16.

World Bank. 2011. "Economics of Adaptation to Climate Change." World Bank. June 6. Accessed July 29, 2022. https://www.worldbank.org/en/news/feature/2011/06/06/economics-adaptation-climate-change.

World Bank. 2012. Turn Down the Heat: Why a 4C Warmer World Must Be Avoided. Washington DC: The World Bank

World Bank. 2020. Reversal of Fortune: Poverty and Shared Prosperity 2020. Washington D.C.: The World Bank Group.

World Bank. 2021. Climate Change Action Plan 2021-2025: Supporting Green, Resilient, and Inclusive Development. Washington D.C.: The World Bank Group.

Xu, Xiaoming, Prateek Sharma, Shijie Shu, Lin Tzu-Shun, Ciais, Francesco N. Tubiello, Pete Smith, Nelson Campbell, and Atul K Jain. 2021. "Global Greenhouse Gas Emissions from Animal-based Foods are Twice Those of Plant-based Foods." Nature Food (2): 724-732.

CHAPTER 7

Emerging Technologies, Risk, Peace, and Conflict

DEFINING EMERGING TECHNOLOGIES

Emerging technologies are those whose potentials are not yet fully recognized or understood. They are characterized by their radical novelty and persistent coherence across different technological streams; fast growth; wide range of impacts across a range of social, economic, and political systems; and the uncertainty of their ambiguous impacts (Rotolo et al. 2015). These technologies often require a high degree of expenditure on research and development and benefit from transdisciplinary approaches. They hold highly transformative potential for creating new industries and for transforming existing ones. Further, these technologies often instigate large-scale social, cultural, and political changes. The printing press, vaccines, antibiotics, airplanes, and the internet were all emerging technology at one point in history, all of which have transformed society.

Throughout history, the net benefits of these technologies have arguably outweighed their harm. However, just because this has been the trend does not mean that a new technology might not carry unforeseen social and ethical implications. An important facet to explore in understanding technologies that do not have a natural precedent and are perceived as highly is what considerations need to be made to prevent an unintended catastrophe before the technology becomes widespread (Bostrom and Ćirković 2011).

© The Author(s), under exclusive license to Springer Nature Switzerland AG 2023
N. B. Taylor, *Existential Risks in Peace and Conflict Studies*, Rethinking Peace and Conflict Studies, https://doi.org/10.1007/978-3-031-24315-8_7

Currently, the term "emerging" is applied to various technologies, from cloud computing to virtual reality (Halaweh 2013). It is often used to refer to artificial intelligence (AI), synthetic biology, nanotechnology, and geoengineering (Alford et al. 2012; Government Office for Science 2014). Since these technologies are "emerging," the question of their timeline becomes a key point of debate. For example, synthetic biology and nanotechnology already exist and can be found in industrial and medical applications. The full transformative potential is thought to lie in the future. The foundations are already present for technologies such as artificial intelligence and geoengineering, but the estimates for their development vary more widely.

An important element to take into account is that emerging technologies have the potential to become even more powerful if they are combined. For example, advancements in nanotechnology can be used to increase the speed of development in biotechnology; one approach to AI development is the use of biotechnology for developing "brain emulations" to simulate the human mind, from which the first artificial general intelligence (AGI) could arise (Eth 2017, Hanson 2016, Baum et al. 2019).

This section discusses emerging technologies in general and outlines the frame for discussing specific technologies in the following sections. The technologies chosen as important topics for Peace and Conflict Studies (PCS) are artificial intelligence, biotechnology, and nanotechnology. These were chosen because they are all novel, rapidly growing with a wide range of impacts, contain uncertainty about their potential uses, and possess both transformative and disruptive potential. A brief overview of the technology will be given for each emerging technology. Each technology will be examined through the lens of Existential Risk Studies (ERS) and PCS to assess the risk's type, scale, and scope, as well as its potential to contribute to drivers of conflict or peace.

Risks from Emerging Technologies

Emerging technologies pose some concerns about existential risks. The concern is especially warranted when the transformative potential of emerging technology is touted as a possible way of addressing an existential risk, such as applying geoengineering to climate change. The worry is that, if done without careful foresight, the same technologies may either pose an existential risk in themselves or contribute to an already existing risk. At this moment in time, more clarity on these issues is needed to understand their impact, mitigate risk, and harness the potential contributions to human flourishing.

In his paper, "The Vulnerable World Hypothesis," Bostrom (2019) likens the development of new technologies to drawing balls out of a container. The majority of the container is "white balls," technologies that are overall beneficial, and many "gray balls," a mixture of beneficial and harmful. This has been the experience of humanity thus far. The fear is that somewhere in that container is a "black ball," a technology that destroys the civilization of those who create it. The risk that such a technology could be developed is a call for careful consideration of policies that guide the development and regulation of technology. When considered in the context of ERS, even if the chances of drawing that black ball are incredibly slim given the level of risk posed, humanity will not be able to rely on learning from mistakes or trial and error; therefore, forward thinking is prudent and required (Government Office for Science 2014).

Peace, Conflict, and Emerging Technologies

An important facet in analyzing an emerging technology through the lens of PCS is whether that technology may be a driver of conflict or peace. When analyzing an emerging technology as a driver for conflict, it is vital to assess the possible weaponization of the new technology. Additionally, given the experiences of the arms race between the USA and the Soviet Union during the Cold War, the possibility of another such race for each of these technologies is an essential consideration for understanding how it may contribute to conflict escalation. Given the far-reaching possible impacts of these technologies, a third element to analyze will be the disruptive social, political, and economic effects they may have. How emerging technologies may be a driver for peace is directly connected to directing the transformative potential of each of these technologies toward beneficial ends.

Weaponization of Technology

It should come as no surprise that with each new powerful technology comes the possibility that someone will turn it into a weapon. Humanity has a long history of weaponizing technology. A positive feedback loop between state warfare and technology can be understood as a significant factor shaping history since the industrial revolution. In his book

Technology, War and the State (2019), Warren Chin argues that this relationship is so vital to understanding warfare that it was one of his main critiques of Carl von Clausewitz's famous analysis of the nature of war.

Regarding the weaponization of emerging technologies, two important facets need to be considered regarding the weaponization of emerging technologies. The first is the kind of agent that/who would have the ability and the motive to deploy such a weapon. The second is the destructive potential of the weaponized technology—could it be scaled to the level of light or heavy armament, or is the potential for it to be used as a Weapon of Mass Destruction (WMD) or even a Weapon of Total Destruction (WTD) (Torres 2018).

A recent example of an existing technology becoming weaponized in a new way was the 2010 Stuxnet worm. This computer virus was a digital weapon that demonstrated the ability to cause destruction in the physical world when it caused centrifuges to malfunction causing significant damage to Iran's Nuclear Enrichment Program (Kushner 2013; Zetter 2014; Kerr et al. 2010). If such a weapon was further enhanced through artificial intelligence, it could become even more destructive.

When powerful technologies are weaponized, accidents or misunderstandings could be disastrous. The story of Vasily Arkhipov is illustrative of how nuclear power, once weaponized and placed into imperfect command and control structure, brought humanity close to a global nuclear war. On October 27, 1962, the world came perilously close to a nuclear disaster during the Cuban Missile Crisis. Tensions between the USA and the Soviet Union were on a razor's edge as nuclear weapons were being transferred to Cuba. Four Soviet B-59 submarines were sent to support military operations in Cuba. Each of these four was armed with a nuclear torpedo on par with what was dropped on Hiroshima. While the crisis was being negotiated, a US warship discovered one of the B-59s captained by Valentin Savitsky and began dropping ordnances as "warning shots" to get the submarine to the surface.

The situation on the submarine was dire; it had been hiding deep in the ocean for days out of radio contact with Moscow. The air conditioning system had broken, and the heat inside ranged from 45°C to 60°C while carbon dioxide was building up, causing many in the crew to lose consciousness. When the US began dropping signaling depth charges, Savitsky thought they were under attack and ordered the nuclear strike saying, "Maybe the war has already started up there, while we are doing somersaults here. We're going to blast them now! We will die, but we will sink them all—we will not disgrace our Navy!" (Gonzalez 2002). Without communication, they did not know if a nuclear war had already started.

Savitsky needed the approval of all three officers on board. He received the approval of their political officer Ivan Semonovich Maslennikov. Luckily for humanity, Vasily Arkhipov, Chief of staff and second-in-command and commander of the entire flotilla, was aboard. Arkhipov did not grant permission to fire and convinced Savitsky to surface and to get in contact with Moscow. No one can know what would have happened if Arkhipov was not present or had acted differently. The nuclear torpedo would probably have been launched, triggering a retaliation, then maybe further escalation and nuclear war (Ord 2020; McNamara 1992; Elisberg 2017; Blanton et al. 2012).

Phill Torres writes that the "question, '*who* would willingly destroy the world if only they were *able* to?'" [emphasis added] (129) is becoming particularly frightening because up until now, the "able to" part of that question dramatically limited the "who" that could be asked that question. This situation is changing; unlike nuclear weapons, which require rare and expensive materials, specialized knowledge, and industrial-level processing facilities, the Weapons of Mass Destruction of the future might be able to be made by a small group of people or even a single individual. The potential that the monopoly of large-scale violence could be taken away from the state for the first time in history necessitates a critical reflection on the connections between technologies and violence.

Additionally, the weaponization of emerging technologies gives rise to the possibility of an arms race. An arms race could come about in at least two different ways. One would be a race between countries to develop a new weapons technology first. Another way would be a race to develop the technology for uses other than military. Both of these possibilities are dangerous. As the world has seen, the nuclear arms race led to stockpiles of weapons bordering on the absurd. Some scholars argue that emerging technologies are potential drivers of conflict escalation, and this potential is increased when the technologies are explicitly weaponized (Miller and Fontaine 2017; Gartzke 2019; Horowitz 2019). A greater number of novel weapons produced in a geopolitical atmosphere of fear will likely be a driver of conflict escalation. Arms races, once started, are challenging to stop. Even the nuclear arms race during the Cold War was predicted but occurred nonetheless (Bostrom 2009). Likely, the future relationship between emerging technologies will not find them to be the only influential independent variable, an exogenous factor sufficient enough to fuel conflict escalation, but instead realize them as intervening variables that make conflict escalation more likely when combined with other factors. The more potent drivers will likely still be long-standing grievances, policy, and politics. The arms race concern is a warranted but tempered concern; it is not the technology that contributes to any particular dynamic, but rather the political and strategic choices regarding that technology that shape its development, regulation, and use (Talmadge 2019).

While competition in technological development may inspire innovation on some levels, it could also lead to a "race to the bottom," whereby safety concerns are eschewed for expediency's sake (Armstrong et al. 2013). Many countries or companies competing to get the coroner on the market for artificial intelligence or synthetic biology might take shortcuts on safety that could result in accidental or intentional misuse of the technologies. Further competition at this level requires attention and resources. These diversions may make other existential risks more likely.

Emerging Technologies as a Driver of Conflict

A critical issue of concern at the nexus between PCS and emerging technologies is the broader economic, social, and political effects they may have. One of the ways emerging technologies may contribute to conflict is through their impact on industry. Emerging technologies are shaping what has been called the fourth industrial revolution (Industry 4.0). Though it had intellectual predecessors, the term "Industry 4.0" was coined by Klaus Schwab in his book *The Fourth Industrial Revolution* (2016). The "4.0" refers to the fourth iteration of the industrial revolution; this designation is a bit of a deviation from the norm. The first, second, and third industrial revolutions were designated after they occurred (Toynbee 1884; Geddes 1915; Jevons 1931; Landes 1969). This era of technological development occurred through manufacturing shifts characterized by automation, data feedback, and adaptive and decentralized decision-making. These were termed "cyber-physical" systems where the digital and physical worlds interact in automated constant data-driven feedback loops (Lee and Matsikoudis 2008). Industry 4.0 will change the nature of production, consumption, and labor markets.

Existing digital technologies have been shown to drive inequality. Inequality results from replacing less-skilled jobs with those requiring more skills, and an increasingly larger share of corporate income goes to companies instead of their workers (Brynjolfsson and McAfee 2011).

Emerging technologies such as artificial intelligence will likely increase the productivity and efficiency of big data analytics, cloud computing, the Internet of Things, and cyber-physical systems. Industry 4.0 (I 4.0) may, directly and indirectly, impact inequality (UNCTAD 2019). If predictions are accurate, then a significant issue of concern for peace research will be the role of inequality as a contributing factor in conflict (Bahgat et al. 2017; Russet 1964; Bartuesvičius 2014; Cederman et al. 2011; Østby 2011; Stewart 2000; Bircan et al. 2017).

If predictions of significant disruptive effects of technology-induced inequality prove to be accurate, large-scale shifts in social, economic, and political life are likely. If, for example, emerging technologies create a world where large numbers of people will no longer be in the workforce, then a large number would be plunged into poverty, or society would have to imagine how to care for people in a radically different way. There is a difference between a world where billions of people no longer *have to* work and a world where they *cannot*.

PEACEBUILDING AND CONFLICT TRANSFORMATION THROUGH TECHNOLOGY

Emerging technologies may become an essential tool for peacebuilding and conflict transformation. One of the hopes in developing emerging technologies in Industry 4.0 is that their transformative potential will be used to realign economies with societies (Herweijer et al. 2018). If this realignment reduces inequality by building trust, stimulating growth, and spurring innovation, then emerging technologies may indirectly contribute to peace (Benioff 2017). Further, emerging technologies such as artificial intelligence and nanotechnology are likely to make more efficient use of resources which is generally better economically and ecologically, which may help decrease other factors contributing to conflict.

Emerging technologies, in particular artificial intelligence, may be used to enhance current technologies used in early warning/early action (EWEA) systems to prevent violent conflict. Projects already exist that use Geographic Information Science (GIS) for monitoring the onset of violent conflict, verification of effects of military conflict, and monitoring population displacement. Machine learning (ML) and Natural Language Processing (NLP) tools are being used to establish more robust quantitative benchmarks for modeling conflicts, conflict forecasting, and documenting human rights offenses. Systems have developed that analyze social media for hate speech and other indicators of conflict. The Armed Conflict Location and Event Data Project (ACLED) has systems for monitoring the media coverage of conflicts in local languages that are then verified by local observers (Panic 2022). It is possible that the efficacy of these existing technologies for their current uses could be enhanced through emerging technologies. Whether they effectively address violence depends on the policy and political structures that link early warning to early action and effective action to mitigate the risks of conflict.

Given their transformative potential emerging technologies may also provide new avenues for building peace. "Peace Engineering" has been proposed as a way for thinking about the interface between engineering and peacebuilding (Vesilind 2005; Özerdem and Schirch 2021; Yarnall et al. 2021). Özerdem and Schirch write on Peace Engineering,

> It might be too early to call peace engineering as the savior of the post-pandemic world, though it is inevitable that it could be pivotal in the realization of a more just and peaceful society. Also, for peace and conflict studies specifically, peace engineering presents a gate to a new world for a more multidisciplinary approach and application to both protracted and new peace and security challenges across the globe. (113)

It will be vital for PCS to participate in multidisciplinary discussions about the research and development of new technologies. Further concerns about peace and conflict need to be a centerpiece in developing how humanity will guide the development of these technologies and mitigate their destructive potential.

Dilemmas Posed by the Intersection of Emerging Technology and Peace and Conflict Studies

Humanity may face the most crucial time in its history for taking actions that will ensure its long-term survival. This notion is particularly true when considering possible existential risks from emerging technology because, arguably, they are still under human control. The decisions humanity makes, or does not make, regarding the governance, regulation, and desired trajectory of these technologies will be pivotal in determining their transformative potential and the ultimate end outcomes (Beckstead et al. 2014; Ord 2020; Boyd and Wilson 2020). The same can be said about how to guide the research and development that may be applied to these technologies, and which may be applied to beneficial and destructive ends.

A significant inception point for the establishment of PCS and ERS was the creation and use of the first nuclear bomb, the *ur*-example of a technology that at the time would have been considered "emerging" and certainly did have transformative and disruptive effects on the planet. In 1942 Robert Oppenheimer was leading the development of the first nuclear bomb. An atomic bomb works by triggering a fission reaction. Before the first atomic tests, there was worry in the development team that the chain reaction may ignite the hydrogen in earth's water or react with the nitrogen in the air, possibly boiling off the seas and setting the atmosphere ablaze. Oppenheimer commissioned a now declassified report examining the possibility of the atmosphere igniting. The report concluded with,

> One may conclude that the arguments of this paper make it unreasonable to expect that the N+N reaction could propagate. An unlimited propagation is even less likely. However, the complexity of the argument and the absence of satisfactory experimental foundations make further work on the subject highly desirable. (Konopinski et al. 1946, 16)

These concerns continued until July 16, 1945, the day of the Trinity Tests, when the atomic bombs were detonated, and the world is still here. It was not until some years later that there was scientific confirmation that such a result was impossible, that humanity did not just get lucky (Weaver and Wood 1979). The weaponization of nuclear research was a novel dilemma for scientific research. For the first time in history, humanity could produce unprecedented amounts of energy in a way that could be weaponized (Elisberg 2017). This episode from history brings with it many questions. Many of the best minds in the world were developing profoundly disruptive, transformative, and destructive technologies, but what were the probability estimates that such a disastrous reaction would not occur? How low should the probability have been? Who would get to decide? Would these decision-makers be elected? Whom would they represent?

The Large Hadron Collider (LHC) is another test-case example of the problems governing the development of new technologies that pose uncertain risks. In 2008 the European Organization for Nuclear Research (CERN) began using the accelerator to speed up ions around a 27 km-long track and close to the speed of light (CEERN n.d.). The intention of the LHC was to conduct experiments into the origin of mass, better understand dark matter, and look for symmetries in the universe. But there were also fears that LHC may create unintended effects such as causing earth to be converted into a "strangelet," an extremely dense piece of matter smaller than a particle. Obviously, this fear was not realized. Many legal cases were filed before the accelerator was turned on, but all failed due to the inability of most legal systems to deal with this type of issue (Adams 2009). This is not to say that the reactor should have been stopped due to concerns for its safety, but rather a way of demonstrating that current legal and regulatory systems may not be well-suited for addressing extremely low-probability, high-impact types of risks.

The Need for Governance and Regulation

Advancements in nanotechnology, bioengineering, and artificial intelligence all stand to create potentially great benefits to humanity as well as to cause disastrous consequences if not used carefully (Wilson 2013). This concern is particularly valid because, unlike a nuclear bomb or a super collider, many of these technologies could be developed by a small group of people with access to fewer resources and infrastructure. Greater powers may, thus, fall into fewer and less controlled hands.

There are many challenges to the governance of emerging technologies. Beckstead et al. (2014) address these regulatory problems, writing that protection from these risks is

> a global public good and, thus, undersupplied by the market. Implementation often requires cooperation among many governments, which adds political complexity. Due to the unprecedented nature of the risks, there is little or no previous experience from which to draw lessons and form policy. Moreover, the beneficiaries of the preventative policy include people who have no sway over current political processes—our children and grandchildren. (3)

At its core, the problems with governing emerging technologies stem from incongruence in time horizons and incentive alignment in our cognitive and political structures. Mitigating existential risks arising from emerging technologies may require making decisions in the present that will bear fruit decades, if not centuries later. This kind of thinking does not fit well with how government policy is made. Jonathan Boston (2021) referred to this as an "intertemporal policy conflict," the kind of risks posed by having to make policy decisions now that may be critical in guiding something like the development of technology like artificial intelligence (1). It may be difficult for a politician to see the near-term benefit of considering such long-term policies, let alone enacting them (Gluckman and Bardsley 2021). This type of governance problem needs to be addressed because, ostensibly, one of the roles of government is to ensure continuity of policy over time. Added to this temporal problem is that the voices of those who would benefit or suffer the most from the consequences of these decisions, hypothetical future people, do not have a voice in the discussion.

There is also an inherent difficulty in that, for the governance of emerging technology to work effectively, it must be done at the global level because it poses a global risk. Any institution charged with global governance of emerging technologies will have to deal with the problems of "centralization/aggregation, coordination, politicization, transparency, adaptation and accountability" (Boyd and Wilson 2021, 21), as well as inequities among countries responsible for creating, mitigating, and suffering the consequences of the potential harm. It is likely that when risks are deeply uncertain different tools of analysis, evaluation, and mitigation are needed. Then, what is the norm both nationally and internationally (Kwakkel et al. 2016)? When it comes to the military applications of emerging technologies, the question of legal justification and logic becomes even more complicated in determining which types of laws would be validly applied (Boothby 2018).

Many of these governance challenges will require a dynamic balancing act. This challenge is true of dual-use research, where both the research and the technologies derived from it have the potential for wide-ranging benefits and large-scale harm. It would not be wise to forsake the benefits these technologies could bring for fear of their dangers. Moreover, it is unclear if the research and development of technology could be stopped if deemed desirable.

QUESTIONS FOR THE FUTURE

How can the risks of emerging technologies be mitigated so that their benefits do not come at the cost of conflict, violence, or catastrophe?

Emerging technologies present unique challenges because they are novel, and with their possibility of resulting in existential risks, they are phenomena that cannot be fully anticipated. In this way, emerging technologies also represent humanity's relationship to the unknown and how humanity can best develop its thinking and institutions to relate to that unknown space. The decisions humanity makes now regarding these technologies may significantly impact their future development, even if the fulfillment of these technologies lies very much in the future. The role of peace research in helping to shape the development and governance of emerging technologies so that society can reap their benefits while not succumbing to their negative costs will be an important area of research. In the following sections artificial intelligence, biotechnology, and nanotechnology will be discussed as examples of the relationships among concerns regarding emerging technology, peace, and conflict.

Emerging Technologies: Artificial Intelligence

The possible applications of artificial general intelligence (AGI) are far-reaching, and research into its safety will be necessary. In the field of ERS, the risks and ethics of artificial intelligence have been a primary focus. A wide range of organizations have developed working on these topics, including the Centre for the Study of Existential Risk (CSER), the Future of Humanity Institute (FHI), the Algorithmic Justice League, Open AI, the Partnership on AI, the Leverhulme Centre for the Future of Intelligence, and the Centre for Human-Compatible AI. Specific attention will be needed to be directed at how developments in the field of AGI may affect conflict and what peacebuilding potential it may hold. The further reaches of AGI development are a horizon that cannot be looked across because nothing like it has happened before. The most dramatic impacts of AGI may be unimaginable. Humanity may be at a critical moment in developing this technology and deciding how progress will be made and who will determine its direction will be vital questions for its future.

Artificial intelligence (AI) is perhaps the most "science fiction-like" technology included in this book. Nils John Nilsson, computer scientist and founder of the field of artificial intelligence (AI), defines AI as the "activity devoted to making machines intelligent. Intelligence is that quality that enables an entity to function appropriately with foresight in its environment" (2010). Generally speaking, AI means human-created, non-biological intelligence. There are different categories of AI. Each category comes with a new stage of technological development, a range of applications, and possible risks. These categories range from currently existing technology to more speculative and are largely differentiated by their caliber. At the less powerful and already existing end of the spectrum is artificial narrow intelligence, or "weak" AI, which can accomplish complex goals within a narrow domain, such as an AI that can play games like chess or go (the board game) and are already found in automobiles and phones. In the middle of the spectrum is artificial general intelligence (AGI) or "strong" AI, which can accomplish complex goals in many domains and is as smart as a person (Urban 2015). Currently, AGI is considered the "holy grail" of AI research because it will be able to use its intelligence across domains like a human can. At the end of the spectrum is artificial superintelligence, which would be vastly more intelligent than the smartest humans in every field which has not yet been realized (Bostrom 2017).

There are several different subfields within the larger domain of artificial intelligence. Within the larger domain of AI is the subfield of machine learning. Machine learning holds that given enough data, systems can learn, find patterns, and make decisions with little human intervention. These learning processes use algorithms that are capable of improving themselves over time. A further subfield of machine learning is using neural nets of deep learning. Neural nets are systems modeled after the human nervous system. This type of approach to deep learning allows for better predictive capacity (Panic 2020).

When discussing the development of AGI, the question of the timeline has been important. There have been several "AI winters," periods where there was no progress in its development. Preceding many of these winters were moments of extreme optimism about how quickly AI may progress. Famously, during a workshop held in 1956 at Dartmouth College, many experts predicted that machine intelligence would rival that of humans within a generation and from these promises were able to raise significant funding for research into AI (Newquist 1994). Humanity may have recently entered into the pivotal moment of AI development, or in another era of optimism with a survey of leading AI experts estimating a 10% chance of AGI being developed in the next 20 years, a 50% chance by 2050, and 90% by 2075. The same survey estimates that once AGI is achieved, there is a 10% chance that superintelligence will be developed in the following 2 years and a 75% chance in 30 years (Müller and Bostrom

2016). Accurately predicting these timelines involves combinations of extrapolation from current technological and industrial trends with methods of forecasting such as horizon scanning and expert elicitation (Brundage et al. 2018).

The exact timeline may not be as important of a question for considering how to mitigate possible risks. Only two reasonable assumptions must be made to conclude that someday humanity will create an AGI that is vastly more intelligent than its creators. The first is that barring extinction or the collapse of civilization; humans will likely continue to develop intelligent machines because of their value. The second assumption is that intelligence is substrate independent, meaning for something to be intelligent it does not need to exist in a human brain. This second assumption is likely to be true, narrow AI already exists, and the operational definition of intelligence used does not preclude such intelligence from becoming a digital being (Kore 2022). The important question to consider is that given that someday humanity will be in relation with infinitely more intelligent beings than themselves, what can be done now to ensure that this will be a beneficial relationship to both parties (Harris 2022).

The hypothetical benefits of AGI are vast and far-reaching. AI is an essential component for the full development of Industry 4.0, and it may allow for improved medical diagnostics, autonomous driving vehicles, and support for personalized education (Panic 2020). Given the ability of AI systems to process large amounts of complex and ambiguous information, AI may be used in many research capacities. AI may be able to remove human error in systems where it is prevalent and dangerous. For example, AI-enabled robots can perform dangerous jobs like defusing bombs or working with hazardous materials. There is current research into the possible applications for AI in peacebuilding and humanitarian response operations (Hsu et al. 2022, Panic 2022, Vinuesa et al. 2020, Seeber et al. 2020, Olsher 2015). AI will likely synergize with other emerging technologies such as bio- and nanotechnology, speeding the development and increasing the overall capacities of those technologies.

Existential Risks and Artificial Intelligence

The wide range of benefits that might come from AGI evokes utopian dreams alongside apocalyptic fears. In the previously mentioned estimates of the timeline of AGI development, the same experts also said that there was a 31% probability that the developments turn out to be "bad or extremely bad for humanity" (Müller and Bostrom 2016, 15). Assessing the dangers posed by AGI is critical for discussing the existential risks enacted by emerging technology because AGI is arguably the topic at the heart of the early development of ERS and is one of the most frequently researched topics. Eliezer Yudkowsky summarized that the most significant danger posed by AGI "is that people conclude too early that they understand it" (2008, 308). The combination of many uncertainties and a high degree of confidence that it is possible leads to a wide range of speculation about AI's dangers.

The popular imagination of the AI threat follows the plot of *The Terminator* movies (Cameron 1984, 1991). Humans create AI, and AI becomes self-aware, decides to rebel, and turns the nuclear weapons against humans. After the mushroom clouds have settled, humanity then faces a protracted war with super-advanced robots to which they are outmatched. A casual search of the headlines will show titles like "AI Is Not Sentient. Why Do People Say It Is?" (Metz 2022), "'I Am, in Fact, a Person': Can Artificial Intelligence Ever Be Sentient?" (Tait 2022), and "'Risks Posed by AI Are Real': EU Moves to Beat the Algorithms That Ruin Lives" (Makortoff 2022). Curiosity and uncertainty about AI seem to be part of the current zeitgeist.

The extent to which AI and AI development might become an existential risk is an essential topic of inquiry. Despite the risk from AI still being speculative, Ord (2020) estimates the risk of AI being the cause of an existential catastrophe in the next 100 years as 1 in 10. There are several avenues by which AI could feasibly become a threat, all involving AI taking control of humanity's future.

Among AI experts, the fear of an existential catastrophe does not come from self-aware robots seeking revenge but rather through philosophical and design problems. Noah Yuval Harari (2018) summarizes a typical threat example with regard to superintelligent AI:

> One popular scenario imagines a corporation designing the first artificial super-intelligence and giving it an innocent test such as calculating pi. Before anyone realizes what is happening, the AI takes over the planet, eliminates the human race, launches a campaign of conquest to the ends of the galaxy, and transforms the entire known universe into a giant super-computer that, for billions upon billions of years calculates pi ever more accurately. (327)

There is no malice toward humanity on the side of the AI, but rather it is doing exactly the job it was asked to do to the best of its ability. Humanity made mistakes in its development; they could not ensure that AI wants the same things humans do. These challenges are called the "value alignment problem," ensuring that AI is aligned with human values and will remain under human control (Gabriel and Ghazavi 2021). Alternatively, in the context of PCS, the question becomes, "how can we design artificial intelligence that can align with the global diversity of human values?" (Panic 2020, 20).

Governance and Regulation of Artificial Intelligence
Governance and regulation of artificial intelligence is a relatively new field and currently exists in a piecemeal fashion. Internationally, new regulation efforts have focused on regulating weaponized AI in the form of Lethal Autonomous Weapons Systems (LAWS), which will be discussed later. This kind of regulation seems not to have garnered sufficient attention because it does not fit clearly into the purview of most large advocacy organizations. Those who have proposed ways of regulating this type of technology have tended to do so in the frame of working for a "killer robot ban," which may not be the most tractable approach to addressing the risks. Other obstacles are the current lack of an international definition of LAWS and the general unwillingness of states to share their cutting-edge military technologies (Surber et al. 2018).

The second trend in AI governance is a focus on AI risk reduction and promoting "friendly AI." Many large technology companies such as Google have begun initiatives like DeepMind's Ethics and Society research unit which was created to ensure that technological innovation is paired with social progress and conducted in ways that protect against harm (Legassick and Harding 2017). This work is also done on the NGO level by organizations such as the Center for Human-Compatible Artificial Intelligence (CHIAI), founded by Stuart J. Russell, an early researcher and coauthor of one of the leading textbooks on AI (Russell and Norvig 1995). CHIAI was founded based on Russell's fears of possible avenues that AI research and development could take and focuses on the value-alignment problem.

AI has become an issue for the United Nations (UN). In 2020 the United Nations High-level Panel on Digital Cooperation reported the findings of a working group that had been tasked with exploring digital cooperation to "address the social, ethical, legal and economic impact of digital technologies to maximize their benefits and minimalize their harms" (UN 2020, 4). Important topics of concern in the report were that some nations might be left behind and not share in the benefits of advanced technological development.

There have also been efforts on the cultural level to develop principles to guide the development of AI. The Future of Life Institute organized a conference of experts in the field of AI in 2017 that resulted in the Asilomar Principles. These 23 principles focused on research, ethics and values, and longer-term issues and were developed to foster a culture of trust, cooperation, and transparency among researchers and policymakers (FLI 2018; Garcia 2019). The willingness of concerned experts to come together to draft these principles indicates the need for continued research and deliberation on which strategies will likely be effective in building and sustaining a global culture of openness and sharing and identifying potential problematic consequences of AI development (Bostrom 2017).

Fears regarding the risks posed by AI should not be a call for banning research and development but rather for caution and collaboration. "Trial and error" based approaches will not be sufficient to guide the safe development of AI; careful foresight will be needed. AI systems need to be robust enough not to fail or become compromised. Legal systems will need to keep pace with changes in technology. Equal distribution of the benefits of AI will need to be considered. Further, because advancements in AI are likely to have a wide range of applications, it is necessary to examine which types of conflict various forms of AI might affect.

Peace, Conflict, and Artificial Intelligence

Artificial intelligence (AI) will be an essential topic for the future of PCS because of its ambivalent nature. It will have transformative and disruptive effects on many areas of life. Its development may take a beneficial path where AI is applied to industry, resulting in incredible increases in wealth and efficiency. AI systems may be used to make legal and financial systems fairer by threatening cases more impartially than humans would. AI could have unintentional harmful effects. AI may increase social and economic inequality, and there have already been examples of AI bias. Further, like all technologies, AI may be used as a weapon, and the race to develop AI could have all the harmful effects of past arms races. PCS might be able to influence the direction of its development to beneficial ends. Further, AI may become an important tool for peace research and practice.

Weaponization of AI

The possibility of weaponizing AI and the likely inevitably that it will happen will contribute to a sense of geopolitical fear of insecurity and vulnerability. Humanity has a long history of weaponizing new technologies. One only needs to recall that dynamite was initially invented for use in construction but quickly found itself weaponized to be reminded of this tendency. AI may augment existing weapon systems (Surber 2018): AI weapons would likely be faster, more accurate, and more efficient. If AI allows the weapon systems to become more autonomous, they would be a force multiplier. Fewer soldiers would be needed in combat, and the efficacy of each soldier would be enhanced through these systems. AI may be able to be used as a weapon to conduct fast and effective cyber-attacks, develop more effective military strategies, or be applied in some not-yet-known fashion.

With all these strategic advantages of using AI to augment weapons or as a weapon, it is likely that someone somewhere will use it as such.

AI may go the way of drones, initially developed for military surveillance use, but quickly turned into weapons. The Tadiran Mastiff is thought by some historians to be the first modern military Unmanned Aerial Vehicle (UAV). It was developed by the Israeli military and was used for surveillance in the 1973 Yom Kippur War (Merrin 2018). The Predator drone was invented in 1996 (Whittle 2013) and was used in the first lethal drone strike in 2002 (Fuller 2015). Since then, their military use has grown substantially. Estimates regarding the use of drones vary. The Bureau of Investigative Journalism (2022) estimates that from 2004 to 2022 there have been a minimum of 14,040 drone strikes with between 8858 and 16,901 people killed. Initially, only a tool of advanced militaries; now, upwards of 100 countries may have military UAVs (BBC 2022). The use of drones has spread beyond state militaries. In 2016, the first known deaths from a nonstate group's use of drones occurred when Islamic State (IS) militants killed two Kurdish Peshmerga fighters and wounded two French soldiers in Mosul (Reuters 2016).

AI would not even need to augment existing physical weapons technology. The Stuxnet worm, as mentioned earlier, is an example of a digital weapon, the efficacy of which could be significantly increased through AI. AI could also automate complex tasks that make other forms of cyberwarfare unfeasible. This change in the cost-effectiveness ratio and the difficulty in assigning blame to specific cyber-attacks may be incentives for the use of AI cyber weapons (Brundage et al. 2018).

In 2018 the Korea Advanced Institute of Science and Technology (KAIST), in partnership with Hanwha Systems, announced a joint project to weaponize AI technology to be "able to search for, and eliminate targets without human control" (Ji-hye 2018). This technology has been called "the third revolution in the battleground after gunpowder and nuclear weapons" (Haas 2018). There are also efforts to ban the use of autonomous weapons or weaponized AI (HWR 2020) and efforts to regulate its development. These efforts have had the support of experts at leading companies interested in developing AI. Elon Musk and Mustafa Suleman, along with 155 other experts, have joined in an open letter to the United Nations Convention on Certain Conventional Weapons calling for international regulation of AI (FHI 2017).

There are also less direct ways in which AI can be weaponized. The application of powerful AGI systems to mass-disinformation campaigns could be extremely dangerous for inciting violence, increasing polarization, and escalating conflicts. Intelligent bots would make the work of large-scale and effective use of propaganda easy. These tools can also be used to generate individually targeted persuasive information such as Cambridge Analytics' "Weaponized AI Propaganda Machine" (Anderson 2017; Hall 2017). AI is likely to improve the quality of "deep fakes" developed by "generative adversarial networks" that could be a powerful tool for a malicious actor. There has already been evidence of such use in the ongoing Russia-Ukraine war (Wakefield 2022).

With the vast potential of AI, there are strong incentives to develop it quickly. There is a real possibility of an AI race as countries and companies seek to seize its financial, industrial, military, and political applications. The possibility of such a race is already on the horizon. The Chinese Government has declared the goal of becoming the world leader in AI by 2030, and Russian President Vladimir Putin has stated that "whoever becomes the leader in [the AI] sphere will become the ruler of the world" (Vincent 2017).

Max Tegmark (2018) stresses that preventing a global AI arms race is one of the key challenges facing humanity. The danger of such a race is further magnified by the current lack of international norms, regulations, and consensus regarding the development and use of AI that, when combined with profit incentives, may lead to a race to the bottom where safety is sacrificed for expediency (Tiku 2018). An AI race is likely inevitable, but the questions are to what degree it will be an AI arms race and whether the race for AI will strain geopolitical tensions, possibly increasing the potential for a Great Powers Conflict.

Influences on Other Driving Factors of Conflicts
There are many ways in which AI may become a direct or indirect factor in driving conflict. As mentioned in Industry 4.0, AI may be at the heart of new industrial systems that drive inequality. This fear was echoed in the recent UN report on digital cooperation (UN 2020). Given the already cited links between inequality and conflict, this is cause for concern.

AI can help remove human bias, but it can also be an instrument for reproducing and scaling up bias. This bias can come intentionally or unintentionally at several stages in its development. Bias can creep in during the problem scoping stage, where the initial frame of the problem is taught to the AI. An AI can also become biased based on the training data learned and the choice of algorithms and parameters given (Luengo-Oroz et al. 2021). The scale of the harm done by biased AI can also come from what tasks the systems are given. There have already been cases where racial or gender bias has been found in AI systems used for hiring (Parikh 2021), health care (Vartan 2019), and predictive policing (Angwin et al. 2016). While each of these examples is harmful in its own right, it is also possible that the effects of these biased systems may be a driver of conflict.

Peacebuilding/Conflict Transformation and AI
The possibilities for AI to enhance peace are already being explored (Yamakawa 2019), as well as possible uses in peacekeeping operations (Independent Commission on Multilateralism 2007). Using AI to analyze existing conflict databases in order to develop deeper insight for peacebuilding and conflict transformation strategies is being explored (Trapple et al. 1995). AI systems could also use these complex datasets to build more accurate conflict forecasting, early warning, and intervention methods (Colaresi and Mahmood 2017). Using AI to develop more sophisticated and accurate conflict models has also been suggested (Lagazio and Marwala 2007). Such AI-developed models may allow for more efficient conflict resolution practices (Olsher 2015). There is ongoing research into the use of AI as a "teammate" in complex disasters and emergency responses where real-time data is beyond what a human can process. And there are hopes that AI systems may allow for more efficient deployment of resources and energy (Seeber et al. 2020).

There are an increasing number of organizations with an explicit focus on AI and peace and conflict issues and using AI to process large data sets to support peace processes (Özerdem and Schirch 2021). AI for Peace was founded by Branka Panic in 2020, to examine AI and PCS from her experiences working on the intersections of machine learning and peacebuilding and seeing the possible ethical implications and unintended consequences of such approaches (Panic 2021). AI for Peace works at the nexus of academic, industry, and civil society to maximize the use of AI to be a driver for peace and mitigate its potential for fueling conflict (AI for Peace n.d.). The PeaceTech Lab at the United States Institute of Peace (USIP) aims to utilize new technologies to reduce violent conflict worldwide.

Questions for the Future

> *What roles may future advancements in AI play in increasing the likelihood, intensity, or specific types of conflicts?*

> *What peacebuilding and conflict transformation opportunities may AI hold?*

At this time AI is going through a renaissance with machine learning algorithms powering advances in many sectors including transportation, medicine, finance, military (Liu et al. 2018), and more. However, current AI is modest in comparison to future expectations. In particular, it has been proposed that AI could eventually surpass humanity in important respects and with transformative consequences (Miller 2019, Bostrom 2016, Hanson 2016, Sotala 2017). Such AI could be superintelligent, with greater-than-human intellectual capacity, and super powerful, with a greater-than-human capacity to effect change in the world. Depending on the details of its design, such AI could transform human civilization by solving many of its problems, creating countless new opportunities, or becoming a driver of inequality, conflict, and perhaps extinction.

At its core, AI will be a profoundly transformative technology. Fears and hopes concerning the future development of AI come from intersections of models for predicting the future and the limitations of those models. The imagined future of AI among experts ranges widely. It may become a kind of "oracle" that answers complex questions. Alternatively, it may become a techno-deity governing humanity's utopia. It might exterminate humanity or keep humans in a zoo. It may empower malicious actors or hybridize with humanity, allowing humans to spread to the stars and become something entirely new.

All these fantasies seem to commit the anthropomorphic fallacy in which humanity assumes how AI will act based on how humans likely would. What is entirely possible is that a superintelligent AI, if it emerges, would act in entirely unexpected ways. The fear of AI may not come from its direct or indirect threats but rather the fear of unintended consequences, the fear of the unknown. It may be that humanity's concerns about AI are a mirror by which it confronts the limitations of its own knowledge. AI, as a mirror, also reflects humanity's own capacities for destruction.

Emerging Technologies: Synthetic Biology and Biotechnology

Biotechnology and synthetic biology emerged from discovering the central importance of proteins for most functions in living cells. The development of genetic engineering techniques allows for modifying pathways that produce these proteins. Synthetic biology and biotechnology are interdisciplinary approaches that combine genetic engineering, biochemistry, and many other subfields of biology. The distinctions between the two fields are not clear-cut nor unanimously agreed upon, but the general characteristics of both fields will be outlined here.

Synthetic biology is the creation of new biological systems or the redesigning of natural ones for a purpose (Schmidt 2012). These biological systems can be those in viruses, bacteria, cells, and other living organisms (DiEuliis et al. 2018). The difference between synthetic biology and biotechnology is primarily the novelty of the function of the new system. Putting human genes into a plant or plant genes into a human, as long as these genes are still producing their initial effect, would not be considered synthetic biology. If those genes were combined in ways that create novel metabolic pathways, it would be considered synthetic biology.

Both fields have been driven by the reduction in the cost of sequencing and synthesizing DNA, the invention of new genome editing tools like CRISPR/Cas9, and advancements in analytical tools. Synthetic biology has increased the accessibility of these techniques for engineering biology and has led to some decentralization of the field. Following these trends, one of the hallmarks of synthetic biology has been increasing the accessibility of using these techniques to engineer biology. This decentralization aimed to "unleash the full potential of biotechnology and spark a wave of innovation" (Schmidt 2008, 1) as more people will be able to access these technologies.

The development of synthetic biology from the genetic engineering approach traditionally used in biotechnology can be seen in the Golden Rice project, one of its earliest applications. This project aimed to address the problem of Vitamin A deficiency worldwide by increasing the amount available in rice, one of the most commonly eaten food crops. Naturally occurring rice does not have high beta-carotene levels, a vitamin A precursor. These levels are even lower in the part of the plant that humans eat, but it does contain the precursor lycopene. The genetic code for a bacterial enzyme was used to increase the plant's natural lycopene. This modification resulted in a strain of rice that produces five times the normal amount of Vitamin A than the previous strains. However, this modification was insufficient to address the problem of Vitamin A deficiency because even at these levels, a significant amount of the rice would still have to be eaten to achieve normal levels. In the second version of the Golden Rice project, two genes from different organisms were introduced to significantly modify the rice plant's metabolism. The pathways for making both lycopene and beta-carotene were enhanced, making the new version of Golden Rice produce approximately 100 times more beta-carotene than the natural plant (Davis 2018).

Biotechnology and synthetic biology have a wide range of current applications. Its current uses include improving agricultural and livestock production; producing industrial chemicals; diagnosing, preventing, and treating diseases; and engineering human cells. One of the first breakthroughs in synthetic biology applications was the synthesis of somatostatin and human insulin in the 1970s (Goeddel et al. 1979). The creation of this artificial insulin was revolutionary in treating diabetes, increasing average life expectancy and quality of life. Katz et al. (2018) write that the future of these technologies is likely to have "broadening impacts on the biotechnology industry to address ongoing issues of human health, world food supply, renewable energy, and industrial chemicals and enzymes" (449).

At the far end of the spectrum of possibilities is the use of synthetic biology to alter the notion of a human being (Tegmark 2018). Its truly transformative potential may lie in its use for altering human nature to make humans more physically fit and cognitively capable (Bostrom and Sandberg 2009). In the far future, if humanity learns to modify its own biology as it travels through the stars, which could result in the eventual splintering of the current human species into different subspecies (Baum et al. 2019).

Governance and Regulations
Similar to artificial intelligence, one of the main challenges to the governance of biotechnology and synthetic biology is that their rate of development often outpaces governance and regulation systems (Garfinkel et al. 2008). While it is common for governance to lag behind technological progress, the increasing rate of development makes the gap between technologies and their control wider than in the past. Governance challenges are further complicated by the fact that a robust and effective approach would have to address both the risks posed by biological weapons and the issue of dual-use research (WHO 2013; Baum and Wilson 2013).

International law is often used for addressing global risks but has not kept pace with the development of synthetic biology (Wilson 2013). The Biological Weapons Convention (BWC) is the highest profile international effort for protection from the risks of biological weapons. It prohibits biological and toxin weapons and entered into force in 1975 (UNODA n.d.). While the BWC has not been effective in eradicating the development of biological weapons, it has played an essential role in establishing an international norm of repulsion against their use (Cross and Klotz 2020). This shift is evidenced by the fact that despite allegations and sometimes evidence of secret biological weapons programs, no country would outright admit to having a program (Guillemin 2007). The BWC faces significant challenges to its ability to achieve its goal. The first is the number of resources the UN member states allocate to it. Ord points out that the convention employs far fewer people than the International Atomic Energy Agency (IAEA) and the Organization for the Prohibition of Chemical Weapons (OPCW) and has "a smaller budget than the average McDonald's restaurant" (Ord 2020, 57). This lack of resources compounds with its second challenge, the lack of effective measures to ensure compliance. It also does little to address the risk of nonstate or individual actors. The articles of the BWC do not cover research on biological weapons but only on weapons development, acquisition, and stockpiling. The implication is that dual-use research can continue under the guise of defense while the same research could be used for other purposes misused (Kelle 2009).

Most of these technologies and the research used to develop them are "dual-use," meaning military and civilian applications. This facet of the technology requires careful attention and international collaboration as the aim is not to inhibit research that could cure diseases or promote human flourishing at the expense of fears of misuse.

There is progress in working on the cultural level to foster trust and cooperation among researchers and industries regarding the potential dangers of biotechnology. These movements focus on defining which research areas are the most dangerous and what kinds of systems could be implemented to sanction those who violate them. In this direction, the US National Academies report, *Committee on Research Standards and Practices to Prevent the Destructive Application of Biotechnology* (2003), has identified seven experiments of concern: (1) demonstrate how to render a vaccine ineffective, (2) confer resistance to therapeutically helpful antibiotics or antiviral agents, (3) enhance the virulence of a pathogen or render a non-pathogen virulent, (4) increase transmissibility of a pathogen, (5) alter the host range of a pathogen, (6) enable the evasion of diagnostic/detection modalities, and (7) enable the weaponization of a biological agent or toxin (Rappert 2014). Research on the efficacy of building consensuses to increase biosecurity is indeed needed. Building consequences among researchers could help to identify risky research areas, build a culture of caution, and bring unforeseen dangers to light.

The existence of information hazards further complicates attempts to mitigate biosecurity risks. These are "risks that arise from the dissemination or the potential dissemination of true information that may cause harm or enable some agent to cause harm" (Bostrom 2011, 44). Information hazards create difficult decisions in Biorisk. A company that supplies genetic supplies may want a list of specific genetic codes that would be dangerous to sell, so they would not allow people to purchase them. While a well-meaning idea, once it is known what materials are not for sale, potential dangerous genetic materials have been identified to anyone looking for them. In another example, the United States Agency for International Development (USAID) has recently launched a new program, Discovery & Exploration of Emerging Pathogens—Viral Zoonoses (DEEP VZN), in 2021. This program aims to "strengthen global capacity to detect and understand the risks of viral spillover from wildlife to humans that could cause another pandemic" (USAID 2021). The program aims to document possible transmission vectors where diseases may move from animal populations to humans to prevent or prepare for possible future pandemics. This type of program may effectively mitigate disease risks, given that the vast majority of pandemics that affect humans cross over from animals. What this program may be overlooking is a significant Biosecurity Information Hazard Risk. With access to the information found through the DEEP VZN program, any person with destructive motivation would have the ability to unleash a pandemic. Esvelt (2022), in his testimony to the Subcommittee on Emerging Threats and Spending Oversight, addressed this threat, "I am reasonably confident that pandemic virus identification represents a greater near-term threat to national security than anything else in the life sciences—and a more severe proliferation threat than nuclear has ever posed" (2). Any practical approach to governance of biotechnology and synthetic biology will likely have to find a way to address these hazards.

The challenge of governing and regulating dual-use technologies and research, particularly biotechnology and synthetic biology, is navigating the balance between potential harms and benefits. This balance is difficult given the extremes promised or feared at each end of the spectrum. The purported potential benefits of these technologies are the level of curing most diseases and ending aging. Its most extreme risks include the development of a world-ending engineered pathogen.

Existential Risks and Synthetic Biology
Assessing the potential for biotechnology and synthetic biology to contribute to an existential or global catastrophic risk is complex. In essence, synthetic biology does add additional elements intentionally to existing pandemic risks and, therefore, could allow for weaponized pathogens to further complicate geopolitics (Pamlin and Armstrong 2015). There are at least three pathways to disaster:

1. The intentional development and use of a bioweapon
2. A laboratory accident resulting in the release of a pathogen regardless
3. Risks from unknown effects and unforeseen consequences

I will begin by discussing risks from unknown effects, accidental release, and finally, intentional use of a bioweapon.

Gene drives are an example of an application of biotechnology that illustrates the possible dangers of unforeseen consequences. Gene drives are methods for ensuring engineered traits would be favored and thus passed down through generations in wild populations (Esvelt et al. 2014). There are many compelling reasons to use a gene drive. For example, a gene drive could be used to eradicate malaria from the planet. In 2018, there were 228 million cases of malaria worldwide, with an estimated 405,000 deaths during the same year (WHO 2019). Of the thousands of species of mosquitos, only a few can transmit malaria effectively to humans.

Using CRISPR/Cas9 techniques to do germ-line editing in mosquitos could spread altered traits through world populations of mosquitos and force genetic changes to an entire species that would limit the spread of disease (Esvelt et al. 2014).

Eradicating malaria would no doubt be positive and reduce human suffering. Moreover, the number of lives saved would likely be a compelling reason to use a gene drive. However, the risks of altering the genetics of wild populations are not well understood, and the potential for many unforeseen or unintended consequences. Further additional questions arise about consent and decision-making. Who would have the right to implement such a technology.

Leaving aside, for the moment, intentional misuse of biotechnology, there is a troubling potential for the accidental release of dangerous biological materials. Historical precedence for such accidents with biological materials exists. In the 1979 Sverdlovsk incident, an aerosol leak from a biological weapons facility in Russia releasing anthrax and killing at least 66 people (Meselson et al. 1994). Furthermore, forgotten smallpox specimens were discovered by the CDC in an unused storage room in 2014 (CDC 2014). The US army accidentally shipped live anthrax in 2015 (Reardon 2015). Accidental release of dangerous stored pathogens is not the only way laboratory accidents could result in catastrophe. Experiments also can have dangerous unintended consequences. For example, in 2001, an Australian researcher significantly increased the fatality rate of mousepox (*ectromelia virus*) even in mice with immunity to the original virus accidentally, despite this not being the aim of the research (Jackson et al. 2001). If a similar accident were to happen with a normally benign virus that affects humans, livestock, or crops, the results could be disastrous.

Most research on the extreme risks of biotechnology focuses on its use as a weapon. The possibilities and consequences of weaponized pathogens will be discussed later. George Church, one of the pioneers of the field of synthetic biology, said that "the consequences [of biological weapons] loom larger than chemical and nuclear weapons, since biohazards are inexpensive, can spread worldwide and evolve on their own" (Church 2004). The risks posed by a bioweapon sit between Great Powers Conflicts and Pandemics. Viable bioweapons could provide a new type of Weapon of Mass Destruction (WMD) to further add to the calculus of Great Power rivalries. These technologies could also increase existential risk by increasing the lethality and virulence of a pandemic disease.

Toby Ord estimates that an engineered pandemic has a 1-in-30 chance of causing an existential catastrophe in the next 100 years (Ord 2020).

Ord's estimates include intentional use of bioweapons regardless of actor and laboratory accidents. Another study by Boddie et al. (2015) examines the risk from nonstate groups, noting significant disagreement among experts on the likelihood of a large-scale biological attack in the next ten years (2015–2025), ranging from less than 10% to as high as 90%.

There are at least three interrelated assumptions in assessing this risk. A viable engineered pathogen can be produced; a country, group, or individual wants to create one; and it is used as a weapon. The harm this pathogen could cause would be significantly affected by the weapon used to spread it and the target. The scale of harm would then follow along the possible pathways of a Great Power Conflict if the weapon was used by a state and provoked an in-kind response. The risk that a pandemic could become an existential threat is connected to the amount of harm the pathogen can do. The level of damage would be determined by the complex interaction of vulnerability and resilience in the systems set up to mitigate the disease and the degree to which international cooperation and coordination would effectively contain the spread.

The Global Challenges Foundation identifies five factors that will affect the likelihood of an existential catastrophe resulting from synthetic biology:

- The destructive potential of the biology developed
- The ability of regulation to control
- Whether the technological developments are weaponized
- The degree to which effective defenses are or can be developed
- The reliability of the biologists in estimating and understanding the risks of their research (Pamlin and Armstrong 2015)

Given the large number of variables and potential for mitigation, an engineered pandemic alone may not be an existential risk, but would certainly be a global catastrophic risk. However, a bioweapon may become an existential threat through the indirect and compounding effects it may have on creating instability, fragmenting, and possibly collapsing society making humanity not able to effectively respond to other existential threats (Maher and Baum 2013).

Peace, Conflict, and Synthetic Biology
Even though pandemics have their roots in nature, it may make more sense to classify them as being caused by humans, anthropogenic risks.

They are best considered an anthropogenic risk, that is, caused by humans. In a globalized world where the food chain is international and travel is frequent, the evolution and spread of diseases are expectedly woven into our technology and way of life. Engineered pandemics are an emerging concern and may soon be one of humanity's most significant risks. Because of the potential for malicious use, advancements in biotechnology are worrisome. The cost of these technologies is decreasing and access to them is increasing, shifting the ability to inflict mass violence from the domain of nations to organizations or individuals (Garrett 2013). This threat became all the more concerning after it was proved that methods of synthetic biology could, intentionally or unintentionally, produce a pathogen with staggeringly high levels of transmissibility and case fatality (Millett and Snyder-Beattie 2017).

Fears regarding the weaponization of synthetic biology, particularly through engineered pathogens, are warranted and have historical precedents. In March of 1995, the religious sect Aum Shinrikyo attacked five subway stations in Tokyo with Sarin gas killing 13 and injuring many more (Smithson 2014). After the attacks, investigators showed that the group tried to develop VX gas (a toxic chemical weapon) as well as weaponize anthrax (*Bacillus anthracis*) (Metraux 1995). This attack was before the advent of more powerful and accessible genetic engineering tools such as CRISPR/Cas9 and other genome sequencing and synthesis. A significantly motivated group or individual may now be able to produce and deploy an even more dangerous weapon. A bioweapon would not even have to target humans to cause large-scale harm to humanity. A biological weapon that was produced through military, commercial, or other non-state means could be used to target a vital food supply such as rice, corn, wheat crops, livestock, or the natural environment.

The international system is highly vulnerable to such a possibility. In 2021 the Nuclear Threat Initiative (NTI) held a wargame simulation with heads of infectious disease control from many countries and representatives from biotechnology and pharmaceutical companies. After the simulation, Jamie Yassif, the senior director at NTI, said, "There is no institution that's set up with the ideal features to really tackle this head-on and move at the pace that needs to happen" (Matthews 2022).

Synthetic biology may also contribute to conflict through many of the same pathways as artificial intelligence. Competition over the development of new synthetic biology may create an arms race and result in a race to the bottom where mistakes are made as safety is sacrificed for expediency. Further, these races may not occur in the open, given the international norms against developing and using biological weapons pushing the race into the shadows and out of the purview of effective oversight and making the possibility of accidental release more likely (Talmadge 2019).

Collaborative opportunities for peacebuilding and conflict transformation exist alongside initiatives to mitigate risks from biotechnology and synthetic biology. Such alliances would likely find purchase due to existing international norms against biological weapons and gain acceptance because the risks are fairly straightforward and readily understandable. With the potential level of danger posed by synthetic biology and biotechnology, fostering international cooperation may be easier to initiate. Approaches to building this cooperation are more effective when working on the issues of unintended consequences of biotechnology or the acquisition of biological weapons by nonstate actors than specifically on state-level biological weapons research. It might be possible to develop cooperation between Great Powers like the USA and China on the issue of biotechnology that could be used indirectly, as a precedent, for mitigating the possible risks from other emerging technologies such as AI. Further, similar to the multitrack diplomacy work of the Esalen Institute during the Cold War, cooperation within the scientific community could be developed between countries in an unofficial capacity. Additionally, the proposed benefits from these technologies stand to address many global problems that drive conflict.

Questions for the Future

> How might current and future advancements in biotechnology affect conflict?

> How might peacebuilding efforts be paired with the mitigation of risks from biotechnology?

Synthetic biology and biotechnology may give humanity unprecedented power over life itself. The ability to alter existing organisms and build entirely new ones has already had transformative effects in many areas of life. The further reaches of this technology's possible applications could lead to dramatic advancements in the ability to cure and treat diseases. At the same time, the world has already seen the effects of the global pandemic and how underprepared the global system was to deal with it. The possibility of future advancements in biotechnology being a driver of conflict and conflict being an opportunity for malicious use of biotechnology should be an area of concern for peace research. Additionally, given the benefits of the best-case scenario with biotechnology alongside the worst, there may be opportunities to combine peacebuilding efforts alongside approaches to mitigate biological risks.

Emerging Technologies: Nanotechnology

Nanotechnology is a third emerging technology to be considered when imagining humanity's long-term future, possible threats, and how it may influence the dynamics of peace and conflict. The reason this technology was developed was to essentially address the problem between all the things humanity wants and what the current physical limits are to having them. It also is the third piece in the trifecta, the emerging technologies to change the world fundamentally: artificial intelligence giving humans the ability to create and control a mind, synthetic biology providing the ability to create and control life, and nanotechnology offering the ability to control and change matter itself.

Nanotechnology is "based on the manipulation of individual atoms and molecules to build structures to complex, atomic specifications" (Drexler 2006, 573). It is already considered to be one of the most transformative technologies in the next 100 years (Ord 2020) as well as a "disruptive" one (Lu et al. 2012). This technology already exists and is used for many applications such as transistors, additives for strengthening materials, intelligent fabrics, medical diagnostics, batteries, and carbon nanotubes. There is concern regarding the potential risks of nanomaterials—their toxicity, bioaccumulation, and environmental persistence—all of which are being researched (Azoulay 2009).

Although nanotechnology is currently used in industrial processes to produce materials on the nanoscale (having or involving dimensions of less than 100 nanometers), its transformative potential lies in using nanomachinery to create large-scale objects. Molecular manufacturing would greatly expand the possibilities and precision by which these items could be produced. These systems would allow for the fast and inexpensive production of objects built on macro and microscopic scales (Bostrom and Ćirković 2011). This advanced "3D printing" would enable the manufacturing of almost anything from digital blueprints. This kind of technology could be one of the most profound shifts in manufacturing, industry, and economics in human history (Ord 2020; Drexler and Pamlin 2013). Similar to artificial intelligence and synthetic biology, elements of nanotechnology currently exist, but its most transformative potential capacities lie in the future.

To understand the effect of manipulating atoms and molecules, consider what can happen if the size of a particle is changed. Changing the size of gold nanoparticles (NPs) increases the melting point from 200°C to 1068°C (Tweney 2006). Current nanotechnology is already being used to create intelligent and resilient materials, more efficient solar power, fuel cells and batteries, and more effective thermal insulation for construction (Roco and Bainbridge 2005; Drexler and Pamlin 2013). Based on existing technologies, it is projected that nanotechnology will soon be used to create carbon neutral fuels, improve cancer treatments, speed up the creation of treatments for emerging diseases, improve the purification of water, reduce toxic emissions, increase data storage capacity, allow for the design of molecular structures, and allow for the scaling up of nanoscale processes for macro-scale production (Pamlin and Armstrong 2015).

Nanotechnology's future lies in High-Throughput Atomically Precise Manufacturing (HT-APM). These artificial (non-biological) systems will be able to build with atomic precision on the molecular level. In theory, such machines, maybe no larger than a desktop computer, would be able to create any object for which it has a blueprint using a generic raw material (Phoenix and Treder 2008). This kind of technology sits between a printer that can print anything and the philosopher's stone. Drexler and Pamlin (2013) describe the transformative potential of HT-APM:

> The world faces unprecedented global challenges related to depleting natural resources, pollution, climate change, clean water, and poverty. These problems are directly linked to the physical characteristics of our current technology base for producing energy and material products. Deep and pervasive changes in this technology base can address these global problems at their most fundamental, physical level, by changing both the products and the means of production. (2)

If fully realized, this technology could catalyze profound changes in civilization. Groups and individuals could manufacture anything with little cost, labor, or waste. The Global Challenges Foundation lays out five key factors that will influence the possible impact that nanotechnology will have:

- The timeframe for its development
- Which aspects of nanotechnology research occur first
- If the advancements in nanotechnology allow for a small group to put together weapons arsenals
- How effective nanotechnology can be applied for defensive purposes or surveillance
- If instrumentalized or weaponized nanotechnology can be independent from human control (Pamlin and Armstrong 2015)

Nanotechnology will likely be a transformative and perhaps disruptive technology. To better understand the trajectories it may take, its risk potential needs to be examined and how it might become a driver for peace or conflict.

Existential Risks and Nanotechnology
Four types of risk are to be analyzed when discussing the risk potential with nanotechnologies. The first is the risks posed by current nanotechnologies. The second is potential risks from future nanotechnologies, and the third is the risks posed indirectly through nanotechnologies. The indirect risks could come from synergies with existing technologies, other emerging technologies, and the disruptive effects that currently speculative nanotechnology may hold. Finally, the risk from nanotechnology could come from unintended consequences of the technology, how it is used in combination with other technologies, or the disruptive effects it may have on civilization. Given that nanotechnology is often used in other technologies, it may be more difficult to precisely estimate its risks than those posed by artificial intelligence or synthetic biology.

Existing nanotechnology's existential risk potential currently seems relatively low (Drexler and Pamlin 2013) and has focused on the potential risks of nanoparticles (NPs) (Drexler and Pamlin 2013). Currently, many NPs are used for industrial purposes and consumer goods. NPs are added to fabrics to increase their strength and to provide them with antimicrobial abilities. The extent to which these particles end up in the environment or within plants and animals is still not fully understood. However, it is feasible that a runaway process could result in harm to human and animal health and the environment (Boyd and Wilson 2020). Accidental release of NPs can occur at any stage of the product's development but is particularly difficult to address when it occurs in the final stage. It is not well understood how current waste disposal methods affect the release of

NPs from products into the environment (Martinez et al. 2021). The impact NPs have on the environment is related to their potential toxicity to cells and their ability to accumulate in organisms (Ma et al. 2010). These particles can enter the body through respiration, ingestion, or the skin. Due to their size, many of these NPs can enter into areas that larger particles cannot, further complicating their possible effects. Studies have shown that common NPs such as those that come from carbon nanotubes can be toxic to mitochondria and silver NPs can change the morphology of cell membranes in some species (Samiei et al. 2020; Xiang et al. 2020).

What is even less understood and potentially more alarming are the larger systems-wide effects the release of these particles may have. From discarded NP-enhanced consumer goods, NPs are released into the environment where it has been shown they can become toxic when they accumulate in soil or seaweed. These particles can also enter the water system and end up being ingested. Additionally, it is not well understood what possible solutions exist for eliminating the NPs already released into the environment. The environmental and health risks from the release of NPs may not be existential, but that is not to say there is no risk at all (Phoenix and Treder 2008).

The catastrophic or existential risk potential of nanotechnologies likely lies in its future developments. One scenario, perhaps the one that most often comes to mind but is very low probability, is the risk of a "grey goo." The grey goo, proposed initially as a hypothetical risk by nanotechnology pioneer Eric Drexler (1990), refers to highly advanced self-replicating nanomachines that would consume their entire environment converting all matter into more nanobots. Drexler later regretted coining the term because, for a while, it became the most known aspect of nanotechnology in popular culture (Giles 2004). The development of grey goo is impossible according to the current understanding of nanotechnology (Phoenix and Drexler 2004).

Further, developments in the field have suggested that there would be little incentive for building such self-replicating systems because nanofactories would likely be more efficient for atomically precise manufacturing than these self-replicating free-range robots. Even as a weapon, grey goo would have little tactical value as it would be difficult to control. The only foreseeable use would be through apocalyptic terrorism (Phoenix and Treder 2008).

It is unknown if advancements in nanotechnology for use in manufacturing will follow previous industry trends or be a massive disruption. If

High-Throughput Atomically Precise Manufacturing (HT-APM) systems are developed, the effects on society would likely be disruptive as many foundational aspects of the current economic system could be called into question. The net benefit versus large-scale harm is difficult to estimate. If these technologies augment other technologies, such as engineered pathogens, they will worsen the risk of that pathogen. They could be used to build new products, creating unforeseen risk potentials. At the same time, they may also be essential in developing viable solutions for addressing other catastrophic risks such as climate change (Phoenix and Treder 2008).

The governance of nanotechnology is even less developed than that of artificial intelligence and nanotechnology. There are few existing systems at the international level that address the governance and regulation of nanotechnology (Wilson 2013). Nanotechnology research and development typically does not require using rare materials that are either regulated, such as nuclear weapons, or that could be regulated, such as synthetic biology. Nor does nanotechnology require large manufacturing facilities which are easier to monitor. Governance and regulation of nanotechnology are likely to be done through specific domains of application such as for military or medical uses, environmental protection, and internally through practices and values developed by the scientific community.

Peace, Conflict, and Nanotechnology

Nanotechnology's potential applications and benefits could create a driving force for peace or conflict. On one level, like all technologies, it could be made into a weapon and make other weapons more dangerous. On a more profound level, it could change the balance of the natural constraints imposed by the physical systems in which humanity lives, fundamentally changing the nature of production and value.

Weaponization of Nanotechnology

Given the wide range of possible uses, it is likely that current nanotechnology is or will be used in military technology. Nanotechnology holds benefits for both offensive and defensive capabilities with uses in armor, camouflage, sensors, communication devices, and energy storage (Nasu 2012). If HT-APM is developed, it will also be used for military purposes. A single nano-factory would allow for easy production of conventional weapons and lead to innovation, creating entirely new weapon technologies, both appealing to militaries (E. Drexler 2006, Phoenix and Treder

2008). The degree to which these technologies could be used to augment existing weapons technologies or as a weapon itself is not well understood.

The militarization of this technology seems as if it would be difficult to control as there are no international treaties that regulate the use of nanotechnology for military purposes except to the extent that nanotechnology might be applied to classifications of weapons that are already regulated (Nasu 2012). There is also the fear that advances in nanotechnology may allow for more efficient extraction and separation of Uranium, making nuclear weapons available to more actors and undermining the strategic logic of nuclear security (Hyatt and Ojovan 2019).

Nick Bostrom, drawing on the work of Erick Drexler, describes what a nano-weapon might look like:

> Theoretically, in its mature form, molecular nanotechnology would enable the construction of a bacterium-scale self-replicating mechanical robots that can feed on dirt or other organic matter. Such replicators could eat up the biosphere or destroy it by other means by poisoning it, burning it, or blocking out the sunlight. A person of malicious intent in possessing of this technology might cause the extinction of intelligent life on Earth by releasing such nanobots into the environment. (Bostrom 2009)

The possible development of nano-weapons, though remote, is cause for concern. Such weapons would likely be challenging to ensure they remain under human control. It is also easier to envision what a nano-weapon could be than what effective defenses against it would look like (Bostrom 2009). Furthermore, if a nano-weapon system was created and used, it is possible that it would remain in the environment, making a recovery more complex. Conversely, the same nanotechnology level could make rebuilding easier after large-scale disasters or destruction (Phoenix and Treder 2008).

Nanotechnology as a Driver for Conflict

On one level, the pathways by which nanotechnology may directly or indirectly be a driver for conflict follow what has been said regarding Industry 4.0. Advancements in nanotechnology are likely to drive other digital and industrial development. Nanotechnology will lead to advancements in AI, and AI, in turn, will allow for more sophisticated nanotechnology. Whether these developments become drivers of conflict will largely depend on policy decisions.

HT-APM would likely be a step-change beyond 4IR. HT-APM molecular manufacturing may allow people to produce whatever they need from an inexpensive generic feedstock. The effects on economic, social, and political systems are likely to be profound. If this technology is developed, many jobs could disappear, but more profoundly, the nature of what work means would change. And if access to this technology is limited to only certain regions or countries, a problematic "north-south nano-divide" would likely result (Azoulay 2009). Dramatic shifts in economies and livelihoods and unequal access to such a transformative technology could indirectly increase other risks like Great Power Conflicts. Socioeconomic turmoil is not often conducive to the coordination and cooperation needed to mitigate those risks. The widespread use of HT-APM could decrease the economic dependence of rich countries on poorer countries, which would likely be a net positive development for global peace. At the same time, it may decrease the economic interdependence between nations which, under the liberal peace paradigm, is part of how peace is made (Copeland 1996). If nanomanufacturing decreases the costs associated with conflict, it could increase the likelihood of war by removing a major deterrent (Bostrom 2009).

Peacebuilding Potentials with Nanotechnology
Nanotechnology may contribute to peacebuilding indirectly. The imagined benefits of nanotechnology would be an asset in solving many of the world's problems. PCS research on nanotechnology should focus on how best to guide its development to avoid its destructive potential. This destructive potential pertains to its possible detrimental effects on biological and ecological systems and its disruptive possibilities for social, economic, and political systems. For example, nanotechnology may become a driver for peace if low-cost general-purpose nano-factories could be used to help reduce poverty and alleviate scarcity problems in impoverished areas. Similarly, because these nano-factories could make it so that nothing was scarce, competition over resources might no longer be a driver for conflict. At the same time, if these nano-factories cause unanticipated shocks to economic systems affecting both supply and demand, changing the nature of how value is determined and changing trading relationships, then the effects could become a driver for conflict.

It is possible to imagine a scenario where most of the world's workforce is displaced and the control of nanotechnology falls into the hands of a few. This shift would make large numbers of people on earth superfluous from an economic perspective. Whatever kind of entity controls the technology then could quickly become a system of oppression spurred on by cheap and ubiquitous mass surveillance, which if augmented with nanotechnology could easily become catastrophic (Phoenix and Treder 2008)

The impacts of such technologies will probably be much more complex than a magic box that ends poverty or oppresses the world. It is unwise to think that without changing the structures and systems that result in and reinforce poverty transforming the structure of economics and value at the ground level could happen without conflict. Theoretically, an HT-APM-based nano-factory could produce anything. If water filters, solar panels, diamonds, gold, antibiotics, opioids, microprocessors, and more nano-factories could all be produced at the atomic level, then the notion of value itself would have to be reimagined. Arguably a technology that would end dependence on scarce resources, allow for the conservation or replacement of raw materials, and allow easy production of whatever is needed could help humanity achieve many of the goals it thinks is necessary for peace.

Questions for the Future

> How can the transformative potential of nanotechnology be guided so that it becomes a driver for peace?
>
> How can profound changes in economic and industrial systems be made without becoming a source of violence?

Once developed, advanced nanotechnologies may, like many emerging technologies, become a mirror for humanity. Given the potential to change largely scarcity-based perspectives on economics and politics to one of abundance, would humanity be able to harness such a gift without finding a way to make it ruinous? Future research and development of nanotechnology would best keep in mind a focus on how to shape the development of the technology so that its benefits can be reaped and its potential negative impacts can be avoided. To get the good while avoiding the bad with nanotechnology involves understanding how a few technological innovations could dramatically affect economic and industrial systems and how best to prepare for such changes.

Emerging technologies will significantly affect the shape and trajectory of the future. These technologies could become a cornerstone for building very different futures through their transformative potential. The list of benefits is vast if humanity can achieve the envisioned benefits of these technologies while avoiding their potential negative consequences. The trifecta of artificial intelligence, biotechnology, and nanotechnology will play a significant role in granting powers over creation, once thought divine to humans and what Noah Yuval Harari describes as an "upgrade from *Homo Sapiens* into *Homo Deus*" (2018, 21). Through the development of artificial general intelligence and perhaps super intelligence, *Homo Deus* will have, for the first time, a new power over the creation of minds and be able to create a conscious being of a wholly different kind, made in its image but with a vastly powerful and likely, alien-seeming, intelligence. AI stands to enhance existing technologies, manufacturing, industrial, and research processes, making everything smarter, faster, and better. Synthetic biology and biotechnology would grant *Homo Deus* power over life itself. With the ability to alter biological organisms and processes at the most fundamental genetic level and create entirely new forms of synthetic biology, humanity may find a way to cure most diseases and radically extend human life. As the final piece in this trifecta, nanotechnology grants *Homo Deus* control over matter itself. With the ability to alter matter at the smallest level, humanity would essentially have the ability to transform anything into anything else. Opening up this world of the "small" gives humans an entirely new domain to explore and perhaps use to secure the long-term survival of the species.

Emerging Technology and the Future

These powers over creation are also powers over destruction. Just as it is likely that the first tools were quickly used as weapons, humanity may decide to use these new powers for destructive ends. AI, biotechnology, and nanotechnology could foreseeably be used as weapons in themselves, used to enhance current weapons technologies, and combined to enhance the destructive potential of each other. Beyond their use as a weapon, because these technologies stand to be powerfully disruptive, they could enhance the forms of structural and cultural violence already entrenched in the world, making them more robust and efficient. These technologies could further inequality and be used to prevent needed healthy change by powerful actors controlling these technologies.

Humanity stands at a precipice in the development of these technologies. Even if the mature forms of these technologies are decades away, the decisions made now about their regulation, governance, and ethics of development will all shape the relationship between humanity and these new tools. Many of these issues are currently being researched, and the structures, practices, and institutions that will guide these technologies will likely be made soon. Given the potential for powerful transformation inherent in these technologies a focus on them is essential for PCS. Peace researchers who better understand the nature of these technologies, the effects they may have, and what ways their risks might be mitigated will be better positioned to understand and practice peace in the future.

References

Adams, Samuel J. 2009. "'Honey I Blew Up the World!' One Small Step Towards Filing the Regulatory 'Black Hole' at the Intersection of High-Energy Particle Colliders and International Law." *Georgia Journal of International and Comparative Law* 38 (131).

AI for Peace. n.d. "About Us." *AI For Peace*. Accessed August 12, 2022. https://www.aiforpeace.org/about.

Alford, Kristin, Stephen McGrail, and Sarah Keenihan. 2012. "The Complex Futures of Emerging Technologies: Challenges and Opportunities for Science Foresight and Governance in Australia." *Journal of Futures Studies* 16 (4): 67–86.

Anderson, Berit. 2017. "The Rise of the Weaponized AI Propaganda Machine." *Medium*, February 13. Accessed August 10, 2022. https://medium.com/join-scout/the-rise-of-the-weaponized-ai-propaganda-machine-86dac61668b#.n8fjxsof5.

Angwin, Julia, Jeff Larson, Surya Mattu, and Lauren Kirchner. 2016. "Machine Bias: There's Software Used Across the Country to Predict Future Criminals. And it's Biased Against Blacks." *ProPublica*, May 23. Accessed August 12, 2022. https://www.propublica.org/article/machine-bias-risk-assessments-in-criminal-sentencing.

Armstrong, Stuart, Nick Bostrom, and Carl Schulman. 2013. "Racing to the Precipice: A Model of Artificial Intelligence Development." *Technical Report #2013-1* (Future of Humanity Institute) 1–8. https://www.fhi.ox.ac.uk/wp-content/uploads/Racing-to-the-precipice-a-model-of-artificial-intelligence-development.pdf.

Azoulay, David. 2009. "Addressing Nanomaterials as an Issue of Global Concern." *The Center for International Environmental Law (CIEL)*. May. https://www.ciel.org/wp-content/uploads/2015/05/CIEL_NanoStudy_May09.pdf.

Bahgat, Karim, Gray Barret, Kendra Dupuy, Scott Gates, Solveig Hillesund, Håvard Mokleiv Nygård, Siri Aas Rustad, Håvard Strand, Henrik Urdal, and

Gudrun Østby. 2017. *Inequality and Armed Conflict: Evidence and Data*. Oslo: Peace Research Institute Oslo (PRIO).

Bartuesvičius, Henrikas. 2014. "The Inequality-conflict Nexus Re-examined: Income, Education and Popular Rebellions." *Journal of Peace Research* 51 (1): 35–50.

Baum, Seth D, and Grant S Wilson. 2013. "The Ethics of Global Catastrophic Risk from Dual-Use Bioengineering." *Ethics in Biology Engineering and Medicine* 4 (1): 59–72.

Baum, Seth D., Stuart Armstrong, Timoteus Ekenstedt, Olle Häggström, Robin Hanson, Karin Kuhlemann, Matthijs M. Maas, et al. 2019. "Long-Term Trajectories of Human Civilization." *Foresight* 21 (1): 53–83.

BBC. 2022. "Combat Drones: We are in a New Era of Warfare—Here's Why." *BBC*, February 4. Accessed September 23, 2022. https://www.bbc.com/news/world-60047328.

Beckstead, Nick, Nick Bostrom, Niel Bowerman, Own Cotton-Barratt, William MacAskill, Seán Ó hÉigeartaigh, and Toby Ord. 2014. "Unprecedented Technological Risks." *Future of Humanity Institute*, September. Accessed August 8, 2022. https://www.fhi.ox.ac.uk/wp-content/uploads/Unprecedented-Technological-Risks.pdf.

Benioff, Marc. 2017. "Four Ways to Close the Inequality Gap in the Fourth Industrial Revolution." *World Economic Forum*, January 18. Accessed August 10, 2022. https://www.weforum.org/agenda/2017/01/4-ways-to-close-the-inequality-gap-in-the-fourth-industrial-revolution/.

Bircan, Cagatay, Tilman Brück, and Marc Vothknecht. 2017. "Violent Conflict and Inequality." *Oxford Development Studies* 45 (2): 125–144.

Blanton, Thomas S., William Burr, and Svetlana Savranskaya. 2012. *The Underwater Cuban Missile Crisis: Soviet Submarines and the Risk of Nuclear War*. National Security Archive, Electronic Briefing Book No. 399. National Security Archive.

Boddie, Crystal, Matthew Watson, Gary Ackerman, and Gigi Kwik Gronvall. 2015. "Assessing the Bioweapons Threat." *Science* 349 (6250): 792–793.

Boothby, William H. 2018. "Regulating New Weapon Technologies." In *New Technologies and the Law in War and Peace*, edited by William H. Boothby, 16–42. Oxford: Cambridge University Press.

Boston, Jonathan. 2021. "Assessing the Options for Combatting Democratic Myopia and Safeguarding Long-term Interests." *Futures* 125.

Bostrom, Nick. 2009. "Existential Risks: Analyzing Human Extinction Scenarios and Related Hazards." *Journal of Evolution and Technology* 9.

Bostrom, Nick. 2011. "Information Hazards: A Typology of Potential Harms from Knowledge." *Review of Contemporary Philosophy* 10: 44–79.

Bostrom, Nick. 2016. *Superintelligence: Paths, Dangers, Strategies*. Oxford: Oxford University Press.

Bostrom, Nick. 2017. "Strategic Implications of Openness in AI Development." *Global Policy* 8: 135–148.
Bostrom, Nick. 2019. "The Vulnerable World Hypothesis." *Global Policy* 4 (10): 455–576.
Bostrom, Nick, and Anders Sandberg. 2009. "Cognitive Enhancement: Methods, Ethics, Regulatory Challenges." *Science and Engineering Ethics* 15: 311–341.
Bostrom, Nick, and Milan M. Ćirković. 2011. *Global Catastrophic Risks*. Edited by Nick Bostrom and Milan M. Ćirković. Oxford: Oxford University Press.
Boyd, Matt, and Nick Wilson. 2020. "Existential Risks to Humanity Should Concern International Policymakers and More Could Be Done in Considering Them at the International Governance Level." *Risk Analysis* 40 (11): 2303–2312.
Boyd, Matt, and Nick Wilson. 2021. "Anticipatory Governance for Preventing and Mitigating Catastrophic and Existential Risk." *Policy Quarterly. In Focus: Social Insurance* 17 (4).
Brundage, Miles, Shahr Avin, Jack Clark, Helen Toner, Peter Eckersley, Ben Garfinkel, Allan Dafoe, et al. 2018. "The Malicious Use of Artificial Intelligence: Forecasting, Prevention, and Mitigation." *arXiv preprint arXiv:1802.07228*.
Brynjolfsson, Erik, and Andrew McAfee. 2011. *Race Against the Machine: How the Digital Revolution is Accelerating Innovation, Driving Productivity, and Irreversibly Transforming Employment and the Economy*. Lexington: Digital Frontier Press.
Bureau of Investigative Journalism. 2022. "Drone War." *The Bureau of Investigative Journalism*. Accessed September 12, 2022. https://www.thebureauinvestigates.com/projects/drone-war.
Butcher, James, and Irakli Beridze. 2019. "What is the State of Artificial Intelligence Governance Globally?" *The RUSI Journal* 88–96.
CDC. 2014. "CDC Media Statement on Newly Discovered Smallpox Specimens." *Center for Disease Control*, July 8. https://www.cdc.gov/media/releases/2014/s0708-NIH.html.
Cederman, Lars-Erik, Nils B. Weidmann, and Kristian Skrede Gleditsch. 2011. "Horizontal Inequalities and Ethno-nationalist Civil War: A Global Comparison." *American Political Science Review* 105 (3): 478–795.
Cameron, James, director. 1984. *The Terminator*. Orion Pictures.
Cameron, James, director. 1991. *Terminator 2: Judgment Day*. Tri-Star Pictures.
CEERN. n.d. "The Large Hadron Collider." *European Organization for Nuclear Research (CERN)*. Accessed August 11, 2022. https://home.cern/science/accelerators/large-hadron-collider#:~:text=It%20first%20started%20up%20on,the%20particles%20along%20the%20way.
Chin, Warren. 2019. "Technology, War and the State." *International Affairs* 95 (4): 765–783.

Church, George. 2004. "A Synthetic Biohazard Non-proliferation Proposal." *Harvard*. Accessed August 12, 2022. http://arep.med.harvard.edu/SBP/Church_Biohazard04c.htm.

Colaresi, Michael, and Zuhaib Mahmood. 2017. "Do the Robot: Lessons from Machine Learning to Improve Conflict Forecasting." *Journal of Peace Research* 54 (2): 193–214.

Committee on Research Standards and Practices to Prevent the Destructive Application of Biotechnology. 2003. *Biotechnology Research in an Age of Terrorism*. Washington, DC: National Research Council.

Copeland, Dale C. 1996. "Economic Interdependence and War: A Theory of Trade Expectations." *International Security* 20 (4): 5–41.

Creighton, Jolene. n.d. "Gene Drives: Assessing the Benefits and Risks." *Future of Life Institute*. https://futureoflife.org/gene-drives-assessing-the-benefits-risks/.

Cross, Glenn, and Lynn Klotz. 2020. "Twenty-first Century Perspectives on the Biological Weapon Convention: Continued Relevance or Toothless Paper Tiger." *Bulletin of the Atomic Scientists* 76 (4): 185–191.

Davis, James A. 2018. *Synthetic Biology: A Very Short Introduction*. Oxford: Oxford University Press.

DiEuliis, Diane, Andrew D. Ellington, Gigi Kwik Gronvall, and Michael J. Imperiale. 2018. "Does Biotechnology Pose New Catastrophic Risks?" In *Global Catastrophic Biological Risks*, edited by Thomas V. Inglesby and Amesh A. Adalja, 107–121. Cham: Springer.

Drexler, Eric. 2006. *Engines of Creation 2.0: The Coming Era of Nanotechnology*. Anchor Books.

Drexler, Eric K. 1990. *Engines of Creation: The Coming Era of Nanotechnology*. London: Fourth Estate.

Drexler, Eric K, and Dennis Pamlin. 2013. *Nano-Solutions for the 21st Century: Unleashing the Fourth Technological Revolution*. Oxford: Oxford Martin School.

Elisberg, Daniel. 2017. *The Doomsday Machine: Confessions of a Nuclear War Planner*. New York: Bloomsbury.

Esvelt, Kevin M. 2022. "Credible Pandemic Virus Identification Will Trigger the Immediate Proliferation of Agents as Lethal as Nuclear Devices." *Senate Homeland Security and Governmental Affairs Committee: Subcommittee on Emerging Threats and Spending Oversight*, August 3. Accessed August 16, 2022. https://www.hsgac.senate.gov/imo/media/doc/Esvelt%20Testimony.pdf.

Esvelt, Kevin M., Andrea L Smidler, Flaminia Catteruccia, and George M. Church. 2014. "Emerging Technology: Concerning RNA-Guided Gene Drives for the Alteration of Wild Populations." *Elife*.

Eth, Daniel. 2017. "The Technological Landscape Affecting Artificial General Intelligence and the Importance of Nanoscale Neural Probes." *Informatica* 41: 453–470.

FHI. 2017. "An Open Letter to the United Nations Convention on Certain Conventional Weapons." *Future of Life*. Future of Life Institute. https://futureoflife.org/autonomous-weapons-open-letter-2017/.

FLI. 2018. "Asilomar AI Principles." *Future of Life Institute*. https://futureoflife.org/ai-principles/.

Fuller, Christopher J. 2015. "The Eagle Comes Home to Roost: The Historical Origins of the CIA's Lethal Drone Program." *Intelligence and National Security* 30 (6): 769–792.

Gabriel, Iason, and Vafa Ghazavi. 2021. "The Challenge of Value Alignment: From Fairer Algorithms to AI Safety." In *The Oxford Handbook of Digital Ethics*, edited by Carissa Véliz. Oxford: Oxford University Press.

Garcia, Eugenio V. 2019. "Artificial Intelligence, Peace and Security: Challenges for International Humanitarian Law." *Cadernos de Política Exterior n°8* (Instituto de Pesquisa de Relações Internacionais).

Garfinkel, Michele S, Drew Endy, Gerald Epstein, and Robert Friedman. 2008. "Synthetic Genomics: Options for Governance." *Biosecurity and Bioterrorism: Biodefense Strategy, Practice, and Science* 5 (4).

Garrett, Laurie. 2013. "Biology's Brave New World: the Promise and Perils of the Synbio Revolution." *Foreign Affairs* 28–46.

Gartzke, Erik. 2019. "Blood and Robots: How Remotely Piloted Vehicles and Related Technologies Affect the Politics of Violence." *Journal of Strategic Studies*.

Geddes, Patrick. 1915. *Cities in Evolution: an Introduction to the Town Planning Movement and to the Study of Civics*. London: Williams and Norgate.

Giles, Jim. 2004. "Nanotech Takes Small Step Towards Burying 'Grey Goo.'" *Nature* 429 (591).

Gluckman, Sir Peter, and Anne Bardsley. 2021. *Uncertain But Inevitable: The Expert-Policy-Political Nexus and High-Impact Risks*. Koi Tū: The Centre for Informed Futures.

Goeddel, David V., Dennis G. Kleid, Francisco Bolivar, Herbert L. Heyneker, Daniel G. Yansura, Roberto Crea, Tadaaki Hirose, Kraszewski, Keichi Itakura, and Arthur D. Riggs. 1979. "Expression in Escherichia coli of Chemically Synthesized Genes for Human Insulin." *Proceedings of the National Academy of Science of the United States of America* 76 (1): 106–110.

Gonzalez, David. 2002. "At Cuba Conference, Old Foes Exchange Notes on 1962 Missile Crisis." *New York Times*, October 14. Accessed September 1, 2022. https://www.nytimes.com/2002/10/14/world/at-cuba-conference-old-foes-exchange-notes-on-1962-missile-crisis.html.

Government Office for Science. 2014. *Annual Report of the Government Chief Scientific Adviser 2014. Innovation: Managing Risk, Not Avoiding It. Evidence and Case Studies*.

Guillemin, Jeanne. 2007. "Scientists and the History of Biological Weapons: A Brief Historical Overview of the Development of Biological Weapons in the Twentieth Century." *EMBO Reports* S45–S49.

Haas, Benjamin. 2018. "'Killer Robots': AI Experts Call for Boycott over Lab at South Korea University." *The Guardian*, April 5. Accessed August 11, 2022. https://www.theguardian.com/technology/2018/apr/05/killer-robots-south-korea-university-boycott-artifical-intelligence-hanwha.

Hanson, Robin. 2016. *The Age of Em: Work, Love, and Life When Robots Rule the Earth*. Oxford: Oxford University Press.

Halaweh, Mohanad. 2013. "Emerging Technology: What is it?" *Journal of Technology Management and Innovation* 8 (3): 108–115.

Hall, Jessica. 2017. "Meet the Weaponized Propaganda AI That Knows You Better Than You Know Yourself." *Extreme Tech*, March 1. Accessed August 10, 2022. https://www.extremetech.com/extreme/245014-meet-sneaky-facebook-powered-propaganda-ai-might-just-know-better-know.

Harari, Yuval Noah. 2018. *Homo Deus: A Brief History of Tomorrow*. New York: HarperCollins.

Harris, Sam. 2022. "How Much Does the Future Matter? A Conversation with William MacAskill." *Sam Harris*, August 14. Accessed August 16, 2022. https://www.samharris.org/podcasts/making-sense-episodes/292-how-much-does-the-future-matter.

Herweijer, Celine, Benjamin Combes, Leo Johnson, Rob McCargow, Sahil Bhardwaj, Bridget Jackson, and Pia Ramchandani. 2018. " Enabling a Sustainable Fourth Industrial Revolution: How G20 Countries can Create the Conditions for Emerging Technologies to Benefit People and the Planet." *Economics Discussion Papers, No 2018-32, Kiel Institute of the World Economy*.

Horowitz, Michael C. 2019. "When Speed Kills: Autonomous Weapons Systems, Deterrence, and Stability." *Journal of Strategic Studies* 42 (6): 764–788.

Hsu, Yen-Chia, Huang (Kenneth) Ting-Hao, Himanshu Verma, Andrea Mauri, Illah Nourbakhsh, and Alessandro Bozzon. 2022. "Empowering Local Communities Using Artificial Intelligence." *Patterns* 3 (3): 100449.

HWR. 2020. "Killer Robots: Growing Support for a Ban." *Human Rights Watch*, August 10. https://www.hrw.org/news/2020/08/10/killer-robots-growing-support-ban.

Hyatt, Neil C, and Michael I Ojovan. 2019. "Materials for Nuclear Waste Immobilization." *Materials (Basel)* 12 (21): 3611.

Independent Commission on Multilateralism. 2007. "The Impact of New Technologies on Peace, Security, and Development." *International Peace Institute Independent Commission on Multilateralism Policy Paper*. May. https://www.ipinst.org/wp-content/uploads/2017/05/New-Technologies.pdf.

Jackson, Ronald J., Alistair J. Ramsay, Carina D. Christensen, Sandra Beaton, Diana F. Hall, and Ian A. Ramshaw. 2001. "Expression of Mouse Interleukin-4 by a Recombinant Ectromelia Virus Suppresses Cytolytic Lymphocyte

Responses and Overcomes Genetic Resistance to Mousepox." *Journal of Virology* 75 (3): 1205–1210.
Jevons, William Stanley. 1931. *The Theory of Political Economy*. Macmillan and Co.mpany: Stuttgart.
Ji-hye, Jun. 2018. "Hanwha, KAIST to Develop AI Weapons." *The Korea Times*, February 25. Accessed August 11, 2022. http://www.koreatimes.co.kr/www/tech/2018/02/133_244641.html.
Katz, Leonard, Yvonne Y. Chen, Ramon Gonzalez, Todd C. Peterson, Huimin Zhao, and Richard H. Baltz. 2018. "Synthetic Biology Advances and Applications in the Biotechnology." *Metabolic Engineering and Synthetic Biology* 449–461: 449.
Kelle, Alexander. 2009. "Ensuring the Security of Synthetic Biology—Towards a 5P Governance Strategy." *Systems and Synthetic Biology* 3 (1–4): 85–90.
Kerr, Paul K., John Rollins, and Catherine A. Theohary. 2010. "The Stuxnet Computer Worm: Harbinger of Emerging Warfare Capability." *Congressional Research Service*.
Konopinski, Emil, C. Marvin, and Edward Teller. 1946. "Ignition of the Atmosphere with Nuclear Bombs [Report LA-602]." *Los Alamos National Laboratory*.
Kore, Akshay. 2022. *Designing Human Centric AI Experiences*. Berkeley: Apress.
Kushner, David. 2013. "The Real Story of Stuxnet: How Kaspersky Lab Tracked Down the Malware that Stymied Iran's Nuclear-Fuel Enrichment Program." *IEEE Spectrum* 50 (3): 48–53.
Kwakkel, Jan H., Warren E. Walker, and Marjolin Haasnoot. 2016. "Coping with the Wickedness of Public Policy Problems: Approaches for Decision Making under Deep Uncertainty." *Journal of Water Resources Planning and Management* 142 (3).
Lagazio, Monica, and Tshilidzi Marwala. 2007. "Modeling and Controlling Interstate Conflict." *Computers and Society*.
Landes, David S. 1969. *The Unbound Prometheus*. Cambridge: Cambridge University Press.
Lee, Edward A., and Eleftherios Matsikoudis. 2008. "The Semantics of Dataflow With Firing." In *From Semantics to Computer Science: Essays in memory of Gilles Kahn*, edited by Gérard Huet, Gordon Plotkin, Jean-Jacques Lévy and Yves Bertot. Cambridge: Cambridge University Pres.
Legassick, Sean, and Verity Harding. 2017. "Why We Launched DeepMindEtheics and Society." *DeepMind*, October 3. Accessed August 10, 2022. https://www.deepmind.com/blog/why-we-launched-deepmind-ethics-society.
Liu, Hin-Yan, Kristian Cedervall Lauta, and Matthijs Michiel Maas. 2018. "Governing Boring Apocalypses: A New Typology of Existential Vulnerabilities and Exposures for Existential Risk Research." *Futures* 102: 6–19.

Lu, Louis Y.Y., Bruce J.Y. Lin, John S. Liu, and Chang-Yung Yu. 2012. "Ethics in Nanotechnology: What's Being Done? What's Missing?" *Journal of Business Ethics* 109: 583–598.

Luengo-Oroz, Miguel, Joseph Bullock, Katherine Hoffmann Pham, Lam Cynthia Sin Nga, and Alexandra Luccioni. 2021. "From Artificial Intelligence Bias to Inequality in the Time of COVID-19." *IEEE Technology and Society Magazine* 40 (1): 71–70.

Müller, Vincent C., and Nick Bostrom. 2016. "Future Progress in Artificial Intelligence: A Survey of Expert Opinion." In *Fundamental Issues of Artificial Intelligence*, edited by Vincent C. Müller, 553–571. Berlin: Springer.

Ma, Xingmao, Jane Geisler-Lee, Yang Deng, and Andrei Kolmakov. 2010. "Interactions Between Engineered Nanoparticles (ENPs) and Plants: Phytotoxicity, Uptake and Accumulation." *Science of the Total Environment* 408 (16).

Maher, Timothy M., and Seth D. Baum. 2013. "Adaptation to and Recovery from Global Catastrophe." *Sustainability* 5: 1461–1479.

Makortoff, Kalyeena. 2022. "'Risks Posed by AI are Real': EU Moves to Beat the Algorithms that Ruin Lives." *The Guardian*, August 7.

Martinez, GuillermoMartinez, Manuel Merinero, María Pérez-Aranda, Eva María Pérez-Soriano, Tamara Ortiz, Educardo VIllamor, Belén Begines, and Ana Alcudia. 2021. "Environmental Impact of Nanoparticles' Application as an Emerging Technology: A Review." *Materials* 14 (166).

Matthews, David. 2022. "How Scientists can Prevent an Engineered Pandemic." *Science Business*, March 24. Accessed August 14, 2022. https://sciencebusiness.net/news/how-scientists-can-prevent-engineered-pandemic.

McNamara, Robert Strange. 1992. "One Minute to Doomsday?" *The New York Times*, October 14.

Merrin, William. 2018. *Digital War: A Critical Introduction*. London: Taylor & Francis.

Meselson, Matthew, Jenne Guillemin, Martin Hugh-Jones, Alexander Langmuir, IIona Popova, Alexis Shelokov, and Olga Yampolskaya. 1994. "The Sverdlovsk Anthrax Outbreak of 1979." *Science* 266: 1202–1208.

Metraux, Daniel A. 1995. "Religious Terrorism in Japan: The Fatal Appeal of Aum Shinrikyo." *Asian Survey* 35 (12): 1140–1154.

Metz, Cade. 2022. "A.I. Is Not Sentient. Why Do People Say It Is?" *The New York Times*, August 5.

Miller, Tim. 2019. "Explanation in Artificial Intelligence: Insights from the Social Sciences." *Artificial Intelligence* 267: 1–38.

Miller, James N., and Richard Fontaine. 2017. *A New Era in US-Russian Strategic Stability: How Changing Geopolitics and Emerging Technologies are Reshaping Pathways to Crisis and Conflict*. Washington, DC: Centre for New American Security.

Millett, Piers, and Andrew Snyder-Beattie. 2017. "Existential Risk and Cost-Effective Biosecurity." *Health Security* 15 (4): 373–383.
Nasu, Hitoshi. 2012. "Nanotechnology and Challenges to International Humanitarian Law: A Preliminary Legal Assessment." *International Review of the Red Cross* 94 (866): 653–672.
Newquist, Harvey. 1994. *The Brain Makers: The History of Artificial Intelligence*. Carmel: Sams Publishing.
Nilsson, Nils J. 2010. *The Quest for Artificial Intelligence: A History of Ideas and Achievements*. Cambridge: Cambridge University Press.
Olsher, Daniel J. 2015. "New Artificial Intelligence Tools for Deep Conflict Resolution and Humanitarian Response." *Procedia Engineering* 107: 281–292.
Ord, Toby. 2020. *The Precipice: Existential Risk and the Future of Humanity*. New York: Hachette Books.
Özerdem, Alpasian, and Lisa Schirch. 2021. "Peace Engineering in a Complex Pandemic World." In *Conflict Resolution After the Pandemic: Building Peace, Pursuing Justice*, edited by Richard E Rubenstein and Solon Simmons, 107–115. London and New York: Routledge.
Pamlin, Dennis, and Stuart Armstrong. 2015. "12 Risks that Threaten Human Civilization: The Case for a New Risk Category." *Global Challenges Foundation*.
Panic, Branka. 2020. *AI Explained: Non-technical Guide for Policymakers*. AI for Peace.
Panic, Branka. 2022. *Can Emerging Technologies Lead a Revival of Conflict Early Warning/Early Action? Lessons from the Field*. New York: NYU Center on International Cooperation.
Panic, Branka. 2021. "Episode 175: AI for Peace, with Branka Panic." *Re-work*, January 7. Accessed August 13, 2022. https://videos.re-work.co/podcast.
Parikh, Nish. 2021. "Understanding Bias In AI-Enabled Hiring." *Forbes*, October 14. Accessed August 11, 2022. https://www.forbes.com/sites/forbeshumanresourcescouncil/2021/10/14/understanding-bias-in-ai-enabled-hiring/?sh=337477177b96.
Phoenix, Chris, and Eric K Drexler. 2004. "Safe Exponential Manufacturing." *Nanotechnology* 15 (8): 869–872.
Phoenix, Chris, and Mike Treder. 2008. "Nanotechnology as Global Catastrophic Risk." In *Global Catastrophic Risks*, edited by Nick Bostrom and Milan M. Cirkovic, 481–502. Oxford: Oxford University Press.
Rappert, Brian. 2014. "Why has Not There Been More Research of Concern?" *Front Public Health* 2 (74).
Reardon, Sara. 2015. "US Military Accidentally Ships Live Anthrax to Labs." *Nature*, May 28. https://www.nature.com/news/us-military-accidentally-ships-live-anthrax-to-labs-1.17653.

Reuters. 2016. "Islamic State Drone Kills Two Kurdish Fighters, Wounds Two French Soldiers." *Reuters*, October 11. Accessed August 11, 2022. https://www.reuters.com/article/us-france-iraq-iraq/islamic-state-drone-kills-two-kurdish-fighters-wounds-two-french-soldiers-idUSKCN12B2QI?il=0.

Roco, M. C, and W. Bainbridge. 2005. "Societal Implications of Nanoscience and Nanotechnology: Maximizing Human Benefit." *Journal of Nanoparticle Research* 7: 1–13.

Rotolo, Daniel, Diana Hicks, and Ben R. Martian. 2015. "What is an Emerging Technology." *Research Policy* 44 (10): 1827–1843.

Russell, Stuart J., and Peter Norvig. 1995. *Artificial Intelligence: A Modern Approach*. Hoboken: Prentice Hall.

Russet, Bruce. 1964. "Inequality and Instability: The Relation of Land Tenure to Politics." *World Politics* 16 (3): 442–454.

Samiei, Fatemeh, Farshad Hosseini Shirazi, Parvaneh Naserzadeh, Faezeh Dousti, Enayatollah Seydi, and Jalal Pourahmad. 2020. "Toxicity of Multi-wall Carbon Nanotubes Inhalation on the Brain of Rats." *Environmental Science and Pollution Research* 27 (11): 12096–12111.

Schmidt, Markus. 2008. "Diffusion of Synthetic Biology: a Challenge to Biosafety." *Systems and Synthetic Biology* 2 (1–2): 1–6.

Schmidt, Markus. 2012. "Introduction." In *Synthetic Biology*, edited by Markus Schmidt, 1–18. Weinheim: Wiley-Blackwell.

Schwab, Klaus. 2016. *The Fourth Industrial Revolution*. Cologny/Geneva: World Economic Forum.

Seeber, Isabella, Eva Bittner, Robert O. Briggs, Triparna de Vreede, Gert-Jan de Vreede, Aaron Elkins, Ronald Maier, et al. 2020. "Machines as Teammates: A Research Agenda on AI in Team Collaboration." *Information and Management* 1–22.

Smithson, Amy E. 2014. "Rethinking the Lessons of Tokyo." In Ataxia: the Chemical and Biological Terrorism Threat and the US Response, edited by Amy E. Smithson and Leslie-Anne Levy, 91–95. Henry L. Stimson Centre.

Sotala, Kaj. 2017. "How Feasible Is the Rapid Development of Artificial Superintelligence?" *Physica Scripta* 92 (11).

Stewart, Frances. 2000. "Crisis Prevention: Tackling Horizontal Inequalities." *Oxford Development Studies* 28 (3): 245–262.

Surber, Regina, ICT4 Peace Foundation, and ZHET. 2018. *Artificial Intelligence: Autonomous Technology (AT), Lethal Autonomous Weapons Systems (LAWS) and Peace Time Threats*. Zurich: ICT4Peace and Zurich HUb for Ethics and Technology.

Tait, Amelia. 2022. "'I am, in Fact, a Person': Can Artificial Intelligence Ever be Sentient?" *The Guardian*, August 14.

Talmadge, Caitlin. 2019. "Emerging Technology and Intra-war Escalation Risks: Evidence from the Cold War, Implications for Today." *Journal of Strategic Studies* 42 (6): 864–887.

Tegmark, Max. 2018. *Life 3.0: Being Human in the Age of Artificial Intelligence*. Vintage.

Tiku, Nitasha. 2018. "Microsoft Wants to Stop AI's 'Race to the Bottom'". *Wired*, June 12. https://www.wired.com/story/microsoft-wants-stop-ai-facial-recognition-bottom/.

Torres, Phil. 2018. "Who Would Destroy the World? Omnicidal Agents and Related Phenomena." *Aggression and Violent Behavior* 39: 129–138.

Toynbee, Arnold. 1884. *Lectures on the Industrial Revolution In England: Public Addresses, Notes and Other Fragments*. London: Rivington.

Trapple, Robert, Johannes Fürnkranz, and Johann Petrak. 1995. "Digging for Peace: Using Machine Learning Methods for Assessing International Conflict Databases." *12th European Conference on Artificial Intelligence* 453–457.

Tweney, Ryan D. 2006. "Discovering Discovery: How Faraday Found the First Metallic Colloid." *Perspectives on Science* 14 (1): 97–121.

UN. 2020. "The Age of Digital Interdependence: Report of the UN Secretary-General's High-level Panel on Digital Cooperation." *United Nations*, June 11. Accessed August 12, 2022. https://www.un.org/en/pdfs/DigitalCooperation-report-for%20web.pdf.

UNCTAD. 2019. *Structural Transformation, Industry 4.0 and Inequality: Science, Technology and Innovation Policy Changes*. Geneva: United Nations Conference on Trade and Development.

UNODA. n.d. "History of the Biological Weapons Convention." *United Nations Office for Disarmament Affairs*. Accessed August 14, 2022. https://www.un.org/disarmament/biological-weapons/about/history/.

Urban, Tim. 2015. "The AI Revolution: The Road to Superintelligence." *Wait But Why*, January 22. https://waitbutwhy.com/2015/01/artificial-intelligence-revolution-1.html.

USAID. 2021. "USAID Announces New $125 Million Project to Detect Unknown Viruses with Pandemic Potential." *USAID*, October 5. Accessed August 16, 2022. https://www.usaid.gov/news-information/press-releases/oct-5-2021-usaid-announces-new-125-million-project-detect-unknown-viruses#:~:text=Discovery%20%26%20Exploration%20of%20Emerging%20Pathogens,that%20could%20cause%20another%20pandemic.

Vartan, Starre. 2019. "Racial Bias Found in a Major Health Care Risk Algorithm." *Scientific American*, October 24. Accessed August 12, 2022. https://www.scientificamerican.com/article/racial-bias-found-in-a-major-health-care-risk-algorithm/.

Vesilind, P. Aarne. 2005. *Peace Engineering: When Personal Values and Engineering Careers Converge*. Woodsville: Lakeshore Press.

Vincent, James. 2017. "Putin Says the Nation that Leads in AI Will be the Ruler of the World." *The Verge*, September 24. https://www.theverge.com/2017/9/4/16251226/russia-ai-putin-rule-the-world.

Vinuesa, Ricardo, Hossein Azizpour, Iolanda Leite, Madeline Balaam, Virginia Digum, Sami Domishch, Anna Felländer, Simone Daniela Langhans, Max Tegmark, and Fuso Fancesco Nerini. 2020. "The Role of Artificial Intelligence in Achieving the Sustainable Development Goals." *Nature Communications* 11 (233).

Wakefield, Jane. 2022. "Deepfake Presidents Used in Russia-Ukraine War." *BBC*, March 18. Accessed August 10, 2022. https://www.bbc.com/news/technology-60780142.

Weaver, Thomas A., and Lowell Wood. 1979. "Necessary Conditions for the Initiation and Propagation of Nuclear-Detonative Waves in Plane Atmospheres." *Physical Review A*.

Whittle, Richard. 2013. "The Man Who Invented the Predator." *The Smithsonian Magazine*, April. Accessed September 12, 2022. https://www.smithsonianmag.com/air-space-magazine/the-man-who-invented-the-predator-3970502/.

WHO. 2013. "Report of the WHO Informal Consultation on Dual Use Research of Concern." *World Health Organization*, February 17. Accessed July 29, 2022. https://www.who.int/publications/m/item/report-of-the-who-informal-consultation-on-dual-use-research-of-concern.

WHO. 2019. "The "World Malaria Report 2019" at a Glance." *World Health Organization*, December 4. https://www.who.int/news-room/feature-stories/detail/world-malaria-report-2019.

Wilson, Grant. 2013. "Minimizing Global Catastrophic and Existential Risks from Emerging Technologies through International Law." *Virginia Environmental Law Journal* 31 (2): 307–364.

Xiang, Qian-Qian, Di Wang, Ji-Lai Zhang, Cheng-Zhi Ding, Xia Luo, Juan Tao, Jian Ling, Damian Shea, and Li-Qiang Chen. 2020. "Effect of Silver Nanoparticles on Gill Membranes of Common Carp: Modification of Fatty Acid Profile, Lipid Peroxidation and Membrane Fluidity." *Environmental Pollution* 256.

Yamakawa, Hiroshi. 2019. "Peacekeeping Conditions for an Artificial Intelligence Society." *Big Data and Cognitive Computing* 3 (34).

Yarnall, Kala, Mira Olson, Ivonne Santiago, and Craig Zelizer. 2021. "Peace Engineering as a Pathway to the Sustainable Development Goals." *Technological Forecasting and Social Change* 168.

Østby, Gudrun. 2011. "Polarization, Horizontal Inequalities and Violent Civil Conflict." *Journal of Peace Research* 42 (5): 143–162.

Yudkowsky, Eliezer. 2008. "Artificial Intelligence as a Positive and Negative Factor in Global Risk." In *Global Catastrophic Risks*, edited by Nick Bostrom and Milan M. Cirkovic, 308–343. Oxford University Press.

Zetter, Kim. 2014. "An Unprecedented Look at Stuxnet, the World's First Digital Weapon." *Wired*, March 11. https://www.wired.com/2014/11/countdown-to-zero-day-stuxnet/.

CHAPTER 8

Totalitarianism Risk and Peace

The dangers from the previously discussed existential and global catastrophic risks will be mitigated or magnified by how humanity governs itself. There are ways in which forms of governance could pose an existential threat to humanity (Borders 2021). Andrew Leigh, in his recent book *What's the Worst That Could Happen? Existential Risk and Extreme Politics*, summarizes the dangers of totalitarianism, "Reducing catastrophic risk is fundamentally a political challenge. Get the politics wrong this century, and our species could face oblivion. Get the politics right, and humanity could endure for millennia to come" (2021, 236). A lack of planning and ineffective cooperation and coordination, particularly at the international level, could exacerbate other risks by increasing humanity's vulnerability and reducing resilience. A global turn toward totalitarianism or the turn of enough powerful states could become an existential risk.

The goal of an authoritarian government is to control its people and suppress, through force and coercion, challenges to its rule (Palouš 2008). Totalitarianism goes beyond the goals and methods of authoritarian governments. In addition to getting into and staying in power, totalitarianism has the goal of establishing total control over the population, not merely enough control to suppress a rebellion. The authoritarian wants to control humans, and the totalitarian wants control over human nature. The methods used by totalitarian governments are aimed at this radical behavior change. To do so, they utilize threats of harsh punishment and carry out enough punishments that the threats are believed. One of the most effective ways of gaining credibility to threats is to carry them out on a large scale. This tactic is further reinforced when the regimes designate specific groups of people to be a problem or a threat based on an identity that cannot change, thus requiring mass murder to remove them (Caplan 2008).

In the last century, there have been many examples of totalitarian rule;:Italy under Benito Mussolini (1922–1943), the Stalin era of the Soviet Union (1924–1953), Nazi Germany (1933–1945), the People's Republic of China under Mao Zedong (1946–1976), North Korea under the Kim regime (1948–), the Khmer Rouge (1951–1999) in Cambodia, Turkmenistan under Saparmurat Niyazov and Gurbanguly Berdimuhamedow (1991–), and Eritrea under Isaias Afwerki (2001–).

Totalitarian regimes generally share a few characteristics: an all-encompassing guiding ideology aimed at controlling and remaking human nature, a single-party state with complete control over the political sphere, a single leader as the head of state to interpret their ideology, the ability to use terror through secret police or the military to enforce their ideology and crush dissent, and control over weapons, the economy, and communications (Freidrich and Brzeziński 1956; Raymond and Ionescu 1968; Pipes 1994).

ERS and Totalitarianism

Many of the previously discussed risks follow two general pathways to catastrophe: a series of events that lead to extinction or the collapse of civilization where recovery is impossible. There is also a third possibility, "a world with civilization intact but locked into a terrible form, with little or no value" (Ord 2020, 153). In this kind of unrecoverable dystopia, humanity may live under a totalitarian state for a very long time that might be arguably worse than going extinct (Farquhar et al. 2017). A society locked in by such a regime could result in a situation where the desirable long-term futures for humanity are no longer possible (Bostrom 2019; Ord 2020; Caplan 2008)

Ord describes three possible scenarios for totalitarian lock-in resulting in an unrecoverable dystopia (Ord 2020). The first scenario is an enforced dystopia, the kind most often found in science fiction plots, where a totalitarian state rises and gains absolute control of the world. In this Orwellian future, a regime along the lines of Hitler or Stalin can harness new technologies to prevent rebellion, creating a stable and enduring authority entity. The second scenario is an undesired dystopia, a situation that is not desired by anyone but nonetheless gets locked in. The pathway to this future could be a tragedy of the commons—a scenario where each individual acts in their own self-interests in a manner that is contrary to the common good and causes the depletion of resources. Another version of the undesired dystopia would be where economic, social, and political forces create a race to the bottom where the quality of human life is not preserved for the sake of another value. For example, if humanity were to optimize the spreading of its genes to create the maximum number of people possible without regard to any other considerations, there could be a future where there is very little quality to the lives that are lived. In this example, people would only need to be provided with the basic resources necessary to ensure survival to reproduction, and the children would only need to be provided for to the extent that they could then grow to produce more people. The third scenario is the desired dystopia, where some sets of ideology or moral theories guide the development and use of powerful technologies to ensure that subsequent generations maintain exactly the same values as the past. In such a world, humanity could at one point halt all technological progress, thereby dooming the species to eventually succumb to a natural existential risk, or humanity could decide to replace itself with a kind of unfeeling machine. Life would hold very little value if there were no one to feel it (Ord 2020).

In all three of these scenarios, locking in specific values also locks out the majority of worthwhile future trajectories that humanity could take. There are two general pathways by which totalitarianism could lead to these scenarios. The first is that an enduring totalitarian hegemon rises to power and controls the globe. This single ridged governing entity maintains pervasive surveillance and control over the globe and is able to stop any possible threats to its dominance. The second is that several large regional totalitarian powers rise, but no specific bloc controls the planet. These different blocs maintain total control over large regions of the globe. Without non-totalitarian system existing to demonstrate an alternative, as generations pass, the idea that a different order could be possible may die out. Assessing the possible threat posed by totalitarianism requires examining both the likelihood of such a regime rising to power, how long a regime would exist, and its ability to contribute to an existential catastrophe.

In his article, "The Totalitarian Threat," Bryan Caplan gives an unconditional probability that a world totalitarian government will emerge in the next 1000 years and last for at least 1000 years at 5%. His estimate breaks down to a 0.5% rise in the next century.

The ability of a totalitarian regime to endure over a long time is a critical determinant in assessing the threat it could pose. Authoritarian regimes tend to last longer than totalitarian ones and may arguably have been one of the most common forms of governance throughout human history. Caplan, writing about the durability of totalitarianism, notes that "the best thing one can say about totalitarian regimes is that the main ones did not last very long" (Caplan 2008, 507). It is unclear whether the short lifespan of history's totalitarian regimes has been related to events of those times or if it is an inherent feature of totalitarian systems.

Technology plays a complex role in governance, with the overall effect of creating the possibility to enhance the power of those who control it. Bertrand Russell wrote in *Authority and the Individual* that technological development enables the possibility of more intense government control (Russell 1949). Technology and power are inexorably interconnected, and the control offered by technological power was essential to the rise of totalitarianism in the twentieth century (van der Laan 1997). Many tensions exist in the relationships between totalitarianism and technology. Technological development is complex and unwise to halt. The profits to be made, improvements to the quality of life, and the ability to mitigate disaster ensure that advancements in most emerging technologies will continue. At the same time, these technologies may enable totalitarian regimes to rise and stay in power. Further, the ability to mitigate many existential risks discussed in this book, such as an engineered pandemic, may require building sophisticated surveillance systems, which, in turn, could be the very technology that allows a totalitarian regime to take control. It may be difficult to garner political will behind the risk of not being able to cure most diseases or increase lifespan for fear of being killed by a possible future regime in the next century (Caplan 2008).

It is possible that the short life of these regimes was due in part to a lack of sufficiently powerful technologies. If totalitarianism aims to control human nature, there are several possibilities for how emerging technologies could grant this power. Caplan highlights how emerging technologies used for control affect the likelihood of a global totalitarian regime coming to power. He argues that developing cheap and effective genetic screening for personality traits could shift the balance of probability. Caplan argues that if this technology comes to pass and humanity maintains reproductive control at the individual level, it would decrease the 5% unconditional probability to 3%, while that same technology in the hands of a government could use it to favor traits amendable to being controlled and raise the probability of totalitarian takeover to 10% (Caplan 2008). Following this line of thought, Caplan argues it can be inferred that if Stalin and Hitler had access to advanced digital technology and biotechnologies, their regimes might have endured much longer.

However, a totalitarian regime could gain and maintain total control without using technology to alter the genes of its population. Advanced smart weapons could be used in lieu of, or in conjunction with, secret police forces. While individual officers may refuse to carry out atrocious acts, an automated system would have no moral objections (Tegmark 2018). Yet unimagined weapons developed through the nexus of AI, nanotechnology, and synthetic biology could lead to a tool for a hegemonic regime to be able to kill their opponents with weapons they did not even know existed (Tegmark 2018).

Propaganda is an essential tool for a totalitarian regime. Through mass media, a regime can influence its population both through the narrative they disseminate and by stating the one acceptable version of the truth, so that even those who disagree with what is being presented know what they are not allowed to say or think (Cassinelli 1960; Kecskemeti 1950; Arendt 1951). Media control has often been shown to make people less critical of political systems (Stockmann and Gallagher 2011).

Digital propaganda and disinformation techniques are rapidly evolving driven by increased computing power, lowered costs, and proof of effectiveness. These tools are no longer used primarily by one state against another, but are deployed domestically by states, nonstate actors, and criminals. One such tool is deepfakes, where Generative Adversarial Networks (GANs) are used to create hyper-realistic synthetic media. Fake audio and video can then be quickly spread through social networks. When applied at a strategic moment, deepfakes have already proven to be destabilizing to governments (Honigberg 2022).

In addition to their effects on governments, deepfakes can slow down the real news as journalists have to determine real sources from the synthetic. While there are currently effective approaches for analyzing and evaluating the validity of deepfakes, it takes time. Often a significant amount of damage has already been done before a deepfake can be identified as such. This technology's larger and more haunting effect is that it diminishes people's trust in authorities, media, and a sense of reality.

Further, deepfakes provide a convenient method for denying real information. Mistrust of the media can be a powerful tool for totalitarianism in its own right, further perpetuating the "liar's dividend," allowing leaders to maintain support in the face of damaging information (Chesney and Citron 2019). Future advances in AI will increase the quality of deepfakes and other synthetic media, further exacerbating the divide between the real and the fake and will likely become a powerful disruptive tool if AI developments for use in deepfakes progress faster than the technology and methods used to detect them (Kietzmann et al. 2020; Anand and Bianco 2021).

Surveillance is another essential tool of the totalitarian regime. To control the human nature of a population, those in control need to know what the people are doing. To stay in power, possible dissent and rebellion must be monitored. Technology increases the research, speed, and effectiveness of surveillance programs. Emerging technologies may continue this trend to a level previously only imagined in science fiction movies. Max Tegmark (2018) describes a possible scenario:

> With superhuman technology, the step from the perfect surveillance state to the perfect police state would be minute. For example, with the excuse of fighting crime and terrorism and rescuing people suffering medical emergencies, everybody could be required to wear a security bracelet that combined the functionality of an Apple Watch with continuous uploading of position, health status, and conversations overheard. Unauthorized attempts to remove or disable it would cause it to inject a lethal toxin into the forearm. (176)

Powerful surveillance systems already exist. One of the many revelations made public by Edward Snowden was that some governments were working to develop "full-take" digital surveillance systems. One of these programs is TEMPORA, a system used by the British Government Communications Headquarters that buffered internet traffic through the fiber-optic cables that make up the backbone of the internet. This information was taken by intelligence agencies in its entirety to be processed later (MacAskill et al. 2013). The aim of such programs may be to develop AI-augmented systems to interpret what these large amounts of data mean in real-time. These advancements are driven by the fact that, generally, computing power improves over time while getting cheaper, making large-scale networking and data mining increasingly feasible. Never before in human history have these technologies been as powerful as they are now, and there is no foreseeable reason why these technologies would not continue to advance (Phoenix and Treder 2008).

It is clear how powerful surveillance systems could empower totalitarian regimes. Similar powerful surveillance systems may, at the same time, be required to mitigate some existential risks. If, for example, future developments in synthetic biology make it frighteningly easy to develop a dangerous pathogen with little skill and resources, this would be the equivalent of discovering that a nuclear bomb could be made by combining common household ingredients in the microwave. Even if the vast majority of people would never consider using this newfound power, it would only take a few individuals to destabilize the world. In such a scenario, governments would have strong incentives to develop real-time global surveillance systems to know what every individual is doing at every moment. Such a system is not impossible, though currently estimated to cost about 1% of global Gross Domestic Product (Bostrom 2019). This system, though developed to safeguard against an existential threat, would be an avenue for the rise of a totalitarian power.

Other emerging technologies initially intended for different uses could also empower totalitarian regimes. Research has already demonstrated the feasibility of using machine learning as a "lie detector" whereby videos of courtroom trials are used to train a program to read micro-expressions and other indicators of deception (Wu et al. 2017). Advanced forms of this technology, if developed initially with questionably benign intent for use in law enforcement, could easily co-opted into a powerful tool for human control, what George Orwell described as "how to discover against his will, what another human being is thinking" (1982, 399). Interest in developing this type of technology already exists. Barring regulation, it is likely that increasingly advanced systems for "knowing what someone is thinking" will be developed (Bittle 2020; Gaggioli 2018). Such a tool would greatly benefit a totalitarian regime that wanted to remake human nature.

One weakness of totalitarian governments has been the problem of succession. When the party leader dies, a power struggle for the leader's successor typically ensues. Often the leader who follows does not hold as stringently to the same system set up by the founder. Nikita Khrushchev followed Joseph Stalin and was later peacefully removed as new leadership came in that was less dogmatic in its adherence to ideology, eventually resulting in Mikhail Gorbachev and his reforms. Then the Soviet Union collapsed in 1991. A similar process occurred in China when Deng Xiaoping succeeded Mao Zedong after his death and reduced the emphasis on Maoist ideology leading to the move toward more free markets (Caplan 2008).

Advancements in biotechnology have already been directed at life-extension and antiaging research (Parrish 2019; Stambler 2019; Abramson 2019). This technology initially developed without the intentions of political control in mind could, in effect, solve the succession problem by ensuring the long or indefinite life of leaders, possibly making their regimes more enduring (Caplan 2008). Additionally, advancements in genetic engineering and behavioral genetics could be used by a totalitarian regime to protect itself from dissent. Some strong components of political orientation may be genetic (Pinker 2002; Dawes and Weinschenk 2020; Hatemi et al. 2014). A sufficiently powerful regime could take these technologies away from their intended uses of treating inherited genetic conditions and use them for screening for dissent or possibly engineering compliance.

The nature of total control defined by totalitarian regimes is also one of their considerable weaknesses in dealing with catastrophes. A rigid governance structure that leads to a single decision-making point can be inflexible and fail to anticipate catastrophe. One reason for difficulty is the tendency in such regimes for aides and advisors to not share negative information with the leadership for fear it would be seen as dissent. Leaders, in this case, would have large information blind spots increasing their vulnerability to risks. When idiosyncratic aspects of the leader's personality inform decision-making and top-level leadership if driven by individual motives or emotions rather than reason, this problem is amplified. These leaders may fail to anticipate and react to catastrophic threats even if they see them coming (Caplan 2008). The centralized control structure of these regimes is likely to lead to society reaching a static equilibrium with little continued technological advancement outside of those technologies of control. On a long enough timeline, this ensures human extinction as a result of any number of natural or manmade disasters is ensured (Cotton-Barratt and Ord 2015).

Totalitarianism increases existential risks indirectly through increasing societal and global vulnerability and decreasing resiliency. A totalitarian regime, like Pol Pot, Hitler, Stalin, or the Kim family, with access to previously described technologies would contribute to geopolitical instability and likely could be a significant factor in a Great Power Conflict.

PCS and Totalitarianism

In part, Peace and Conflict Studies formed as an academic discipline as a reaction against totalitarian governance systems. The development of liberal peace philosophy is a further development of this historical root holding the belief that liberal democratic countries that trade together are less likely to go to war against each other.

Globally, in the past 15 years, democratic freedoms have declined, while authoritarianism has been on the rise (Freedom House 2022). Populism, a political perspective that positions a group identified as "the people" against "the elite," has also been on the rise worldwide (Rodríguez-Pose 2020; IDEA 2021; Berman 2019). Donald Trump's "Make America Great" campaign and the Tea Party in the USA, the rise of Boris Johnson and the Brexit movement in the UK, the election of Narendra Modi and the rise of the Bharatiya Janata Party in India, Rodrigo Duterte and Bongbong Marcos in the Philippines, Prabowo Subinto and Joko Widodo in Indonesia, and Jair Bolsonaro in Brazil are all evidence of this trend.

Scholars debate the relationship between populism, totalitarianism, and democracy. Some see populism as a direct threat to democracy (Urbinati 1998), as a critique of it (March 2007), as ambiguously related to democracy (Panizza 2005; Mény and Surel 2002), and others as a valid form of democracy in itself (Albertazzi and McDonnell 2008).

Totalitarian systems have historically fallen from power either by being destroyed by an outside force, internal revolt from the masses, or the rise of a sufficiently powerful discontent middle class or by losing their own ability to govern (Orwell 1982, 170). If a regimen could guard against these forces efficiently, they could likely maintain control for a long time.

Where populism as a type of proto-totalitarianism becomes a concern as an existential risk is through some of the key traits populist movements share. In addition to positing politics as a struggle between the masses and a corrupt elite, these movements also tend to be "anti-intellectual, anti-institutional, anti-international, and anti-irenic." These tendencies work against the "strong science, effective institutions, global engagement, and sense of cooperation and order" needed to mitigate existential risks (Leigh 2021, 182). A totalitarian system that was able to lock in all these "anti-" values would easily become an existential disaster.

Mitigating the risks of totalitarianism involves three core components: reducing the likelihood that a single global totalitarian power or several blocs rise and take control, reducing the likelihood that such regimes become robust enough to create a lock-in scenario, and mitigating the damage they could cause.

Almost tautologically, one of the safeguards against global totalitarianism is the existence of non-totalitarian countries. Historically when totalitarian regimes exist alongside more moderate ones, the comparison between the two systems motivates forces that cause regimes to fall. Caplan (2008) refers to this as the "totalitarian dilemma" where "as long as totalitarian states co-exist with non-totalitarian ones, they have to expose potential successors to demoralizing outside influences to avoid falling dangerously behind their rivals" (509). The converse of this relationship is also likely true that totalitarian states would become more politically stable if there were no other non-totalitarian states in the world.

In addition to ensuring alternatives to totalitarianism on the geopolitical stage, efforts to reduce poverty and inequality would likely create buffers to prevent populist movements from becoming totalitarian governments. Most, if not all, existential risks require large-scale international cooperation. Climate change and the COVID-19 pandemic have already shown that current abilities for international cooperation are not as effective as will likely be needed to deal with an imminent threat to human extinction. Since one foreseeable way a totalitarian power could rise to global control would be through efforts to solve the global coordination problem, improving global governance systems is also a potential safeguard against pathways by which totalitarianism could rise.

Nick Bostrom (2006) posits this scenario in his "Singleton Hypothesis." His idea is that governance structures have generally become more complex and are further reaching over time. He hypothesizes that "earth-originating intelligent life will (eventually) form a singleton" (52), which he defines as a "single decision-making agency at the highest levels" (48). This singleton would then be able to prevent any threats to its own power or existence and exert control over the entirety of its domain (Bostrom 2006). The idea of a world government that would put a limit on the power of the nation-state and nullify the practice of interstate war has been suggested by many thinkers, including Albert Einstein, Bertrand Russell, Albert Schweitzer, George Bernard Shaw, Thomas Mann, H.G. Wells, and Mahatma Gandhi (Crockatt 2016). Bostrom's singleton could take different forms, a planet run like a country, several regional units that form together into a single decision-making body, or an AI that has either taken or been given control of the planet.

A planet governed by a single decision-making body could have many appealing benefits. Such a system could prevent arms races and races for other powerful technologies. It would be a solution to the coordination problem for addressing global risks. If humanity does become a space-faring species, it could help to address the expected "tragedy of the commons" but in space (Hanson 1998). The distribution of powerful emerging technologies could be controlled so that no single group has exclusive access and control over them. If humanity does find a way to survive for millions of years, it would likely need to start guiding its genetic evolution because there would be no reason to believe that the evolutionary pressures of the past would be sufficient for such a future (Bostrom 2006).

It is clear that the coordination problem exists and is central to safeguarding the future of humanity. These threats are impetus enough to decide how effective global governance systems should be built before a bad singleton finds its way to the seat of power. The future is time sensitive. Efforts toward global governance could prevent a small group from developing powerful technologies and leveraging themselves into a totalitarian singleton. If this group were to get those technologies beforehand, stopping them would likely be difficult. If humanity may soon need to deal with the issue of black ball technologies and turn-key totalitarianism is a possible solution, it is important to have considered this problem on the global level ahead of time.

Questions for the Future

How to most efficiently promote good global governance and address the global coordination problem?

How to safeguard against the lock-in of destructive values?

Given recent human history, the possibility of totalitarianism becoming an indirect existential risk is imaginable. Other possible threats from Great Power Conflicts and climate change could be made much worse through the rise of robust totalitarian governments. Further, it is possible to see how efforts to mitigate existential risks, such as those posed by emerging technologies, may empower a totalitarian regime. Suppose humanity is to survive the challenges ahead and be able to respond to the challenges we do not yet see. In that case, global governance and coordination questions need to be at the center of peace research.

References

Abramson, Maria Entraigues. 2019. "To Age, or Not to Age: That Is the Question." In *The Transhumanism Handbook*, edited by Newton Lee, 355–361. Cham: Springer.

Albertazzi, Daniele, and Duncan McDonnell. 2008. "Introduction: The Sceptre and the Spectre." In *Twenty-First Century Populism: The Spectre of Western European Democracy*, edited by Daniele Albertazzi and Duncan McDonnell, 1–11. New York: Palgrave Macmillan.

Anand, Alisha, and Belén Bianco. 2021. *The 2021 Innovations Dialogue Conference Report: Deepfakes, Trust and International Security*. Geneva: United Nations Institute for Disarmament Research.

Arendt, Hannah. 1951. *The Origins of Totalitarianism*. New York: Schocken Books.

Berman, Sheri. 2019. "Populism is a Symptom Rather than a Cause: Democratic Disconnect, the Decline of the Center-Left, and the Rise of Populism in Western Europe." *Polity* 51 (4).

Bittle, Jake. 2020. "Lie Detectors Have Always been Suspect. AI Has Made the Problem Worse." *MIT Technology Review*, March 13. Accessed August 31, 2022. https://www.technologyreview.com/2020/03/13/905323/ai-lie-detectors-polygraph-silent-talker-iborderctrl-converus-neuroid/.

Borders, Max. 2021. "The Paradox of Turnkey Totalitarianism." *American Institute of Economic Research*, September 10. Accessed August 18, 2022. https://www.aier.org/article/the-paradox-of-turnkey-totalitarianism/.

Bostrom, Nick. 2006. "What is a Singleton?" *Linguistic and Philosophical Investigations* 5 (2): 48–54.

Bostrom, Nick. 2019. "The Vulnerable World Hypothesis." *Global Policy* 4 (10): 455–576.

Caplan, Bryan. 2008. "The Totalitarian Threat." In *Global Catastrophic Risks*, edited by Nick Bostrom and Milan M. Ćirković. Oxford: Oxford University Press.

Cassinelli, C. W. 1960. "Totalitarianism, Ideology, and Propaganda." *The Journal of Politics* 22 (1).

Chesney, Robert, and Danielle Keats Citron. 2019. "Deep Fakes: A Looming Challenge for Privacy, Democracy, and National Security." *107 California Law Review 1752*.

Cotton-Barratt, Owen, and Toby Ord. 2015. "Existential Risk and Existential Hope: Definitions." *Future of Humanity Institute*. Accessed August 18, 2022. https://www.fhi.ox.ac.uk/Existential-risk-and-existential-hope.pdf.

Crockatt, Richard. 2016. *Einstein and Twentieth-Century Politics: 'A Salutary Moral Influence*. Oxford: Oxford University Press.

Dawes, Christopher T., and Aaron C. Weinschenk. 2020. "On the Genetic Basis of Political Orientation." *Current Opinions in Behavioral Sciences* 34: 173–178.

Farquhar, Sebastian, John Halstead, Owen Cotton-Barratt, Stefan Schubert, Haydn Belfield, and Andrew Snyder-Beattie. 2017. *Existential Risks: Diplomacy and Governance*. Global Priorities Project.

Freedom House. 2022. *Freedom in the World 2022: The Global Expansion of Authoritarian Rule*. Freedom House.

Freidrich, Carl J., and Zbigniew K. Brzeziński. 1956. *Totalitarian Dictatorship and Autocracy*. Cambridge: Harvard University Press.

Gaggioli, Andrea. 2018. "Beyond the Truth Machine: Emerging Technologies for Lie Detection." *Cyberpsychology, Behavior, and Social Networking* 21 (2): 144.

Hanson, Robin. 1998. "Burning the Cosmic Commons: Evolutionary Strategies for Interstellar Colonization." *George Mason University*. Accessed August 18, 2022. http://hanson.gmu.edu/filluniv.pdf.

Hatemi, Peter K., Sarah E. Medland, Robert Klemmensen, Sven Oskarrson, Levente Littvay, Chris Dawes, Brad Verhulst, et al. 2014. "Genetic Influences on Political Ideologies: Twin Analyses of 19 Measures of Political Ideologies from Five Democracies and Genome-Wide Findings from Three Populations." *Behavior Genetics* 44 (3): 282–292.

Honigberg, Bradley. 2022. "The Existential Threat of AI-Enhanced Disinformation Operations." *Just Security*, July 8. Accessed August 31, 2022. https://www.justsecurity.org/82246/the-existential-threat-of-ai-enhanced-disinformation-operations/.

IDEA. 2021. *International Institute for Democracy and Electoral Assistance*. November 22. Accessed September 1, 2022. https://www.idea.int/news-media/news/democracy-faces-perfect-storm-world-becomes-more-authoritarian.

Kecskemeti, Paul. 1950. "Totalitarian Communications as a Means of Control: A Note on the Sociology of Propaganda." *The Public Opinion Quarterly* 14 (2): 224–234.

Kietzmann, Jan, Linda W. Lee, Ian P. McCarthy, and Tim C. Kietzmann. 2020. "Deepfakes: Trick or Treat." *Business Horizons* 63: 135–146.

Leigh, Andrew. 2021. *What's the Worst that Could Happen?: Existential Risk and Extreme Politics*. Cambridge: MIT Press.

MacAskill, Ewen, Nick Hopkins, Nick Davies, and James Ball. 2013. "GCHQ Taps Fibre-Optic Cables for Secret Access to World's Communications." *The Guardian*, June 21. Accessed August 20, 2022. https://www.theguardian.com/uk/2013/jun/21/gchq-cables-secret-world-communications-nsa.

March, Luke. 2007. "From Vanguard of the Proletariat to Vox Populi: Left-Populism as a 'Shadow' of Contemporary Socialism." *SAIS Review* 27 (1): 63–77.

Mény, Yves, and Yves Surel. 2002. *Democracies and the Populist Challenge*. New York: Palgrave.

Ord, Toby. 2020. *The Precipice: Existential Risk and the Future of Humanity*. New York: Hachette Books.

Orwell, George. 1982. *1984*. New York: Buccaneer Books.
Palouš, Martin. 2008. "Totalitarianism and Authoritarianism." In *Encyclopedia of Violence, Peace, and Conflict*, edited by Lester Kurtz. Cambridge: Academic Press.
Panizza, Francisco. 2005. "Introduction: Populism and the Mirror of Democracy." In *Populism and the Mirror of Democracy*, edited by Francisco Panizza, 1–31. London: Verso.
Parrish, Elizabeth. 2019. "Extending Healthy Human Lifespan Using Gene Therapy." In *The Transhumanism Handbook*, edited by Newton Lee, 423–431. Cham: Springer.
Phoenix, Chris, and Mike Treder. 2008. "Nanotechnology as Global Catastrophic Risk." In *Global Catastrophic Risks*, edited by Nick Bostrom and Milan M. Cirkovic, 481–502. Oxford: Oxford University Press.
Pinker, Steven. 2002. *The Blank Slate: The Modern Denial of Human Nature*. New York: Viking Press.
Pipes, Richard. 1994. *Russia Under the Bolshevik Regime*. New York: Vintage Books.
Raymond, Aron, and Valence Ionescu. 1968. *Democracy and Totalitarianism*. London: Weidenfeld and Nicolson.
Rodríguez-Pose, Andrés. 2020. "The Rise of Populism and the Revenge of Places That Don't Matter." *London School of Economics Policy Review*.
Russell, Bertrand. 1949. *Authority and the Individual*. London and New York: Routledge.
Stambler, Ilia. 2019. "What Do We Need to Know to treat Degenerative Aging as a Medical Condition to Extend Healthy Lifespan." In *The Transhumanism Handbook*, edited by Newton Lee, 381–397. Cham: Springer.
Stockmann, Daniela, and Mary E. Gallagher. 2011. "Remote Control: How the Media Sustain Authoritarian Rule in China." *Comparative Political Studies* 44 (4): 436–467.
Tegmark, Max. 2018. *Life 3.0: Being Human in the Age of Artificial Intelligence*. Vintage.
Urbinati, Nadia. 1998. "Democracy and Populism." *Constellations* 5 (1): 110–124.
van der Laan, James M. 1997. "Education, Technology and Totalitarianism." *Bulletin of Science Technology and Society* 17 (5): 236–248.
Wu, Zhe, Bharat Singh, Larry S. Davis, and V.S. Subrahmanian. 2017. "Deception Detection in Videos." *arXiv:1712.04415v1*.

CHAPTER 9

Conclusion

Humanity has learned from the horrors of the past as well as future hopes and fears. The disillusionment after World War I led to the development of International Relations and many institutions were charged with preventing such a disaster from happening again. Peace and Conflict Studies came about similarly, from insufficient answers to the problem of war not preventing World War II. During these same moments in history, humanity discovered that our extinction is possible and may well be in our own hands. Grand narratives that explain the order of the past and the future trajectory are no longer sufficient to inspire trust, let alone faith. Without such orientation, understandings of peace became plural and relational. No longer having to hold solely to truth, justice, or security to define the meaning of peace, peace can be understood in relation to one another and the harmony therein. Even a small, every day, and local peace is important. Indeed, this makes up the vast majority of peaces in the world. Peace is about this and more, the relation to the one in front of you in space and those behind and before you in time.

The historical moment humanity finds itself in may now be pivotal. The current nexus of the climate crisis, pandemics, technological advancement, rise of proto-totalitarian politics, and the rumblings of a Great Power Conflict are all a call for a vision of a "big peace" where peace and the long-term survival of humanity are in center place and interrelated. Peace and survival are not to be understood as a monological perspective but rather as a platform from which future conflicts can be continued to be transformed into peaces.

To ask questions about peace and survival is also to ask what is important and why. Humans are limited in time, space, and resources. Living is dangerous, and many threats do lurk out in the dark. To navigate precarious moments in history it is incumbent to ask what is most important and in what order should things be done to ensure peace and survival. These practical considerations also give way to their foundational assumptions. The old question: what is the purpose of human life? What is the nature of a good life? What is peace, and why should it be sought after?

It is not a radical proposition to take the side of humanity, peace, and survival. There can be nothing more basic or rational than favoring the survival of one's species. Of course, what kind of survival it is and how it is ensured are more nuanced questions. To contemplate the far trajectory of the human species is as much a transrational question as it is a rational one—the rational to refine the vision and give it concrete steps that connect the day to the forever, and the transrational to give meaning to what existing along a vast time horizon might mean and how we should feel about a premature end in fire or ice.

The experiences of a world at war influenced the development of Peace and Conflict Studies (PCS) and Existential Risk Studies (ERS). Of all the risks discussed in this book, this is the one humanity can claim the most familiarity with. It is the quintessential anthropogenic risk. Over a long enough timeline, the climate may have changed or a virus evolved that pushed humanity to extinction even if we were not the primary cause. A Great Power Conflict can only happen if humanity goes to war on a scale and with weapons such that the earth becomes uninhabitable. If such a war can be started, so too can it be prevented. The preamble to the UNESCO constitution holds that it is in human minds that war is created, and so too is it the location for the defenses of peace to be constructed. Humanity has learned a lot from war; unfortunately, it has learned this from experience. Let us hope that since the likely toll of war is easier to imagine now than before Hiroshima and Nagasaki, we continue to develop and strengthen systems of governance and ways of de-escalating conflicts so that whoever is left after World War III does not need to consider a new approach for avoiding World War IV.

I hope that the fear, suffering, death, and loss the world has experienced through the COVID-19 pandemic can serve as an example of what an existential risk could look like, what it may feel like, and how underprepared humanity may be. The COVID-19 pandemic turned out not to be an existential risk, whether through the nature of the virus, mitigation efforts by governments, institutions, and people around the world, or both. It was horrible, but we, as a species, got lucky. Imagine a virus as contagious as COVID-19 but as deadly as Ebola. Then remember how well the world, overall, responded to COVID-19. Not everyone alive has a living memory of World War II or the fear associated with the Cold War. There is no one alive who has not experienced a global pandemic. The common ground that can be found through that alone may be quite the gift. Just as humanity will live with the repercussions of this pandemic for years to come, so may we use that experience to appreciate problems on such a global scale and develop better ways of responding.

In 2014 the Okjokull glacier in Iceland was declared dead at 700 years old. Its ice was no longer thick enough to move. Four years later, a plaque was installed. The inscription ended with words from Andri Snaer Magnason, "This monument is to acknowledge that we know what is happening and what needs to be done. Only you know if we did it." Written in copper, this is a letter to an uncertain future. The central problem of climate change for humanity is that we experience time in a vector that moves in a line from the past to the future. The planet and the climate do not. Another world war may not happen. The probability of another severe global pandemic is likely but uncertain. We are already in a changing climate. Serious inquiry now asks questions about how bad it will be, how soon, and what the effects will be. The question of what can *still* be done evokes both hope and trepidation. A changing climate threatens fire and then ice.

With the technologies of the past, we built the world we live in. Simultaneously, it is the means by which we can live in prosperity, make nuclear bombs, cure diseases, and pollute the environment. If experts are correct, then humanity will eventually possess technologies that could imbue us with almost divine powers. When humankind creates artificial intelligence (AI), a mind in its own image, then for the first time, people will be in relation to a whole other type of being. Biotechnology already allows us to change life according to our will; future advancements will enable entirely new things to be created. Nanotechnology may grant the power of creation and control over matter itself. Building at the level of the very small will change the world in a very big way. It can be argued that some of these technologies lie far in the future. It may very well be true. A timeline is important when planning. But it is also reasonable that as long as they do not violate some fundamental laws of the universe on a long enough timeline, any advancements in these technologies will exist. Thinking through how we want these technologies to be developed and used now will be easier than when they have become widespread.

Neither fire nor ice is inevitable, but for humanity, politics might be. The upper limit of how long humanity may exist for stretches until close to the time that the last stars fall dark. Until then, humanity's path is left up to choice and chance. Our ability to organize in groups around common goals united in shared stories is a hallmark of our species. This feature of us likely has saved us from many unknown moments in history where our entire existence was in peril. Just as in recent history, humanity has experienced Great Power Conflicts, pandemics, a changing climate, and rapid technological growth; we have also experienced what happens when governments seek total control over their populations. It is hard to imagine what the systems of governance and political issues will be in 500 or 10,000 years. Politicians tend to think in terms of election cycles and policy in terms of governments. It may not be possible or even wise to precisely define the long-term goal of our species' political ambitions, but it is essential to agree what is not desired and what is dangerous. A system, by whatever name, that locks in the wrong set of values could ensure existential ruin, either through direct action, negligence, or building a world no one wants to live in.

There may be plenty of cause for despair but little reason to do so. The specifics of many of the risks discussed in this book are yet to be understood. What is known, most generally, is what is needed. Whether it be de-escalating a Great Power Conflict or building systems of diplomacy so that they do not happen, reducing the risk of or responding to the next global pandemic, working on what can still be done about climate change, or mitigating its most disastrous effects, developing a powerful new tool or using that tool as a weapon, or finding ways to govern ourselves that acknowledge human dignity, there is not an effort that would not be better served by peace. Not one that violence would not make worse.

"Solving" the global coordination problem would go a long way to reducing the risk potential of the threats discussed in this book. At the abstract and global level, the "problem" is daunting to the point of overwhelming. But it is also just people together on a planet. Trust and cooperation build relationships, families, communities, countries, peoples, and planets. In this jeweled net of people connected across space and time, we come into and out of harmony, become both the just and unjust, find truth and lies, hurt, and are injured. The task we find ourselves at the intersection of PCS and ERS is that we need to find a way to make our survival an enduring cultural and political value. Peace is a part of that, part of what peace is, may *be* that. We are not driven by the obvious as a species. Endowed with a conscious and discerning mind, we can choose to think of peace and survival in the same breath, not the same but not separate. Peace and survival, not as a goal to ever be reached, a paradise on a distant shore, but a practice, a vehicle of our spirit that continues until that final breath.

Index[1]

A
Adaptive Peacebuilding, 18
Agenda for Peace, 9, 13, 99
AI for Peace, 159
Algorithmic Justice League, 150
Allison, Graham, 74
AI winter, 151
Anti-Ballistic Missile Treaty, 8
Arkhipov, Vasily, 142
Armed Conflict Location and Event Data Project (ACLED), 146
Artificial intelligence, 150, 155
Asilomar Principles, 155
Aum Shinrikyo, 167
Authoritarianism, 59, 191

B
Ban on chemical and nuclear weapons, 8
Beard, Simon, 20, 22, 23, 25
Bethe, Hans, 7
Biological Weapons Convention (BWC), 162
Biotechnology, 160–169, 207
Black ball technology, 141
Black Death, 85
Blainey, Geoffrey, 92
Boring Apocalypse, 31
Bostrom, Nick, 23, 24, 27–29, 32, 141, 174, 200
Boulding, Kenneth, 8, 56
Bulletin of the Atomic Scientists, 69

C
Caplan, Brian, 193
Centre for Human-Compatible AI, 150
Centre for the Study of Existential Risk (CSER), 27, 150
Čirković, Milan, 24

[1] Note: Page numbers followed by 'n' refer to notes.

Climate change, 43, 109–111, 113, 114, 118, 120, 121, 128, 200
  likelihood, 113
  risks from climate change, 113
Cold War, 8, 9, 13, 41, 57, 65, 66, 68, 77, 79, 97, 100, 114, 141, 143, 168, 207
Collaborative Learning Projects (CDA), 47, 100
Collingridge Dilemma, 43
Conciliation Resources, 119
Conflict escalation, 73
Conflict management, 5, 9–11, 41
Conflict Resolution, 8–11, 77, 97
Conflict Transformation, 9–11, 14n2, 17, 19, 77, 145–146, 158–159
COVID-19, 2, 27, 58, 59, 72, 85, 86, 90–99, 118, 200, 206
CRISPR/Cas9, 160, 165, 167
Curle, Adam, 6, 55
Cuvier, Georges, 23

D
Darwin, Charles, 23
Desired dystopia, 193
Dietrich, Wolfgang, 14, 53, 76
Diplomacy, 9, 45, 75–77, 97, 168, 208
Direct carbon capture, 125
Doomsday Clock, 8
Drake Equation, 52
Drexler, Eric, 172
Drones, 156
Dual-use, 149, 162, 164

E
Effective Altruism (EA), 25, 26, 29, 35, 44
Einstein, Albert, 7, 200
Elliot, T.S., 4, 28

Emerging technology/technologies, 43, 44, 58, 69, 70, 139–146, 148–150, 152, 168, 169, 171, 176, 194, 196, 197, 201
  defining emerging technology, 140
  risks from emerging technology, 140–141
Emissions reduction, 125
Energetic understandings of peace, 14, 15, 53, 54
Esalen Institute, 76, 77, 168
Eschatology, 21, 23
Everyday Peace, 13
Existential catastrophe, 25, 27, 43, 50, 69, 71, 72, 75, 78, 153, 165, 166, 193
Existential Risk Studies (ERS), 5, 19–35, 68–73

F
Fermi Paradox, 52
Founders Pledge, 68, 69, 125
Future of Humanity Institute (FHI), 23–24, 150
Future of Life Institute, 155

G
Galtung, Johan, 6, 53, 56
Gene drive, 164
Geoengineering, 128
Global Challenges Foundation, 86, 113, 166
Good Food Institute (GFI), 122
Governance, 148–149, 154–155, 162–164, 173
Great filter, 52
Great Powers
  defining Great Powers, 66
Great Powers Conflict, 63–80, 118

likelihood of a Great Power
Conflict, 69
risks from Great Powers
Conflict, 67
Grey goo, 172

H
Hanso, Robin, 52
Harari, Noah Yuval, 153, 177
High-Throughput Atomically Precise Manufacturing (HT-APM), 170, 173, 175, 176
Hybrid peace, 13

I
Industry 4.0, 144, 145, 152, 158, 174

K
Kuhlemann, Karin, 29, 30
Kyoto Protocol, 122, 123

L
Lederach, John Paul, 11, 49, 56
Leverhulme Centre for the Future of Intelligence, 150
Liberal Peace, 13
Liberal peacebuilding, 13, 18
Longtermism, 29, 44

M
Machine learning (ML), 145
Manhattan Project, 7
Maxipok rule, 24
Migration, 111, 112, 115–119
Modern understandings of peace, 15, 54
Moral understandings of peace, 15, 54

N
Nanoparticles, 170, 171
Nanotechnology, 24, 58, 140, 145, 148, 150, 152, 169–177, 195, 207
Natural Language Processing (NLP), 145
Necessity, Tractability, and Importance Framework, 29
Negative peace, 53
Nuclear Non-Proliferation Treaty, 8
Nuclear Threat Initiative (NTI), 167

O
Open AI, 150
Oppenheimer, Robert, 7, 147
Ord, Toby, 26, 68, 165
Orwell, George, 192

P
Pandemics, 85–98, 165
likelihood of Ppandemics, 86
risks from pandemics, 89
Panic, Branka, 159
Paris Agreement, 121, 123, 124
Pax Epidemica, 92
Peace and Conflict Studies (PCS), 2, 5–19, 41, 48, 73–79, 95, 99, 146–149, 199, 205
Peace inhibiter, 117
Peace writ large, 47
Peloponnesian War, 5, 74
Populism, 199
Post-apocalyptic, 21
Post-liberal Peace, 13
Postmodernism, 12
Postmodern understandings of peace, 15, 54
Prioritization
In Existential Risk Studies, 45
in Peace and Conflict Studies, 48
Pugwash movement, 7, 8

Q

Questions for the Future
  Climate Change, Peace, and
     Conflict, 128–129
  Emerging Technologies, 149–150
  Great Powers Conflict, 79–80
  Peace, Pandemics, and
     Conflicts, 100
  Totalitarianism, Peace and
     Conflict, 201

R

Risk multiplier, 116–118
Risks
  anthropogenic risks, 43, 166
  global catastrophic risk, 29, 87, 96,
     113, 166
  natural risks, 26
Russell, Bertrand, 7, 194, 200
Russell-Einstein Manifesto, 7

S

Sagan, Carl, 24
Schwab, Klaus, 144
Sexy risks, 29
Singleton Hypothesis, 200
Societal collapse, 22, 112
Sulfur aerosols, 127
Superintelligence, 28, 30, 151
Surface albedo modification (SAM),
  126, 127
Surveillance, 59, 72, 90, 96, 97,
  156, 171, 176, 193, 194,
  196, 197
Synthetic biology, 160–169, 177
Systems thinking, 13, 16–18, 29
Szilard, Leo, 7

T

Tegmark, Max, 157, 196
Thucydides, 5, 74
Thucydides Trap, 74
Torres, Phil, 20, 22, 23, 25
Totalitarianism, 57, 191–201
Totalitarian lock-in, 72, 192
Total Utilitarianism, 24
Tragedy of the commons, 193, 201
Transhumanism, 24, 25, 35
Transrational, 14, 15, 53–56, 206
Transrational Peace Philosophy, 14, 53
Transrational understanding of
  peace, 54
Trinity Tests, 147

U

Undesired dystopia, 193
United Nations, 27, 46, 65, 67, 91,
  110, 122, 123, 154, 157
Unmanned Aerial Vehicle (UAV), 156
Unsexy risks, 30, 31

V

von Bertalanffy, Ludwig, 8, 77
Vulnerabilities, 25, 31, 32, 34, 35, 57
The Vulnerable World
  Hypothesis, 141

W

Weaponization of technology, 144
Wells, H.G., 91
World War I, 6, 63, 80, 86, 205
World War II, 7, 19, 23, 57, 63, 65,
  67, 68, 71, 76, 80, 99, 205, 207
World War III, 67, 206